THE
PURSUED

OTHER TITLES BY COREY MEAD

The Hidden History of the White House

The Lost Pilots

Angelic Music

War Play

THE
PURSUED

A TRUE STORY OF STALKING, MEMORY,
AND MADNESS IN AMERICA'S HEARTLAND

COREY MEAD

Little
a

Published by Little A, New York
www.apub.com

Amazon, the Amazon logo, and Little A are trademarks of Amazon.com, Inc., or its
affiliates.

EU product safety contact:
Amazon Media EU S. à r.l.
38, avenue John F. Kennedy, L-1855 Luxembourg
amazonpublishing-gpsr@amazon.com

ISBN-13: 9781662527814 (hardcover)
ISBN-13: 9781662527821 (paperback)
ISBN-13: 9781662527807 (digital)

Cover design by Jack Smyth
Cover image: © autsawin uttisin, © Wilqkuku / Shutterstock; © George Marks /
Getty

Printed in the United States of America

First edition

For my family, as always. And for the Reporter.

Contents

1

THE CALL

It was a humid June evening in 1978, the sky bright with stars, and forty-eight-year-old Ruth Finley was alone in her basement when the Poet made his first appearance. In the front yard, the wind rustled the leaves of the elm tree, and the plastic sheet covering the living room window flapped softly against the glass.

Ruth was seldom alone in her house at night. Usually after dinner she and her husband, Ed, sat in the basement working on their hobbies. Ruth knitted or worked on ceramic pieces—frogs, owls, bulldogs—at her kiln in one corner, while Ed painted landscapes at his easel. When the two took breaks, they sat on the couch, leaning in together, and watched television. The large basement also held a pool table and an organ that Ed, who couldn't read music, played by the numbers. A gun rack stocked with unused rifles hung on one wall.

—⁂—

Married for twenty-eight years, Ruth and Ed were comfortable with the long periods of silence that punctuated their evenings. They knew how to adjust to the contours of each other's moods. Both of their boys,

Brent and Bruce, were grown and out of the house, and Ruth and Ed were enjoying being empty nesters. They were best friends.

But that night, Ruth felt uneasy. She sipped coffee and watched television at a low volume alone in the basement, listening to the plastic sheet tapping against the upstairs window. Ed had hung the sheet earlier that week to protect the window from the cement he was pouring to patch up the front porch. The sound reminded Ruth of a tin sheet her father had once hung to cover the south side of their Missouri farmhouse after a tornado had ripped away the wall. The tornado had sprayed glass over her mother and sister and ripped off the chicken house roof, sucking the eggs right out of their chickens. Bundled in a terry-cloth robe, Ruth distractedly watched the ten o'clock news, feeling worried and worn out.

The previous night, as she and Ed had been watching television, Ed had tried to light a cigarette and the matchstick's flaming head had flown right off. He'd lurched sideways to avoid it and felt a stab of pain in his chest. He gasped for breath, then rose from the sofa, clutched the front of his shirt, and collapsed on the floor.

Ruth and Ed were certain he had suffered a heart attack. Ed was a heavy smoker who rarely exercised, and he sported a growing paunch on his otherwise lanky frame. Preliminary tests at the hospital, however, had shown no indication of a heart attack. The doctor wanted to keep Ed overnight as a precaution, and so Ruth had returned home at 3:00 a.m. by herself, trembling as she walked from the car to the front door. She felt afraid to be alone, although she knew that was foolish. That first night, she had barely managed to sleep.

Tests the next day revealed that Ed's pain had been the result of an unhealed tear in his rib cartilage, an injury from a car accident the previous Christmas Eve. Lifting heavy blocks of concrete earlier that day had aggravated the injury. The doctors wanted Ed to stay in the hospital for another night, out of an abundance of caution.

As the TV news anchor cut to a commercial, Ruth yawned and rose from the couch. Fatigued though she was, she knew any attempt at sleep would be futile, so she headed up the stairs to make another cup of coffee.

The phone rang before Ruth had finished climbing the stairs. Friends and family had been calling all day for updates on Ed's health, and Ruth was eager for a familiar voice.

As she entered the kitchen, Ruth could see her reflection in the sliding glass doors that framed the backyard. She tightened the sash of her robe and picked up the phone.

"Hello?" she said.

"Is this Ruth Smock from Fort Scott, Kansas?" an unfamiliar male voice asked.

The question startled her. Smock was Ruth's maiden name, and she had not lived in Fort Scott for decades.

"Yes, it is," she answered.

"I know all about that night," he said, low and ominous. Ruth instantly knew which night he meant.

The caller began reading out loud from an October 15, 1946, article from the *Fort Scott Tribune*: "'Branded on both thighs by a hot flatiron, apparently by a sex maniac, Ruth Smock, sixteen-year-old Fort Scott High schoolgirl, . . . was resting today at the home of her parents . . . following an attack upon her early last night.'"

It had been almost thirty-two years since that night. The man on the line asked Ruth if she still wore her "brand."

"I don't know what you're talking about," Ruth lied. Why was this stranger bringing up that terrible incident from so long ago?

The man told Ruth he worked for a construction company that was tearing down old houses in Fort Scott, and he'd found a number of yellowing newspapers in the walls. The article about Ruth was among them. If she didn't give him money, he said, he would spread the news of her teenage attack. "I know where you work," he warned.

Alarmed, Ruth slammed down the phone. Her temples throbbed, and she felt overwhelmed by exhaustion. Dragging herself to bed, she fell almost immediately into a lengthy slumber.

—⁂—

The Finleys lived in a single-level, yellow brick-and-wood house at 8125 East Indianapolis Street, a tree-lined residential block on the far east side of Wichita, Kansas. Their house resembled most of the others on the street—trim and modest, with a small, neatly kept front yard, a spacious backyard bordered by a chain-link fence, and a two-car garage. The similar architecture and the close proximity of the houses—just a few feet apart from each other—created a warmly familiar environment for residents.

Though two large shopping malls and a Hilton hotel occupied the busy intersection just one block north, East Indianapolis Street felt secluded. When traffic was light, Ruth and Ed could drive their black Oldsmobile to downtown Wichita in just ten minutes.

With a population of three hundred thousand residents, Wichita was the largest city in Kansas. The city was home to the Boeing Military Aircraft Company as well as Beech, Cessna, and Learjet. Offsetting this sleek modernity, the central downtown area was full of beautiful older buildings and scenic parks. Wichita was first settled in 1863, when fifteen hundred Wichita Indians set up camp in the groves of cottonwoods and willows where two rivers, the Arkansas and the Little Arkansas, joined, and they still wound through its heart. But by the late 1970s, Wichita's life had drifted to the perimeters, the inevitable outcome of a decades-long post–World War II economic boom. Towne East and its companion mall, Towne West, now anchored the city on either side and drew most of the shoppers away from its increasingly hollowed-out center.

On the far east side, where the Finleys lived, residents felt removed from any threat of violence. Ruth and Ed and their neighbors could settle in for the night without fear of anyone intruding on their peaceful turf.

—m—

Two weeks had passed following Ed's return from the hospital and Ruth still hadn't told him about her disturbing phone call. She didn't want to add to Ed's burden after his health scare. What if the news upset him enough that he ended up back in the hospital?

But, by the end of June, Ruth couldn't hold it in anymore. Early one morning, she lay beside Ed in their four-poster bed and watched as the summer sunlight filled the room. Robins chirped in the backyard. What a nice morning, Ruth thought. She hated to spoil it, but she couldn't keep things bottled up any longer.

Ruth tried to keep her manner casual. When Ed woke up, she mentioned, "If some guy calls, I want you to talk to him."

"Okay," Ed responded groggily. "Why?"

Ruth hesitated.

"I got a phone call," she finally said. "The second night you were in the hospital. Some guy asked if I used to be Ruth Smock." She could still hear the lascivious voice in the receiver. "Then he asked me about the brands."

Ed, more awake, turned and watched his wife as she spoke.

"I didn't say anything," Ruth continued. "I just froze. Then he said he knew I still had them, and he asked me if I had any mental problems about it. He said he knew about the brands because he had the paper from Fort Scott. He said he'd send me the paper if I paid him some money, and he'd keep quiet about it."

Ed tried to process this information. "How much money?" he said helplessly.

"Didn't say. But can you imagine? Trying to get money to keep quiet about something everybody knows about?"

"Has he called back?"

"No."

Ed wanted to be reassuring. "Probably just some crank," he offered.

"It didn't seem worth bothering you about, not with what you were going through—the hospital and all," Ruth said.

"How about the police?"

"I don't see any reason for that. Do you?"

"Maybe if he calls again," Ed said.

"Maybe," said Ruth. But privately she thought, No way.

They lay in silence for several minutes. In her mind, Ruth could hear the crude obscenities of a man in overalls, the sound of his knife blade slapping against her bare thighs. She could almost feel the man's knee on her pelvic bone again and taste the handkerchief he'd shoved in her mouth. Lying in bed in Wichita three decades later, she felt again as if she was about to gag. She rose quickly to get herself moving and to clear her head.

Ed was puzzled and disturbed. Ruth had never talked much about the attack, even though he'd met her in the boardinghouse where it occurred. When they'd first started dating, Ed's friends had told him about the incident, which had received splashy publicity in Fort Scott, but the two times he had raised the subject with her she'd refused to discuss it. He'd never mentioned it again. There was no reason to, he figured. She never showed any signs that it bothered her. Their marriage was smooth, their lovemaking frequent and passionate.

How would anybody know where she was, Ed wondered, after all those years? Ruth had married, changed her name, and moved states.

Ed tried to tell himself that it was only a crank call. Some creep had taken a lucky shot.

He certainly hoped so. After twenty-eight years, Ed loved Ruth deeply, and he didn't want her to ever have to think about the terrifying Fort Scott assault again.

—⁓—

Ed was nineteen years old and freshly out of the navy when he'd first met Ruth.

By 1978, Ruth and Ed's life had settled into an inviolate routine. Ruth began the day by fixing cereal, juice, coffee, and English muffins while Ed read the newspaper. After breakfast she showered and dressed, and Ed helped her do the dishes. Then the couple climbed into their

Oldsmobile for the drive downtown. Ed dropped Ruth off at the Southwestern Bell building on North Broadway, where she worked as a clerk in the merchandising division, and then he drove to the Halsey-Tevis office.

When Ruth's shift was over, she would walk two blocks south to Henry's, a clothing store, where Ed would pick her up. After crawling home through the rush hour snarl, Ruth would fix dinner and serve one of her homemade pies for dessert. Then she and Ed would descend to the basement to work on their hobbies. Ruth, an early riser, would often crash out on the sofa while Ed, a night owl, stayed up watching *The Tonight Show* or classic movies.

Ruth's family had resettled in Wichita. Her sister, Jean, had moved to Wichita years after Ruth, and she had also taken a job with Southwestern Bell. They worked in the same building and met frequently for lunch and coffee. Ruth's mother, Fay, had moved to the city from Richards, Missouri after Ruth's father, Carl, had died in 1974. She lived alone in a large white house on English Street, east of downtown. Ruth did Fay's laundry every weekend and visited occasionally, but Fay always had the sense that her daughter didn't want to open up to her. It was hard to ever know what was really going on in Ruth's mind.

Habit had made Ruth's and Ed's lives serene and uncomplicated; it soothed them with its predictability.

But after that first call from the stranger demanding money, the telephone began to disturb their carefully curated peace. Often, it would ring but go dead when they picked it up—something that had never seemed to happen before. Other times there would be only silence on their end. Ed sometimes heard footsteps and voices echoing in the receiver, as if the call had been placed from a large hallway in a busy public building. Once, bursting with frustration, he whistled and shouted into the receiver for forty-five minutes, until a man came on the line and said, "This is the weirdest thing. I was just walking by and I seen this phone dangling here."

Ed thought the calls were the work of some solitary crank who would eventually lose interest and find someone else to harass. The calls were annoying but, to his way of thinking, nothing to worry about.

He would soon change his mind.

2

FANTASIES AND NIGHTMARES

Ed had come to Fort Scott, a bustling railroad town in southeast Kansas, to attend junior college on the GI Bill. He and a friend had moved into the boardinghouse where Ruth lived with her roommate in the fall of 1947. Ruth was beginning her senior year of high school, which was a young age to be living on her own. She had finally recovered from the previous year's assault; the bouts of vomiting were behind her, and she had learned to live with the taunts and snickers of her classmates. Ruth was shy and pretty, and Ed fell for her right away.

Ruth couldn't say the same. Ed was tall and gangly, with large, bulging eyes and an already receding hairline. And she knew all about servicemen. They had been raising hell at the junior college, which shared a building with the high school, since their victories over Germany and Japan.

When Ed asked Ruth out on a date, she surprised herself by accepting. She didn't know why, except that he seemed so kind. After her assault, dating had been the last thing on her mind.

Returning from their first date, Ruth and Ed agreed to stop seeing each other as long as they lived under the same roof. Their elderly landlady did not approve of that sort of thing. But Ed moved out in the spring to live with his widowed aunt who needed assistance, and he and Ruth began seeing each other regularly.

Ed often picked Ruth up after she had finished bowling with her high school team. Sometimes they went to the movies, but other times they went to the Land Inn, a south side bar that was popular with ex-servicemen. Ed had a wild streak, and he drank an impressive amount of beer while Ruth sipped Cokes. But Ed never became rowdy; it was simply not in his gentle nature. He was gallant to Ruth, in a way she had never before experienced. She was thrilled for Ed when he was elected student-body president at the junior college, after running on a platform that consisted almost entirely of a pledge to hold more parties.

In those days Ed was aimless, lacking goals and only in school because all his navy buddies had enrolled to take advantage of the GI Bill. But he was having the time of his life. Attending junior college was like being back in high school, except now he could legally drink. Fort Scott was a party town for ex-servicemen, and Ed conformed to the mold. Still, Ruth glimpsed in Ed's sincerity and inner intensity the potential to be much more.

After weeks of dating, Ruth wasn't sure how to sort out her feelings. She admired Ed, but she didn't know if she was in love with him. She was positive it wasn't the storybook love-at-first-sight she had witnessed in movies, at least. But given her assault the year before, she doubted she would ever feel that way with any man. She only knew that Ed was passionate about her, and she was surprised and pleased by how good that felt. It proved she wasn't dead to romance.

Following junior college, Ed attended Pittsburg State University in nearby Pittsburg, Kansas, in order to remain close to Ruth. He took business courses and earned strong grades. Ruth graduated high school and took a job in Fort Scott as a telephone company operator, a position she had started back in Richards when she was only thirteen.

In January 1950, Ed asked Ruth to marry him. She said yes right away, which both delighted and shocked him. Ed pointed out that he wasn't a great catch: He didn't have much money, and Ruth would need to keep working at the phone company in order for them to make it.

Ruth countered by asking Ed if he knew about her assault. She wanted to be up-front with him. Ed said he had heard something about it. "Fine," Ruth answered. "Just so you know."

They were married six months later in an informal ceremony at a Fort Scott Presbyterian church. Forty relatives and friends cheered them on. The reception was held at the Smock farm in nearby Richards.

Twenty-eight years later, one sweltering July afternoon, Ruth ended her shift and crossed a busy intersection in downtown Wichita on her way to Henry's to meet Ed. Broadway and Douglas was the city's most crowded intersection during rush hour; Ruth sometimes felt as if the entire population of Wichita was squeezed into the crosswalk with her. That day, as the commuters jostled to fit inside the white lines, Ruth felt a bump on her shoulder and heard a man's voice behind her.

"You've done such a good job working this week," the voice said. "You can take the weekend off."

Startled, Ruth spun around. The man was in his late forties, five feet nine and skinny, and he wore a plaid sport shirt, jeans, and white canvas shoes. His black hair was graying at the temples.

"You work for the phone company, don't you?" the man asked. Ruth turned around and kept walking, doing her best to ignore him, but he persisted. "What do you do there? Are you an operator?"

When Ruth didn't answer, the man told her he'd recently won some money in Las Vegas. "Would you like to go to Las Vegas sometime?"

Ruth held her silence and kept walking.

Switching conversational gears abruptly, the man announced, "The camera reflects the true quality of one's soul."

Ruth was both annoyed and frightened. "I'm waiting for my husband," she said. She hoped her voice sounded as icy as she intended, but she doubted it.

"Are you still married?" the man asked. When Ruth failed to respond, the man's tone grew menacing. "I like your face," he said.

His eyes twinkled for a moment and then went dead. "I'll see you again, you can count on that. Some people's fantasies are other people's nightmares." Then the man spun on his heel and strode off.

—⚋—

Ed listened as Ruth described the incident on their drive home. Though the phone call had happened several weeks earlier, Ed's first thought was that it must be the same man. Ruth wasn't sure. Smiling, trying to shrug it off, she said, "I think it was just some guy looking for a quick pickup." Ed, not wanting to alarm Ruth, let the subject go.

Still, Ruth watched for the man on her daily walk to Henry's. After two weeks, the man's face, which Ruth had assumed she would never forget, began to fade in her memory. Then an envelope addressed to her arrived at the phone company.

Two things about the writing on the envelope stood out to Ruth immediately: the large, clumsy letters looked like they had been printed by a child, and the *n* in her last name was backward.

When Ruth opened the envelope at her desk, a yellow scrap of newspaper fell out. It was the banner from the October 15, 1946, edition of the *Fort Scott Tribune*. Nothing else: no headline, no story. But Ruth got the message. She didn't need to reread the story of her teenage assault.

—⚋—

Ruth had just returned to her boardinghouse from buying groceries that long-ago night when she heard the screen door open behind her. A stranger's voice cried, "Hi, Sis! Why have you got all the lights burning?" Suddenly Ruth was grabbed from behind by a tall man who began tearing at her clothes. The intruder wore dirty bib overalls and looked about fifty years old. His left arm appeared maimed.

Struggling to break free, Ruth jabbed the man's eyes with her thumbs. Enraged, he pushed her down. "I'll fix you so no one will look at you again!" he spat. In one hand the man held a rag, which he shoved over Ruth's mouth and nose. The rag was apparently doused with chloroform; Ruth began to fade into unconsciousness. Her final hazy image before passing out was of the man heating a flatiron on the stove. When she awoke, she had first-degree burns on both thighs. Blood oozed from scratches on her face, arms, and legs.

What the article didn't mention, Ruth remembered, was how poorly the police had treated her at the boardinghouse that night. They were short with her and radiated the clear impression that she was lying. One officer had even reached out his foot and lifted her leg with his boot to inspect the wounds on her thighs. She heard the policemen mumbling that her knife wounds looked like light scratches from a bobby pin.

The *Tribune* had followed the case for several days, but Ruth didn't read the follow-up stories. By the time they were published, her mother had taken her back to the farm in Richards for privacy.

The *Tribune*'s second-day story had delved more deeply into Ruth's background. Miss Smock was a "quiet and unassuming, pretty brunette," the paper reported, "religious and . . . popular with her girl companions." An official at the phone company, where she worked after school, had praised her as a steady, conscientious employee.

The following day the *Tribune* reported that on the night of the attack, an upstairs tenant in the boardinghouse had gone outside to look for a paper at 6:00 p.m., and then done the same thing twenty-five minutes later, but had not seen anything unusual. A neighbor who was looking out their window at the time of the attack also saw nothing.

The Fort Scott police were having poor luck rounding up suspects. They had two reports of suspicious men with maimed left arms, but one man was dismissed after police learned his left leg was also impaired. The other man simply disappeared.

One of Ruth's aunts told the *Tribune* that Ruth had retracted her claim about her assailant's maimed arm. She now remembered the man wore leather gloves.

Four days after the attack, the *Tribune* ran a front-page photo of Ruth with the word "branded" underneath. Ruth's father, Carl, raised hell with the paper's editors for such a tasteless display.

The *Tribune* also reported that "rumors [were] floating thick and fast" about the boardinghouse attack. Doctors at the scene had not smelled any chloroform or anesthetic on Ruth, who had since said she must have simply fainted from shock. The police also told the newspaper that Ruth's shoes had been found "neatly arranged" under the stove, and the kitchen showed no signs of a struggle. Ruth's leg had been evenly slashed at one-inch intervals, the paper reported, "indicating the perpetrator was in no hurry in consummating the workmanlike task."

The police were frustrated. They had rounded up several convicted child molesters and window peepers, but all had solid alibis. They wanted to bring in the FBI. Meanwhile, Ruth was planning to return to the boardinghouse soon "in the belief that it is the only way to overcome her fear."

No arrest was ever made. The case had faded into memory, and Ruth had moved on with her life.

Thirty-two years later, in her office at Southwestern Bell, Ruth swept the yellowed *Tribune* banner into her top desk drawer so nobody would see it. After a week passed, she threw it in the trash.

—m—

Ruth and Ed did not want to involve the police or tell their family, friends, and neighbors. They continued to hope the problem would simply go away. They kept to their routine. Each weekday morning, Ed dropped Ruth at the phone company at 7:55 a.m. She left her office only for coffee breaks at 10:00 and 3:00, and for lunch at noon. She usually spent her breaks in the eighth-floor cafeteria with her sister, Jean, and a few friends. At five, Ruth would leave her office and walk to Henry's.

One day in late August, Ruth decided to do some shopping during her break. She walked to Macy's department store, across the street from Henry's, browsed the women's section, and then left the store via a revolving door that led into an adjacent alley. She was heading for the street when she felt a hand clutch her arm.

"Ruth!" a man's voice said in a loud, venomous whisper. Ruth tried to break free, but the man held on tight.

Ruth managed to pull loose and run back to the revolving door.

"Get back here, you stupid bitch!"

Frightened and disoriented, she pushed her way inside the store and then rode the escalator all the way to the fifth floor. Panting at the top of the escalator, she tried to collect herself. After a few minutes, she rode back down to the ladies' lounge on the first floor and called Ed from a pay phone. Glancing at her hand as she held the receiver, Ruth saw that her watchband was broken.

Ed knew the time had come to finally contact the police. He left work and drove to city hall on North Main Street, which housed the police department. Ed was bounced from desk to desk until an officer took his statement and promised to contact Ruth soon.

Ed and Ruth waited for days, but nobody called. Apparently the police were busy with more pressing matters, and they didn't consider Ruth's reported harassment a priority.

Finally, Ed suggested that Ruth try calling the police herself. Ruth was passed off to an officer who recommended she change her phone number and be extra careful when walking alone.

Ed was infuriated by this simpleminded advice. So much for the police, he thought.

—✺—

Three weeks later, on September 23, Ruth found a rolled-up sheet of paper stuck between the boards of the back porch. The paper contained a message that had been neatly stenciled on wide-lined notebook paper:

Fuck you, fuck the cops, fuck the tele. ofs. You all make me mad. I didn't no they would watch your phone for so long. You must have lie to them for I never say any bad things to you. I hope you are not dum enough to tell them about this note because in case you didn't no it, there is not wrong in sending a letter. You make me mad for you are a real snob-ass female to me. I saw you smile and talk to a nigger but you won't talk to me. I can make poems. Did you no that? I do them when I am mad. You should not make me mad. I want you to answer my question about the brand. In all my collection that is the only one like that.

When Ed showed the letter to Police Lieutenant Bernie Drowatzky in the Major Crimes office on the fifth floor of city hall, he felt reassured that Ruth's case was finally in the right hands. Drowatzky was compact and tough, with powerful shoulders and thick forearms. His dark, sunken eyes gazed evenly from a deeply scarred face. His thinning black hair was combed back slickly with product. Drowatzky looked like a gangster, and yet Ed found his presence soothing.

Ruth, however, felt apprehensive as she settled into a chair next to Drowatzky's desk. Despite the threatening letter, she still had not wanted to contact the police. "They'll just accuse me like they did in Fort Scott," she told Ed.

"Nonsense," he had responded. The police in Wichita would be more professional than those in her small town. At last Ruth had relented. Now she watched uneasily as Drowatzky read the letter.

When Drowatzky finally looked up, his face was unreadable. He showed only the cool detachment of a veteran police officer.

"You know why anybody would be so angry with you, Mrs. Finley?" he asked.

Ruth shook her head.

"He says he wants to know about a brand. What's that all about?"

Ruth glanced at Ed, who nodded. She told Drowatzky the story of the 1946 assault.

Drowatzky listened impassively, sizing up the couple in front of him. The Finleys looked like your average middle-aged couple, he thought. Solid people, good citizens. Ruth was attractive. She must have been a knockout in her younger days.

Ed's appearance was more unusual. His head was almost completely bald, with large eyes that seemed to bug out of his skull. But he was pleasant and friendly. Salt-of-the-earth type, Drowatzky thought.

Both Ruth and Ed seemed nervous, but Drowatzky knew this was common in law-abiding people who were asking for help.

When Ruth was finished, Drowatzky asked bluntly, "Were you raped?"

Taken aback, Ruth replied, "No."

She and Ed told Drowatzky about the other events that summer: the phone call, the run-ins with the man downtown, the newspaper banner in the mail.

Drowatzky asked about former boyfriends or high school classmates who might have been warped enough to develop a fixation on her brands. Ruth said she had known strange kids, but she was positive she had never seen this man before.

Drowatzky handed Ruth his business card and stood up, signaling the meeting's end. "Usually people like this disappear," he told the Finleys as he walked them from his office. "I'll put a couple of men on it, and one of them will call you soon. Try to think back on people you knew in Fort Scott. Don't worry about this too much."

―⚭―

After the Finleys left, Drowatzky returned to his desk and stared at the letter. For a moment, he allowed himself to think about the BTK serial killer, who had been stalking Wichita since 1974. Drowatzky had been fighting the urge to become obsessive about the BTK case, but the Finleys' letter had him wondering. He hoped he had kept his face neutral in front of Ruth and Ed.

BTK—which stood for Bind, Torture, Kill, the serial murderer's self-appointed code name—had also written letters. They were typed, not handwritten, and bragging of murder, complete with vivid and accurate descriptions of his horrifying deeds. But madness could take many forms, Drowatzky knew from his years on the force. Maybe BTK had more than one personality. Or maybe he had decided to focus his attention on a single victim. Maybe he had somehow heard about Ruth's brands and become obsessed with them. He had stalked his prey before, trailing them, learning their habits before he killed them. But he had never tipped his hand. He wrote his letters only after he murdered someone. Ruth Finley was still very much alive.

Drowatzky sighed, frustrated. The case weighed on the entire department. Drowatzky headed the special team investigating BTK, and his inability to solve the case haunted him. When had the police last heard from BTK? February? Almost a year ago. BTK had thrown the city of Wichita into a panic from which it, understandably, had yet to recover.

Ruth and Ed, however, had not paid much attention to BTK. The story was disturbing, of course, but they generally ignored it, neither one having interest in the gory details. Their street and neighborhood were safe, and they couldn't imagine BTK intruding on their suburban sanctum.

3

THE DETECTIVE AND THE SERIAL KILLER

The brutal killings had started on January 15, 1974. BTK murdered four members of the Otero family, who had only recently moved to Wichita from Puerto Rico: Joseph Sr., 38; Julia, 33; Joseph, 9; and Josephine, 11. The killer then masturbated while watching Josephine's body dangle from a noose in the basement.

After the murders, the police had received a letter that stated, "I can't stop it so the monster goes on and hurt more as well. It a big complicated game my friend of the monster play putting victims down, follow them, checking up on them, waiting in the dark, waiting, waiting . . . Maybe you can stop him. I can't. He has already chosen his next victim or victims . . . The code words for me will be 'Bind them, torture them, kill them,' BTK, you see he at it again. They will be on the next victim."

Three years passed before BTK was heard from again. This message was a poem on a three-by-five card that began, "Shirleylocks, Shirleylocks." It had been sent to the *Wichita Eagle and Beacon* newspaper, but the poem was never printed. The sorters in the paper's mail room assumed it was a Valentine's Day poem meant to run in the personals, but since the sender had not included a name or address, the paper had no way to bill them. The card contained the initials BTK, but that reference failed to register with the sorters, given the years that had passed since his last communication.

BTK was furious with the paper for not printing his poem. He next sent a letter to a local station, KAKE-TV, in which he complained about the newspaper's slight. He also described what he called the "Factor X" inside of him, comparing it to the monster that triggered the murderous impulses of the Son of Sam killer in New York City and the Hillside Strangler in Los Angeles. And he claimed credit for two more murders: that of twenty-five-year-old Nancy Jo Fox, who had been found in her bedroom with a nylon stocking around her neck on December 9, 1977, and Shirley Vian, twenty-six, who had been found in March 1977 with a plastic bag over her head and a cord around her neck.

The police obtained leads from both murders. Someone had called from a pay phone to tip them off about Nancy Jo Fox shortly after her murder. The call had been placed through an operator to the police dispatcher, so it was recorded by an automatic trapping device. But the police didn't know that the caller was BTK. When they got the letter, they listened to the recording again; the tape had been too garbled to air on radio or TV for possible identification by the public.

Shirley Vian's three young children had actually seen the murderer, whom they described as a paunchy, dark-haired male between thirty and forty years old. The killer had locked the children in the bathroom before strangling their mother. They had seen him up close, but the children's young ages, combined with the trauma they had suffered, made it difficult for the police to evaluate the reliability of their description.

BTK's letter ended by taunting the police, asking them to figure out who else he had killed. The four Oteros, Fox, and Vian made six victims. BTK claimed he'd killed seven. Allegedly there was another victim between Fox and Vian.

Studying their files of unsolved murders, the police settled on the case of nineteen-year-old Karen Bright, which had similarities with the other killings BTK had claimed. There was one significant difference: Karen Bright had been stabbed, not strangled. Still, the Bright murder seemed the most likely possibility.

Wichita Police Chief Richard LaMunyon held a news conference to inform the public of BTK's return. He appealed for both caution and information. A BTK trademark—one of the few the police shared with the public—was his habit of cutting the phone lines outside his victims' houses before he entered. LaMunyon also established a task force of police investigators to hunt for the killer. Street patrols were beefed up to reassure residents, and work on all nonviolent crime was halted so that as many officers as possible were available to field the hundreds of calls that poured into a BTK hotline.

The city's residents were terrified. Baseball bats were hauled from closets. Locks were checked and double-checked. Gun sales skyrocketed. Every night, people checked their phones to make sure their lines hadn't been cut. In the days following LaMunyon's press conference, if a Wichita resident picked up a receiver and didn't hear a dial tone, they reported it to the police department instead of to the telephone company.

Despite the deluge of calls, the police received no substantial leads. The hundreds of tips and rumors regarding strange neighbors and coworkers and relatives all dead-ended in a wash of misinformation and speculation.

Drowatzky was the lead detective on the case, and his failure to catch BTK grew more painful with each passing month. Ed Finley's initial impression of him as a tough, no-nonsense officer had been accurate; Drowatzky was tenacious and possessed a fiery temper. Failure infuriated him. Born in Wichita, Drowatzky had grown up in Blackwell, Oklahoma. After an unfulfilling year at the University of Oklahoma, Drowatzky dropped out to join the air force. He then returned to Blackwell and became part of the police force. He served eleven years in nearby Ponca City before relocating to Wichita in 1966. His twelve-year career with the Wichita Police Department had been marked by success, his heroic endeavors praised. He was one of the most respected and decorated officers on the force.

—⁓—

Over the years, Drowatzky had learned to control his temper and use it to his advantage, but his early years were marked by fights with suspects in the "asshole" bars where they hung out. He knew most of the robbers and druggies by name, but he seemed unable to arrest them without first getting into a brawl. His superiors disapproved. Drowatzky eventually realized that he would never advance in rank until he kept his violence in check, which he managed through sheer bulldog determination.

In 1968, Drowatzky's first wife took their two children and ran off with a car thief. Drowatzky took a leave of absence from the Wichita force and spent eight months tracking the runaways through the dive bars of Texas and Mexico before locating them in El Paso. He arrested the thief and offered his wife plane fare back to Oklahoma. When she refused, he picked up his two children and took them home to Wichita. His wife had kidnapped the kids; Drowatzky kidnapped them back.

Upon his return, Drowatzky made detective in 1969, worked in vice for two years, and then requested a transfer to the special investigative unit that handled major crimes. In 1973, a routine missing persons case he had been assigned to ended up being a murder case. He tracked down the killer and compiled enough evidence to convict him not only of that murder but of three other murders committed ten years earlier. That same year, he smashed an interstate fake credit card ring. Drowatzky was named Officer of the Year.

Three years later, Drowatzky and a sheriff's officer were working a hostage situation in which a man had been holding his wife and four children at gunpoint in their home in Haysville, just south of Wichita. Drowatzky and the officer voluntarily gave themselves up as hostages to protect the family. For five hours, the man screamed and raved to them about society's injustices. Drowatzky was convinced he was going to die. Finally, the man walked in front of a window, where he was hit by a sharpshooter's bullet. Drowatzky leaped on the man as he fell, sliding across the floor on his expiring body. For his efforts, Drowatzky received the department's highest award, the Gold Medal of Honor, which had not been bestowed on an officer in thirty years.

—∞—

At age forty-nine, Drowatzky was a more settled individual than he'd been in his youth. Drowatzky's second marriage was considerably happier. Investigative work challenged him, and he enjoyed nothing better than cracking unsolved cases and seeing them through trial. His inability to resolve the BTK case pained him deeply.

With the Finleys' visit, Drowatzky now had another sick and twisted letter on his hands. On the surface there weren't many similarities between BTK and the man who was threatening Ruth, but still . . . what if? He knew madness could mutate into more malignancies than he could imagine.

Drowatzky reread the letter one more time and then placed it in a drawer.

For a town this size, he thought bitterly, we sure have our fair share of assholes.

—∞—

As the weeks following the meeting with Drowatzky passed without incident, Ed felt greater peace of mind knowing he had taken the initiative to get help for Ruth. He was sure she must be more bothered by the harassment than she'd let on. Ed thought she was handling the situation well, much better than he would have if somebody had been stalking him for no obvious reason. Ruth rarely talked about the harassment, and when she did, she often chuckled, seemingly finding the man's obsession with her amusing. It was Ruth's way to be humorously self-deprecating; in fact, it was one of the qualities that had first drawn him to her. He loved the twinkle in her eye when she talked about herself and the girlish giggle that inevitably followed. Still, he knew Ruth well enough to see past that, and he believed she must be anxious and upset inside.

In truth, Ruth *was* upset, and she was far less certain than Ed that her stalker would eventually lose interest. A little over a month since the letter on the porch, on November 3, she received another letter. The opening lines were written with a stencil, the remainder printed in a childish scrawl: "I won't be caught in yur goddam trap. I need some money. I will get in touch with you before the end of the year."

4

THE ABDUCTION

Later, Ruth would not remember anything unusual about the morning of November 21. She typed letters for the phone company, did payroll work, paid checks for expense vouchers, and paid company bills. She enjoyed this type of busy morning. The merchandising department was a happy place: good people, good friends, satisfying work. It was a close-knit office. Most of her colleagues were married women like herself, with children and husbands to joke about. One of these colleagues was retiring that day, and Ruth needed to sneak out after lunch to buy a card for the retirement party.

Her coworkers reminded her that it was cold, damp, and misty out. Ruth wore sandals, black slacks, a black pullover sweater, and a red vest. Not the warmest outfit, but the card store was only a short walk away. She rode the elevator to the lobby and stepped out into the frosty afternoon at 2:00 p.m.

—m—

Two and a half hours later, Ed received a call in his office from one of Ruth's coworkers.

"Had Ruth planned to take any time off today?" the friend asked.

"No," Ed said.

"Have you heard from her?"

"No. What's up?"

"Well, we're hunting high and low for her. We're turning the place upside down."

Ed felt a chill. His wife was a responsible, diligent employee, and she would never simply disappear from the office. When he learned she had been missing for hours, his stomach seized. Fear turned to panic as Ed thought about the man who had been stalking Ruth. Still clutching the receiver but no longer listening to the voice on the other end, Ed had the sickening feeling that Ruth was dead.

He thanked the caller and hung up. Then he picked up the phone again and dialed Drowatzky's number. The detective was out, but one of the officers Drowatzky had assigned to the case, Richard Zortman, was in. Ed told Zortman the news. Zortman told Ed to sit tight.

"Drive by where you usually pick her up," Zortman urged Ed thirty minutes later. "Maybe she's there. If not, swing by the phone company and see if she's waiting there. If she isn't there either, go home and give me a call."

Ed drove his Oldsmobile through the slow-moving downtown traffic to Henry's, pausing in front of the south entrance where he met Ruth every day. She wasn't there. Ed's nausea increased.

He drove north to the phone company, feeling little hope. Ruth wasn't waiting there, either. Ed turned around and made the slow drive home, feeling lonelier than he had ever felt in his life. He held out the slight hope that Ruth would be waiting when he arrived at their house. No such luck.

Overwhelmed by despair, Ed phoned Zortman. The detective reported that a check of local hospitals had also failed to locate Ruth.

Ed phoned Ruth's sister, Jean Jones, who also worked at the phone company, but Jean knew nothing of Ruth's whereabouts. He phoned his boss, Dan Tevis, to explain the situation. Tevis rushed over to help Ed stand vigil; Jean and her husband, Bill, followed close behind. This was the first time in their twenty-eight-year marriage that Ed did not know Ruth's exact location.

—⚉—

In late December, after Ruth and Ed married, Ed drove to Wichita to look for work. He quickly landed a job as an accountant at Beech Aircraft. He disliked the notion of being a cog in such a large machine, but, remembering the Depression and the long breadlines outside his father's drugstore in Kansas City, he took it. He was terrified of unemployment.

Ed and Ruth drove to Wichita in an exhaust fume–filled 1939 Dodge and rented an apartment for seventy-five dollars a month. The phone company offered to transfer Ruth's operator job.

Children followed soon after: Brent Finley was born in 1952, after which Ruth quit her job, and another son, Bruce, arrived two years later. The family moved into their brand-new house on East Indianapolis in 1957. When they had agreed to purchase it the previous year, the lot was nothing more than a hole in the ground.

Ed eventually landed a job at the specialty contracting firm of Halsey-Tevis, where he was the chief bookkeeper, secretary, treasurer, and accountant. At Beech, Ed had hated working in a large room full of desks and people and noisy machines. He loved keeping the books for the much smaller Halsey-Tevis. It was like recording the firm's history in numbers.

Ed and Ruth became active in church, school, and Boy Scouts. Ruth was a homeroom mother at Stearman Elementary, just one block south of their house, as well as a den mother. Once Brent entered high school and Bruce junior high, Ruth returned to work, eager to earn money for the boys' college and anxious to leave the house after so many years of full-time mothering.

Ruth could not imagine two sons more different than Brent and Bruce. Brent, who became a resident in obstetrics and gynecology at the

University of Kansas Medical School, was studious and withdrawn. He had excelled in school and graduated magna cum laude from Wichita State University with degrees in mechanical engineering and chemistry.

Brent was a tough act for Bruce to follow in school. Teachers couldn't avoid making comparisons, with Bruce on the losing end. Ruth attended countless parent-teacher conferences in which the theme was the same: Bruce just wasn't the student his brother had been. Bruce hated school.

But Bruce was lovable and endearing. He was outgoing and fun. He took chances. Bruce was the Boy Scout who always came back from camping trips with poison ivy. He broke his arm once jumping off a stack of bricks onto his bicycle. The cast was barely off when he impaled his leg on a stick he had been throwing to knock leaves out of trees. Ruth and Ed loved both their sons dearly, and through their ups and downs together, Ruth and Ed always felt solid, like a pair of pillars holding up their family unit. One could not work without the other. When Ruth went missing, Ed felt his entire existence toppling.

—⁓—

Earlier that afternoon, after buying her colleague a retirement card, Ruth had been crossing North Market Street on her way back to the phone company when her path was suddenly blocked by a blue-green 1964 Chevrolet Bel Air that came screeching to the curb. The only other person in sight was an elderly woman far up the street.

Ruth froze in horror as the same man from outside Macy's leaped from the car. This time he wore wire-rimmed glasses, a jean jacket, and a sweater. "Have you got my money?" he asked.

"No," Ruth said, backing away. The man grabbed her arm.

"Forget it," he said, delivering a sharp kick to her shin. Ruth folded over in pain, and the man shoved her into the car's tattered, junk-filled back seat. He climbed in next to her and slammed the door. "Let's go get it," he said.

In the driver's seat another man was swigging from a bottle wrapped in a paper bag. Ruth's attacker called him "Buddy." Ruth looked frantically for a means of escape, but the door handle on her side was broken. On the floor she saw a red gas can, pieces of concrete, chains, rags, and a board. The car's rear left window was covered with plastic, and the torn-up dashboard was crisscrossed with white tape. A white terry cloth sat on the front seat.

Ruth's abductor told her to give him her purse. Pawing through it, he found twenty-seven dollars in cash, Ruth's paycheck from the phone company, her checkbook, and the key to her safe deposit box at First National Bank. "We've struck it rich!" the man cried. But his mood turned grim as he came across Drowatzky's business card, which he showed to Buddy. Cursing, he picked up a chunk of concrete from the floor and slammed it into Ruth's head. "You damn stupid bitch!" he said. "You've been to the cops. I'll get you for this." Dazed, Ruth collapsed in her seat. "You notice I didn't hit you with my hand," the man said.

The car sped off, heading northwest, then pulled into the Farmers Market and turned back in the other direction. The two men jabbered back and forth so rapidly that Ruth found it difficult to follow their conversation. Her abductor made up nonsense poems: "Bernie bee, Bernie bee," went one. At a certain point Buddy stopped at Twin Lakes Shopping Center and yammered on about Sears's inability to properly fix his car. "We'll get rid of her, but not here," her abductor said at another time, sending an added jolt of fear through an already terrified Ruth. She thought of the Mace can she always kept hidden at the bottom of her purse, but she felt too scared to reach for it.

Outside the car, the weather grew colder as the afternoon turned to dusk and then night. Buddy continued driving a seemingly random route around the city. "Do you like beer?" Her abductor leered. "We'll get some beer and have a party. I'll be real nice to you." He told her—as he had on the phone—that he had found the 1946 article about her attack at an old construction site.

At one point Buddy drove too fast over a bump in the road, and Ruth's abductor cursed at him. "Can't you see where you're going?" he yelled. "You shouldn't be driving. You're going to wreck Frank's car. He's going to be mad, and he won't let us have the car anymore!"

Finally, four hours into her ordeal, Ruth summoned the courage to speak. "I have to pee," she said, but the men just laughed. Ruth forced herself to gag. "I'm going to throw up if I don't go to the restroom!" she said.

"You won't do that," Ruth's abductor replied, but he told Buddy to stop next to a small park near West Twenty-First Street and Salina.

"This is going to be fun," Ruth's abductor said as he escorted her into the park. "I'll watch you, and you'll watch me. Don't that sound like fun?" Ruth, walking next to him, dug her hand inside her purse until she found her can of Mace.

When they reached a little lake, the man let go of Ruth's arm, saying he would pee first. He made her remove her sandals and sweater so she wouldn't run away. As the man unzipped his fly, Ruth withdrew her can of Mace and pressed the nozzle, aiming it at the man's face. The man collapsed, coughing, as Ruth bolted off into the park.

Spotting a large bush behind which she could hide, Ruth crouched, fearful and shivering, listening for the sounds of the man tracking her. "You'll freeze if we leave you here!" she heard the man shout. "Come get your shoes and your sweater, and we won't bother you anymore!"

Though her feet were turning numb from the cold, Ruth stayed crouched in the dark until long after the man stopped shouting. When her numb feet and aching body grew overwhelming, she scrambled to the top of a small rise. Looking down, she couldn't find the men's car anywhere. Had they driven off?

Exiting the park, Ruth dashed into a liquor store across Twenty-First Street. "Someone's after me," she told the store's owner between gasping breaths.

The owner immediately called the police. "Please, can you call my husband too?" Ruth asked him.

At 7:00 p.m., the phone in Ed and Ruth's kitchen rang. "I've got your wife here," said a man's voice on the other end.

"You let me talk to her!" Ed shouted into the receiver.

"Yes, sir," the man responded, sounding rattled. "Just a minute."

Ruth was crying when she came on the line. She told Ed that she was at a liquor store in the northwest part of the city.

"Stay there. I'm on my way," Ed said. He was so relieved that Ruth was alive that he forgot to ask her what had happened.

Bill Jones, his brother-in-law, drove him to the liquor store, which was twenty minutes away. By the time they arrived, the police had already taken her downtown, the store owner reported. Bill grabbed Ed's arm and the two men sped to city hall.

Ed found Ruth in an interview room in the Criminal Investigations Bureau (CIB) on the building's fifth floor. Her appearance at once frightened and angered him. She was wet and her clothes were disheveled and soiled. She wore no shoes. Her hair clung like tentacles to her head. Her face was scratched and her right cheek was already showing a swollen bruise. She gripped a Mace can in one white-knuckled hand.

Whoever did this to her is going to pay, Ed thought.

Ruth managed a weak smile when she spotted him. She stood, but as Ed reached out to hug her, Ruth broke into sobs. The two held each other for a long moment, ignoring Drowatzky and Zortman, who had entered the room to take Ruth's statement. Ed felt his wife's arms tight around him, the familiar feel of her waist in his arms, her tears on his neck. Ruth was hurt, but she was alive.

—⁂—

After Ed and Ruth left city hall, Detective Zortman drove to the park on Twenty-First Street where she had escaped. He found Ruth's sandals and sweater exactly where she reported having left them, about sixty feet into the trees. Returning to the station, Zortman told Drowatzky that everything was as Ruth had described.

Zortman and Detective George Anderson—the other officer Drowatzky had assigned to the case—spent the next several days sitting in an unmarked car near the phone company, on a stakeout to catch the man Ruth had described. They also made repeated circuits through the Twin Lakes area looking for a blue-green 1964 Chevrolet Bel Air.

Both Zortman and Anderson were experienced and respected investigators. The forty-three-year-old Zortman had been on the force for seventeen years and had once tracked down a rapist who had been haunting Wichita's east side for two years.

Anderson, thirty-nine, had spent fifteen years with the WPD. He'd joined the Criminal Investigations Bureau one year earlier, taking over the BTK case after the murder of Nancy Jo Fox. Both he and Zortman possessed gentle natures but were fiercely determined when it came to solving cases. They had risen to the elite investigative unit through endless hours of dogged work. They also had the patience required to sit in a car for days on end as they sought Ruth's abductor.

During those long hours, the two detectives kicked around some of the questions raised by Ruth's account. When her kidnappers had parked at the Twin Lakes shopping mall, a bustling area on any afternoon, why hadn't Ruth screamed for help? "I guess I just didn't think about it," she'd said during the interview the night of her abduction.

—⁂—

Ruth and Ed spent Thanksgiving Day at Jean's house, surrounded by Ruth's family—her mother, her brother, Morris, and his wife and children. Any mention of Ruth's abduction was studiously avoided at the table. Turkey and trimmings were devoured amid the polite chatter.

The siblings took their lead from Ruth. As the children of a hardworking, devoutly Christian farm couple, Ruth, Jean, and Morris had been taught that no load was too heavy to carry by yourself, if you accepted God's help. If Ruth didn't want to talk about her abduction, her siblings trusted that she could handle it. (Ruth and Ed had not told their own children because they didn't want to worry them.)

Their mother, Fay, wasn't sure what to do. She hadn't known about Ruth's problems until after the kidnapping, and the whole situation bewildered her. Sitting at the dinner table, Fay noticed a large black bruise on Ruth's temple and scratch marks on her right arm. They reminded her of how Ruth had looked after her attack in Fort Scott.

Ruth had kept to herself about that incident, too, Fay recalled. She'd kept waiting for her daughter to say something, but Ruth never wanted to talk about it. She was just like her father, Carl—they both kept everything inside. As Fay saw it, Ruth was in God's hands, like everyone else, and God's will would prevail.

Fay Smock believed deeply in that sentiment. Her own parents had taught her the same thing. Fay had passed it to her children and, as a schoolteacher, to her students in Missouri.

In contrast to her brother and sister, who could both be a handful, Ruth almost never got in trouble—she was the perfect one in the family. Fay's family, the Duncans, doted on Ruth and thought the world would be a better place if there were more children like her. Fay could remember Ruth swearing only once as a child, right after she had finished sweeping the house. As Ruth was fetching the dustpan, Jean and Morris had scattered the dirt pile back over the floor. When Ruth returned and saw the mess, she uttered an oath so mild that Fay could no longer even remember what it was.

Though she didn't press the subject, Fay watched Ruth closely during the Thanksgiving meal. As always, she found it hard to read her sweet, affable daughter.

Ed was used to his wife's family. While he found their passive attitude puzzling, he kept quiet at the Thanksgiving dinner, too.

Inside, Ed was battered by feelings of helpless rage. He had considered buying a handgun. He had hunted as a child, but his collection of rifles was just mounted for show at home; he had never intended to shoot them, nor had he thought about purchasing a handgun until now.

Ed reminded himself of something Zortman had told him after Ruth's kidnapping. Zortman believed her kidnappers would flee town now that they knew the police were involved. "Boy, if that was me," Zortman said, "I'd be across the Mexican border by now."

In reality, Zortman and the other detectives weren't counting on Ruth's kidnappers having fled. After a week of searching for the kidnappers' car, Anderson drove 158 miles east to Fort Scott. He hoped to locate construction sites where Ruth's abductor might have been working when he found the 1946 newspaper article. He also wanted to learn exactly what had happened to Ruth in that boardinghouse.

When Anderson learned that the boardinghouse had been torn down recently to make room for a bank, he thought he'd caught a break. Maybe this man had worked on the site. But the contractor could not remember any employee who matched the description of the assailant.

More disappointment awaited Anderson at the Fort Scott police department. No records still existed of the investigation into the 1946 assault.

There was only one senior officer who remembered the case. After probing the officer for details, Anderson asked if anybody had suspected Ruth of making up the story. Could she have shoved the flaming-hot iron against her own leg and cut herself up?

Sure, that had been a popular theory for the first few days, the officer said, but he didn't think Ruth was the culprit.

"Why not?" asked Anderson.

"We had a pretty good suspect," the old man said. "He was a transient. We'd picked him up before. People had seen the guy in the neighborhood just before Ruth got home that night. Never could prove nothing. But we kept an eye on him. Lived in a nursing home here until a while back. Dead now."

Three weeks after Thanksgiving, on December 12, Ruth received another letter in her mailbox: "You acted OK in the car. I am glad you not tell on me & that is because you didn't want to get me in trouble. I like you for that, but you were mean. You will go home with me next time & maybe we could cash the check. You get paid pretty much for a female . . . How many brands do you have."

The Finleys turned the letter over to Drowatzky, who had just received his own letter from Ruth's stalker:

> *Bernie Bee, Bernie Bee*
> *Friend to all females is he.*
> *One thing is plain to see*
> *I don't like you & you don't like me.*
> *No dum female can make a fool out of me.*
> *Something else I ought to do:*
> *Hold her under water & watch face turn blue*

Downtown Wichita had long possessed a steady crop of transients who filled the lobbies of its aging hotels and bars, as well as two parks that provided grassy refuge from the pavement. As the autumn of 1978 wound to a close, Zortman went undercover with this roughshod group. With the weather growing increasingly icy, Zortman prowled the bars, hotel lobbies, and public library looking for men matching Ruth's description. But the description was so vague—a man of average build with dark hair graying at the temples—that many of the men he saw matched it in some way. When pedestrian traffic was heavy, Zortman's eyes couldn't keep up with the passing suspects. He would snap his head back and forth as if he was being manipulated by some mad puppeteer.

Zortman sometimes followed men who fit the description for blocks, hoping to find out where they lived. But mostly he walked and watched, the frigid Kansas wind cutting through the thin garments of his transient's disguise.

Ruth and Ed, meanwhile, stayed cozy in their basement. Ruth spent time filling her kiln with clay figures, or sewing, while Ed painted with acrylics. He preferred them to oils or watercolor, finding the results more vivid and clean. Ed liked things that way: neat, clean, tidy.

He liked anything he put on paper—including his accounting work at Halsey-Tevis—to be immaculate. He liked paintings that were neat and easy to understand. He liked music that had a recognizable melody, and he liked books that told a straightforward story.

The basement walls were lined with his paintings. These were landscapes depicting images of rural tranquility, scenes he'd sketched on vacations in Colorado, and a few that were drawn from the memory of his childhood. One was of a farmhouse with a barn and a river and a stone bridge, set deep in a field of snow. Another showed the Rocky Mountains and a river as seen from one of his favorite fishing holes in Gunnison, Colorado. Another was of a ghost town near Aspen.

But Ed's favorite was a painting he had recently hung at the foot of the stairs leading down from the kitchen. It was of a large, one-lane suspension bridge. The foreground was dominated by a pickup truck and a man and boy walking toward a riverbank with their backs to the viewer. In the background, a dirt road wound up a hill and disappeared over the rise. Sunflowers, trees with green leaves, and a pale blue sky filled the rest of the canvas.

He and Ruth often drove over that same bridge on visits to Missouri. The road was pocked and rutted, and the bridge's corrugated metal underside rattled noisily as cars rolled over it. It was only four miles from the farmhouse where Ruth was raised.

—∿—

As the holiday season approached, Ruth began to feel more secure. Ed, who never again wanted to experience the acute sense of loss he had felt on the day of the abduction, kept a keen watch over her, but Ruth didn't chafe under his vigilance. Instead, she found it comforting.

January and February 1979 passed without incident. Ruth, Ed, and the police began to entertain the notion that Ruth's ordeal was over.

Then, on March 3, Ruth's stalker broke his silence with another letter:

There once was a girl name Smock
Whose door she forgot to lock
& if she don't pay like I say, your head can be under a rock
Changes wrought on body & face
if my demands are not embraced
Against your knife scarred breast a tender male hand might
be pressed
to ease bad memories in your mind
—all the blood & pain of passed years left behind.
Over the meadow or in the grass
Bernie will protect the females ass
Bernie, Bernie go away
Cut & brand teach girls that don't want to play.

The letter was written in pencil on wide-lined notebook paper. The *n*'s were backward, as usual, and some of the misspellings were the same as in other letters, but the police could find little that would help them speed up the investigation.

Detectives hadn't found prints on the letters, and the twisted Mother Goose–like verses, although eerie and scary, didn't provide any clues that would move them closer to identifying a suspect.

The author's central themes were getting old. He wanted money from Ruth to keep quiet about the brands; he was paranoid about the police and the phone company; he loved taunting Drowatzky. He had written about trying to get Ruth to give him money again but hadn't made a move against her since the kidnapping in November, even though he supposedly needed money urgently.

The kidnapping hadn't left the police with much, either. Nearly four months later, and the car still hadn't been found, even though it was distinctively marked with tape and a rear window covered by a plastic sheet. Nor could police find anyone who had witnessed the abduction or seen the car at Twin Lakes. Nobody had seen a beat-up vehicle with two men and a woman sitting inside in the middle of the afternoon at a crowded shopping mall.

5

THE REAPPEARANCE

As March gave way to April and the kidnapping incident receded into the past, interest in the case within the Criminal Investigations Bureau continued to decrease. Drowatzky, Zortman, and Anderson had trouble finding time to work on it as more-pressing cases were dumped in their laps. They continued to care about Ruth—Drowatzky had learned that he attended the same church as the Finleys and felt even closer to them now—but priority had to be given to matters of greater urgency.

Ruth's case faded into the background and almost disappeared.

Then two events shoved it back into the foreground. The first was a letter, the second a third-rate burglary.

The letter was sent to the city's newspaper, the *Wichita Eagle and Beacon*, on April 3, 1979. It was addressed only to the "Crime Ed." Because the paper had no crime editor as such, the envelope was opened by a newsroom assistant who sorted the mail and made decisions about where improperly addressed mail should be delivered.

This letter appeared to be the work of a crank. Inside the envelope was a short note asking the paper to pass another enclosed envelope to "Lt. Bernie." Inside that envelope were several sheets of wide-lined notebook paper. The printing was in pencil. Part of it was traced with a stylus; the rest was scrawled freehand in childish letters. The message, in poetry, made no sense to the editors because the Finley letters, not to mention the entire Finley case, had not been made public. But the editors had seen BTK's poetry, and they were immediately struck by the similarity. They quickly delivered the envelopes to the police department.

Drowatzky was furious when he learned the newspaper had opened the envelope addressed to him. It contained three drawings of streets that were identified by name, perhaps indicating where the man would strike next, and a poem in rhyming couplets that made obvious references to BTK. In short, the letter was a bombshell. Drowatzky hated that the media had seen it first.

The letter was clearly from Ruth Finley's attacker. "I have tried to get in touch with you," it began. "I don't like surprise." The street diagrams were titled Plan 1, Plan 2, and Plan 3. The first showed two streets marked Amidon and Waco, the area where Ruth's abductors had taken her on November 21. Plan 2 was a drawing of two parallel streets, Woodlawn and Rock Road, on the other side of town. Plan 3 showed a single straight line marked "54 E.," indicating the highway that ran just north of the Finleys' street.

The poem began:

> In the long run, fame finds deserving man
> Whether in bus or van.
> If any had a brain
> No one would have pain.
> I unnoticed go my way
> I may just prosper for 1 day.

The next part made Drowatzky's neck prickle:

> For someone you might be searching I will guide.
> Some have parts of bodies broken
> Before words of greeting can be spoken.

How fast time flies.
You should look at people's eyes.
Some try to get out of sight.
It's easy when there is no light.

BTK had not been heard from in more than a year. Was he finally making contact? The letter concluded: "Police protect bitches too much, I think. They should work on robberies & things more. I told you in the mail I don't like police or females or the tele. ofs. They cheat people all they can & they won't listen to yur side & some of them don't even anser."

Drowatzky would have loved to answer this guy. Just send me your address, pal, he thought. But his first job was to handle the reporters who had brought him the letter—after blasting their bosses for reading it first.

No, he told the reporters, this is not BTK. This is just some man harassing a woman. Anyone could read the papers and write a letter pretending to be BTK. The author probably just wanted some attention. There was no connection.

Privately, he was far less sure of that.

—⁂—

Less than a month later, BTK reappeared. On April 28, a sixty-three-year-old woman returned from a square dance to her home on South Pinecrest and discovered she had been robbed. A few articles of clothing, some inexpensive jewelry, and thirty-five dollars in cash were missing. But several odd things about the robbery stood out to her: A clothesline had been brought upstairs from the basement, and the telephone line had been cut. She knew enough about BTK to know the significance of a clothesline and severed telephone wires. She phoned the police from a neighbor's house.

At the time, the Wichita Police Department operated on a team-policing concept. The city was divided into six quadrants, with teams of detectives and street patrolmen assigned to each quadrant. The unit that investigated major crimes in the city—murders, rapes, robberies, aggravated assaults—was a separate entity. Burglaries, like the one on South Pinecrest, were handled by the teams.

Two months later, in June, BTK wrote another letter. This time, there was no doubt it was from him: the letter was typed, single spaced, and the errors in spelling and grammar were consistent with previous BTK letters. It came in a package that contained pieces of clothing stolen from the woman's house.

When they saw the letter, Drowatzky and the other officers in the Major Crimes office, who had been unaware of the April burglary, cursed in frustration that the house on South Pinecrest had not been blanketed by officers immediately that night.

BTK's letter was composed of several rhyming verses. One spoke of the author's regret that his intended victim hadn't been home when he dropped by to visit. Another began with the phrase "Curly locks, curly locks." Another seemed to concern Nancy Jo Fox.

The police held a news conference to inform the city that BTK had returned. A wave of new guns and new locks were purchased; the BTK hotline returned. Frightened residents phoned in more unhelpful tips, more rumors, and more reports of suspicious uncles, cousins, and neighbors, sending officers scrambling on more wild-goose chases.

The police also rounded up the usual psychologists. "Quiet, unassuming, never arouses suspicion," the doctors said of the strangler. "Probably a loner, maybe an only child, has severe sexual problems and a highly developed fantasy life."

One doctor was asked why BTK caused such panic among Wichita residents. "It's the unpredictability of the whole thing that makes it so frightening," he said.

—m—

Ed and Ruth Finley could certainly identify. A feeling of unpredictability hung over their own situation like a heavy fog. Since the phone call the previous summer, their lives had formed a pattern of fear and forgetfulness, caution and carelessness, as Ruth's harasser appeared and disappeared, wrote and withdrew.

In May he wrote again, demanding money and asking Ruth to tell him about her brands. One week later, he told Ruth in another letter to place one hundred dollars under the seat of Ed's yellow pickup truck.

Two days after BTK's letter was made public, Drowatzky received another message. This time, the subject was not Ruth but BTK's victims:

> *There once was a lt. named Bernie*
> *Who wundered about a fox & a shirley*
> *The letters of names may be part of the game.*
> *Little Nancy folded her petticoat neatly on a chair.*
> *Time for her to get up, presto she wasn't there.*
> *A female like a winter rose*
> *Will disappear when the wind blows.*
> *Some females have pretty faces.*
> *I'd like to mark them with a knife, like laces.*
> *Bind them up & choke the lady.*
> *No one will find her, it's true, not maybe.*
> *Little Bo Peep lost her arm*
> *Trying to keep herself from harm.*

Drowatzky felt another tingle as he read the lines. It was true that BTK was in the news again, and the killings of Nancy Jo Fox and Shirley Vian had been rehashed in the media, so it would have been easy to dismiss the reference to "a fox and a shirley" as mere taunting, or as an attempt on the part of the author to have himself taken more seriously. Except for one thing: Police had never told the public that they had found one of Nancy Jo Fox's undergarments folded over the back of a chair near her body.

Four weeks passed before Ruth received another letter.

"Dear Ruth," the author began, with unprecedented formality. "I am going to go and not see you. I told you in July that I like yur face & still want to see where yur brand is. You still should not run off. I am not going to write anymore. I am getting tired of you & the lt. & righting & everybody."

Not nearly as tired, Ruth thought, as she was getting of him.

—⁓—

By July 1979 Ruth and Ed were once again growing hopeful that her tormentor had moved on. They even felt comfortable enough to plan their annual summer trip to a dude ranch in Colorado. Ruth wanted a new pair of jeans for the trip, and on August 13, she told Ed she was heading to Dillard's department store at the Towne East mall after work. Ed felt nervous about Ruth venturing out by herself, but Ruth said she would be fine.

By the time Ruth walked out of Dillard's with her new jeans, the summer dusk had settled in, casting shadows over the enormous, nearly deserted mall parking lot. Ruth, aware of her vulnerability, hurried to her vehicle, eyes scanning the lot for potential danger. She was almost to her Oldsmobile when she heard a voice call, "Hey, Ruth, I didn't know you were going to make this so easy!"

She turned around and recognized with horror the man who had kidnapped her the previous fall. Ruth ran for her car, but before she could unlock the door, the man came up from behind and grabbed her wrist, then shoved her head against the window. "Get in," he ordered, saying he wanted to take her to a bridge near Augusta Airport Road. He threw a brown paper shopping bag through the partially open rear window onto the back seat. "We'll go to a nice little place where it says 'Keep Out,'" he said as Ruth struggled.

Ruth broke free and tried to step around the car. The man withdrew an eight-inch boning knife from his pocket and stabbed her—twice in the back and once in the side. On the third stab, the knife stuck in Ruth's side and the man lost his grip. Ruth ran to the passenger side, got in, slammed the door, and began rolling up the window. The man tried to reach in after her, but his hand got caught in the window; as he withdrew it, his brown cotton glove remained stuck between the window and the doorframe. Ruth drove off with the glove still dangling there. In her rearview mirror she could just make out the man behind her in the twilight.

Ruth felt woozy as she turned from the parking lot into the street's heavy traffic. When she stopped at a red light, she finally noticed a burning pain in her left side; looking down, she saw the knife was still jutting from her body. Her energy was slipping. Blood from her wounds dripped onto the car's seat.

At the corner of Douglas and Rock Road, Ruth spotted a gas station and pulled into its driveway, stopping in front of the station's pay phone. Staggering from the car, she dialed 268-4181, the only police number she knew.

At police headquarters Captain Al Thimmesch, Drowatzky's boss, picked up the phone. Ruth began to introduce herself.

"I know who you are," Thimmesch cut her off. "What's going on?"

"I've been stabbed."

An alarmed Thimmesch said he would send an officer over immediately. Ruth, however, was frightened that her attacker might show up at the gas station. After hanging up the phone, she returned to her car and, feeling increasingly weak, drove the five minutes back to her house, certain that at any minute her attacker might pull behind her. She was so distracted and in so much pain that she almost missed her street.

In the meantime, Thimmesch had called Ed. When Ruth pulled to the curb, a panicked Ed was already waiting in front of the house. He ran to the driver's side of the car to take Ruth to the hospital. But he quickly saw a dilemma: with a knife in her side, Ruth could not slide over to the passenger seat. Ed had to help her out of the car and take her around to the other door. The process was awkward; Ruth was hunched over in severe pain, and the knife handle wobbled in the air as she walked. Ed was too afraid to attempt to remove the knife himself.

At last Ruth was in the passenger seat, her face pressed against the window, her back turned toward Ed to accommodate the knife handle. She moaned intermittently.

Ed sped toward St. Joseph Medical Center, the closest hospital. From the corner of his eye, he saw his wife's blood seeping onto the passenger seat. He tried to quell the rising panic, but every time Ruth moaned, that panic threatened to overwhelm him. He stepped on the gas pedal and ran through stoplights.

Ruth felt nauseated and desperately wanted to sleep. Ed refused to let her. "Don't go to sleep," he said, thinking of the line he had often heard in movies whenever somebody was wounded.

Ruth stared at the night sky. A thin line of clouds smudged the horizon, but the rest of the sky was clear—vast and dark and somehow almost inviting, like the deep black pond she used to swim in when she was a child. She wanted to jump into the sky and swim until she disappeared.

"Just stay awake," Ed kept repeating.

Ruth felt as if a hole as wide as a cave had opened in her back. She felt as if she had been split in two. She forced herself not to cry.

Ed spun the car into the emergency drive-up at St. Joseph, slammed on the brakes, and leaped out. Suddenly, all was efficient commotion; orderlies rushed a wheelchair up to the car, but turned around when they realized the knife handle would make it impossible for Ruth to sit in the chair.

An aluminum gurney appeared out of nowhere, and Ruth was lifted out of the car and placed upon it face down.

Ed started to walk with the gurney toward the emergency room doors, but a hospital guard moved in front of him and ordered him to stop. In his alarm, it took Ed several seconds to notice that the guard had one hand on the butt of a revolver in his holster. Ed stared at the man in disbelief—he was keeping Ed from his wife in a moment of crisis. He felt a deep rage building. Then it hit him: the guard thought Ed was the assailant.

As Ruth was wheeled inside, Ed explained the situation. When he mentioned Drowatzky's name, the guard relented and motioned Ed into the hospital.

Ruth lay quietly on the gurney behind a curtain, watching nurses and orderlies gather around her. She felt somebody snip off her jeans and blouse. The pain throbbed in waves. Why don't they take out the knife? she wondered. Everything would be okay if they just took the knife out. She heard a man's voice speaking, saying something soothing. Nurses charted her vital signs. She could hear Ed asking questions.

The knife, she thought. Please, somebody, just take out the damn knife and make the pain go away.

Suddenly, Drowatzky was standing beside her. "Ruth, where did you get stabbed?" he said. His voice was soft, distant.

Misunderstanding his question, Ruth lifted a hand and tried to indicate her back.

"No," said Drowatzky, "I mean—"

"Towne East," Ruth said.

"Where at?"

"Dillard's, north parking lot."

"Upper or lower level?"

"Upper."

"Was it the same man?" Drowatzky asked.

"Yes," said Ruth.

A nurse stepped in and told Drowatzky to leave. Ruth had to be moved quickly.

Suddenly Ruth felt the knife slip out of her side. She heard it fall onto the gurney with a soft plunk. But the pain did not lessen. She listened to the puffing of the orderlies as they rushed the gurney down various hallways. There was an elevator ride and then another hallway, until finally the gurney bumped through a swinging door and came to a stop.

Ruth felt a rubber mask being fitted over her mouth and nose. Slowly—blissfully—the sky, the cave, the hole opened up and she felt herself falling at last into the deep black pool.

—∾—

Ruth and Ed had come to Drowatzky for help, and he had let them down. He and his wife had become friends of the Finleys over the last year. Sometimes they ate dinner together. They saw each other at church. He thought he had done everything he could for Ruth. That offered little solace now. Whatever he had done, it had not been enough.

Drowatzky's mood did not improve when Ruth's brother, Morris, arrived at the hospital and started chewing him and his men out for failing to protect her. Morris and Ruth had always been close, despite Morris being a hell-raiser as a child.

When Ruth was a child, the only blemish on Ruth's face was a small scar above her nose, which had been Morris's fault. When their mom told him not to jump around on his bed, he did it the instant she left the room. On one occasion, an infant Ruth had made the mistake of trying to imitate him by bouncing on her own bed, and she smashed her head on the railing. She broke into tears, bringing Fay back into the room in a rage. That was the beginning of a tight relationship between Ruth and her brother. Morris raised hell, Ruth went along with him, and Morris caught the blame.

Until Jean's birth four years later, Morris and Ruth were inseparable. They shot at squirrels and field mice with a popgun. They killed sparrows in the barn's hayloft. They rode bicycles and their dad's plow horses. They frolicked in the creek that fed a pasture pond across the road from the main house. They shared each other's toys; Morris let Ruth play with his tiny cars and trucks and ride his tricycle and bright red wagon, and Ruth let Morris play with her dolls.

Their play often turned mischievous. Most of the time, the mischief was as harmless as sneaking through the barbed wire that protected the pond to splash in the muddy water. But occasionally it became dangerous. Once, they put a lid on a well that contained gas fumes and threw a match down to see how high they could blow the lid.

Whenever their cousins visited the farm from Kansas City, ninety miles to the north, Ruth and Morris took it upon themselves to make their stay as unpleasant as possible. Their mildest prank was removing the toilet paper from the outhouse. One time, she and Morris took the cousins for a walk along the railroad tracks, arriving at a trestle just as the train pulled into sight. Their plan had been to jump off the trestle at the last minute, but when the time came, the cousins were paralyzed with fear. She and Morris had to fling them off before the train ran them over.

Morris sometimes got punished three times a day. Carl Smock often made him cut the thin branches he was to be whipped with.

Morris had turned out fine—he worked as an assembly foreman at Cessna Aircraft in Wichita. But Morris himself had always said he was a worthless kid. He had dropped out of high school in the eleventh grade, mercifully ending a relationship with school that had been unhealthy for both sides. He used to light matches and throw them out school windows to try to set the grass on fire. The school in Richards was a small wood building that was highly vulnerable to flames. Ruth always figured the school was glad to see him go.

Morris and Ruth had drifted apart a bit in their adulthood, but Morris still felt a fierce protective bond with her. When he showed up at the hospital, fearful for his sister's life, he let all of his frustration and terror fly straight at Drowatzky, who tolerated the scolding. In addition to being angry at himself, and frustrated, Drowatzky was genuinely afraid for Ruth's life for the first time.

The stabbing upped the ante on the case. This went beyond threatening letters, harassing telephone calls, even a kidnapping and assault. It had been difficult for Drowatzky to convince some officers to take the case seriously, to treat it as more than simple harassment. But now they would have to listen to him, Drowatzky thought. This time, the son of a bitch actually had tried to kill her. Awful as that was, Drowatzky could not help feeling a sense of vindication.

Drowatzky saw the X-rays himself. Ruth had been stabbed twice in the back and once in the side. The deepest thrust had nicked a kidney. "She was lucky," a doctor told him. "If she had been inhaling when she was stabbed, the knife would have punctured the lung."

Drowatzky, with Anderson in tow, strolled outside to smoke a cigarette just as lab officer Stephen Munsell arrived. "Ruth's in surgery," Drowatzky told Munsell. He pointed to the black Olds. "Let's start with the car."

The first thing Drowatzky, Anderson, and Munsell found was a brown work glove on the console, between the front seats. Then they saw a paper sack in the back seat. Drowatzky lifted the sack and placed it in a plastic evidence bag. He peeked inside. His throat constricted. The sack contained a metal knife with the blade missing, two pieces of material that appeared to have been cut from a red bandanna, a roll of adhesive tape, a roll of clothesline rope bound by adhesive tape, and a half-empty bottle of Almaden wine.

Drowatzky wondered if he was staring at the tools of BTK.

A smaller paper sack lay bunched at the bottom of the larger bag. Drowatzky lifted it out and peered inside. He found a tiny sliver of newspaper that had been scissored out of a story with painstaking care. It contained just three words: "Lt. Bernie Drowatzky."

—⚇—

Ruth awakened in the night to a dull, throbbing pain in her back. The only sound was the occasional clicking of stretchers rolling past the ICU door. The sound reminded her of the creaking railroad cars that had drifted past the farm in Richards every night.

She remembered the exchange she and her mother often had in the darkness of her bedroom after her mother had tucked her into bed.

"Will any nasty things get me tonight?" Ruth would ask.

"No, dear," Fay would tell her. "Don't you worry like that."

"Will we all still be here in the morning?"

"Of course. Now be still and go to sleep."

But Ruth knew she wasn't safe. She knew nasty things were indeed out there, and that some morning she might be gone.

She also knew now, beyond any doubt, that the stranger who was after her—a person whose motives she could not begin to fathom—was going to kill her.

6

LOTS OF PAIN

The hospital bed felt like some cruel torture device. Every move Ruth made sent a jolt of sharp pain up her back. When it wasn't on fire, her back throbbed with a dull, persistent ache. She tried not to show the pain to Ed or Jean or Morris when they visited, or even to the nurses. (Ruth and Ed hid the news from their sons, not wanting to worry them.) She wanted to cry, but she could not bring herself to do it even when she was alone.

The presence of police officers was nearly as bad as the pain. They had been assigned to protect Ruth twenty-four hours a day in the hospital. She knew she should be grateful, but every time one of them stuck his head into the room to see if she was all right, she felt only fear. One glance at a policeman's uniform would remind her of the danger she was in, and she would have visions of the man with the knife and his horrible grin. She could still feel his rancid breath on her neck.

The doctors told her she was out of immediate danger. The stab to her left kidney had grazed the organ but done no permanent damage. They had drained the wound and sewed it back together, although the threat of infection remained. Ruth was lucky—if the knife had entered just a hair's breadth to the side, she would have been dead.

The doctors had treated two more stab wounds on the lower left side of her back, plus a three-and-a-half-inch laceration on her left arm and a bruise on her forehead.

Lying in bed, Ruth felt sore all over. She hated pain. As a kid, she couldn't even stand having splinters removed.

When Ruth was stable, Ed brought his art supplies to the hospital to work on a sketch of the man's face for the police. He and Ruth spent hours on it, and when it was finished, Ruth thought it was remarkably accurate. The drawing revealed the man's face in three-quarter profile, with high cheekbones, a weak jaw, thin lips, and a pair of glasses. The most arresting feature was the man's hair, which was parted low on the left side and swept over the top, bangs falling over the forehead like a wave.

His face was expressionless. Ruth would have preferred to have the man grinning the way he always did when he confronted her, but this was close enough.

—⁂—

Meanwhile, the police were having little luck with the investigation. Scouring the Towne East mall in search of witnesses to the stabbing, they located one woman who remembered seeing a man raising a fuss by a black car at about the time Ruth was stabbed, but she could provide no description or details.

Anderson and Zortman had, in private, questioned Ruth's account of her kidnapping, but there could be no question about multiple stab wounds in the back. On top of that, Anderson had come to know Ruth as a polite, soft-spoken person who wasn't the type to draw attention to herself. What's more, the doctors said the locations and depths of the wounds meant an assailant would have had to be behind her—it would have been impossible to inflict them from any other position. There was absolutely no chance that Ruth could have stabbed herself.

But after a week of canvassing the shopping mall for witnesses, the investigation had no leads. Lab officers had found no prints on the items in the paper sack, the sack itself, the brown glove that had been found on the car's console, or the knife. They were nowhere.

—ᴍ—

The stabbing forced the police to make the case public. Drowatzky released information about the assault to the news media, along with Ed's drawing of the assailant, and he appealed to the public for help finding the man who had stabbed Ruth. The response was underwhelming. The police received a few unhelpful phone calls, most of which came in to the BTK hotline.

The day after Ruth's stabbing, the police allowed a radio station to play a recording of BTK's voice. The recording, which lasted only seven seconds, had been made when BTK phoned the emergency number to report the murder of Nancy Jo Fox in 1977. New technology had been developed since then to enhance the sound of the poor-quality recording. The station played the recording throughout the day at the request of the police, who were hoping somebody would recognize the man's voice. Calls poured in to the hotline. Amid that deluge were a few about Ruth. People were confusing the two cases.

Five days after the stabbing, Halsey-Tevis, Ed's employer, offered a three-thousand-dollar reward for information leading to the arrest and conviction of Ruth's assailant. A new sketch of the man, this time by a professional sketch artist, was released. The suspect's cheekbones were less prominent than in Ed's drawing, the lips fuller. The frames of his glasses were wider, and his eyes were sadder, less startled than in Ed's drawing. But the biggest difference was the hair, which was neater and shorter in the new sketch.

The man's appearance was so bland, he might be anybody. Ruth had described him as being between forty-five and fifty-five years old, with black hair graying at the temples. The police realized that you could put a pair of wire-rimmed glasses on almost any white man of that age and build and he would look similar to the sketch.

Nine days after the stabbing, Ruth was released from the hospital. She was escorted home by Ed, Morris, and Drowatzky. Her back still burned, but she was thrilled to return to the comforts of home. Jean and her husband, Bill; Drowatzky's wife, Dorann; and Ed's boss, Dan Tevis, came over for an impromptu welcome home party. The group ate fried chicken and chatted in the living room, Ruth perched delicately and uncomfortably on the sofa.

A little more than an hour into the celebration, a police officer came to the house. "Just dropped by to see if everything is all right," he said. Then he pulled Drowatzky aside and whispered in his ear. Drowatzky looked stricken. The lieutenant turned to the others and told them that a man had come to St. Joseph looking for Ruth a short time after Ruth had checked out. A nurse told police the man had matched the sketch of her attacker.

"We gotta get Ruth out of here fast," Drowatzky said.

Ruth's stomach twisted. She rose from the sofa and went into the bathroom to throw up.

By the time she returned to the living room, Drowatzky had developed a plan. Ruth would spend the next week at Jean's house, and then she and Ed would take their delayed vacation to Colorado—the one that Ruth had been shopping for when she'd been stabbed. Meanwhile, a police officer would spend the week with Ed at the Finleys' house. If the assailant intended to pay a visit, Drowatzky wanted the police officer to give him a greeting he would not forget.

The detective suggested that Ed go with Ruth to Jean's house.

"Nope," Ed declared. "I've been pushed far enough. I'm staying."

"Good. I don't blame you," Drowatzky said.

Ruth spent a few minutes gathering clothing, and then she climbed into the back seat of Morris's car and lay down. She would make the trip across town hidden under a blanket.

Morris followed a winding route to Jean's house just in case anyone was trying to follow him. Beneath the blanket, Ruth felt as if her brother was driving down every street in Wichita. The car turned this way and that, sped up and slowed. Ruth felt like she was trapped in a bad movie.

That night, Ruth and Jean shared the main bedroom, while Ruth's brother-in-law, Bill, slept on the living room floor with a shotgun.

But over the next seven days, Jean was pleasantly surprised by how relaxed Ruth appeared. The two sisters spent the hot summer afternoons by the pool in Jean's spacious backyard, sipping strawberry slushies and chatting for hours. Jean was worried for Ruth but also thrilled to be spending so much time with her. She and Ruth had not always been close; Jean was about five years younger than Ruth, and by the time that age difference no longer mattered, Ruth had married and moved away.

Jean's career had followed the same path as her older sister's. As a teenager, Jean worked as an operator for the phone company in Richards, and then she moved to the Wichita office of Southwestern Bell after marrying Bill. Like Ruth, Jean had stopped working to raise her children, and then returned to Southwestern Bell when they were grown.

As a child, Jean had worshipped Ruth. Jean was feisty and opinionated and given to mischief; she envied Ruth's serenity, brains, and looks. Jean was cute and didn't mind flirting with boys, but Ruth had a composure that set her apart from the other girls. She never had to work to catch boys' eyes. Jean would have resented her sister except that Ruth had always made Jean feel good about herself. After Ruth moved to Fort Scott for high school, she regularly sent Jean five-dollar bills, which always managed to arrive when Jean was feeling depressed. She didn't know how Ruth possessed such a perfect sense of timing.

Both Jean and Morris, who was thirteen months Ruth's senior, were constantly in trouble as children, unlike Ruth. On the rare occasions when Ruth did something wrong, she never received blame. Jean might have resented Ruth for that, too, but Ruth's almost ethereal charisma led Jean to idolize her instead. She wanted to be just like her.

Jean loved Ruth, but she didn't always understand her. Ruth was so quiet. Jean thought of her sister as the heroine of a romantic novel, someone who passed through the world beautiful and bewitching, cloaked in an aura of secrecy.

Jean was shocked when one afternoon, as she and Ruth sat by the pool, her sister mentioned the long-ago assault in Fort Scott. Ruth had never spoken of it to Jean before.

Now, in the wake of her stabbing, Ruth had a question: "Why didn't anybody ever ask me about it?"

Jean remembered the night it happened. It was her eleventh birthday. She remembered how horribly scared Ruth had seemed when she came home that night, how Ruth stood trembling and looking forlorn in a pale green, polka-dot dress, before their mother led her to the parents' bedroom. Ruth wasn't crying—Ruth never cried—but Jean found it terrifying to see the sister she idolized badly shaken.

The door to that bedroom remained closed for a week.

Now, the sun bobbed on the surface of Jean's pool as Ruth's question hovered in the heat.

"Mother told us not to," Jean answered.

—⁓—

At the end of the week, Ed and Ruth drove out of Wichita, heading for the mountains of Colorado, with Anderson following them to the city limits in an unmarked police car. Ruth's attacker had not appeared at the house, and the police wanted to protect her as long as she remained in the city.

The Finleys spent the week at a dude ranch near Gunnison, where the high mountain air provided cool relief from the oppressive Kansas heat. Ruth sewed, swam in the ranch's pool, and—despite recovering from her wounds—hiked some of the easier trails, while Ed fished for trout. They had been coming to Colorado twice every summer for eight years, always to the same two places: Estes Park in June, and the dude ranch in August. Ruth and Ed ran into the same couples every year, people from Texas, Denver, and Chicago, and they always looked forward to sharing drinks and playing cards with them. The week passed blissfully normally.

When Ruth and Ed returned to Wichita, they were greeted at the city limits by an officer who escorted them home.

—⁂—

The police became a central part of the Finleys' lives. A mobile home leased by the department was parked up the street on East Indianapolis. Anderson and Zortman spent eight hours a day either in the mobile home or in the house. Drowatzky had decided that at least one officer was to be with Ruth and Ed at all times.

Ruth, who remained at home while trying to gather the strength to return to Southwestern Bell, tried to be a good hostess, baking pies and cakes for the officers. But she and Ed soon began to show signs of strain. Ed, feeling angry and helpless, became irritable at work and began snapping at coworkers over matters of little significance. Ruth would jolt awake at night and complain of nightmares.

Ruth finally returned to work two weeks after the Colorado trip. The phone company had assigned her to a new position as secretary to the chief of security for southcentral Kansas; the WPD couldn't have asked for a more ideal position for a woman who required protection. The job brought Ruth into regular contact with law enforcement officials. She coordinated employee investigations, ran checks for toll fraud, and helped authorities locate missing persons.

Ruth's new office was on the twelfth floor of the Southwestern Bell building. Her boss, Joe Horvat, spent much of his time on the road, but Ruth felt perfectly safe in the building. There was only one door to Ruth's office, and it was built of thick hardwood and secured by a sturdy dead bolt. Ruth and Horvat were the only two people who had keys.

—⁂—

The Finleys' lives were arranged into a pattern ruled by paranoia. Ed took Ruth to work in the morning, she ate her lunch in the building, she never ventured outside alone, and Ed picked her up at the phone company in the late afternoon. A police officer stayed at their house every night.

But twenty-four-hour protection is costly. After two weeks passed without any sign of Ruth's attacker, the officers assigned to the overnight shift at the house began leaving at 3:00 a.m. After three weeks, the night shift officers were pulled completely.

Leaflets containing the police sketch of the suspect and a description of the kidnappers' car were distributed at Towne East, but drew no response. No leads were developed from the phone calls that had come in after the story appeared in the media.

By the end of September, the investigation had petered out.

Ed decided to take his wife's case into his own hands. He bought space in the personal ads of the Wichita newspaper to get in touch with the attacker. Drowatzky didn't think the approach would work, but he saw no harm in it. If it would make Ed feel better, then the attempt was worthwhile.

Because Ruth's assailant had written letters in rhyming verse, Ed called him the Poet.

The message in the personal ads was short and simple.

"Poet: Tell me what you want. RSF."

Drowatzky and the other detectives decided it was time for a gamble of their own. They figured the man was probably spooked by all the protection Ruth was receiving, and that he was biding his time until the heat died down. They wanted to flush him into the open.

One day in early October, Zortman met Ed at Halsey-Tevis after work. Suspecting the man might be watching Ed, waiting for a chance to strike against Ruth, Zortman climbed into the back seat of Ed's Oldsmobile and lay down. After Ed drove home and pulled the car into the garage, Zortman climbed out and joined the Finleys for dinner. After dinner, he returned to the back seat and stayed there while Ruth drove the car to Towne East. Wearing a radio transmitter, Ruth retraced her path on the night of the stabbing as eight undercover cops stood watch throughout the mall.

Ruth was supposed to speak into the transmitter to let the officers know where she was as she moved throughout the mall. But she felt so embarrassed talking to herself in a crowd of people that the officers couldn't hear her low murmur. Less than thirty minutes into the operation, it had to be scrubbed.

On October 15, Drowatzky received another letter from the Poet at his office. It made no mention of Ed's ad.

> *Rage in my mind gives thots to kill*
> *Kindled strife wrought conquering skill.*

The next part of the letter intrigued Drowatzky.

"I can't call for I no the tele. Ofs. The last time I use a phone I think yur force saw me. I put the phone up & ask buddy for change and they left & I left but I bet she didn't use telephone for awhile. I don't no how fast they are. Yur force looked at me though & scared the hell out of me using the phone."

Had his men really seen this guy?

The letter continued:

> *One great wrong judgement I made was using a knife with*
> *too short a blade.*
> *No hope for the female does remain.*
> *Sudden horror to her, and lots of pain.*

A week later, the *Wichita Eagle and Beacon* received a letter from the Poet. He was irate over a story about the BTK hotline, which noted that some of the calls to the hotline were in fact about the Finley case.

"Yur editor make a bad journalistic error when you refer to BTK & other in same report," the Poet wrote. "Make sure you don't confuse the executioners again."

But reporters who had covered the BTK case were struck by what followed the stern admonition. The psychological jargon reminded them of BTK's own letters.

Impulses are set off by brain waves that are uncontrollable when they get released. The deeds must be done before the brain waves control. No one can be manipulated by society & outside agents. Completeness to deeds is transmitted from nerve fibers to muscles that control power. Our social system will work when individuals play by the rules. Disunity is caused by competitive conflict and communicative neglect. The brain waves have all the control.

The pursued are sought out by:

A. You do not like appearances.

B. Debts.

C. Some are just opportunities.

D. Other.

The reporters quizzed Drowatzky about the references to other victims besides Ruth Finley, but Drowatzky downplayed them.

"There's nothing to indicate he's done it before," the lieutenant said, meaning they had no physical evidence to link the Poet with any previous killings. "But it indicates he fancies himself an executioner. I think he feels in his own way that that's what he is, or is intending to be."

And, no, there was no substantial reason to believe that the Poet and BTK were the same person.

But privately, Drowatzky and many others in the department still thought it was possible.

To clear the doubts, Police Chief Richard LaMunyon and the new officer in charge of the Criminal Investigations Bureau, Captain Mike

Hill—who started the job in October 1979—sent examples of the BTK and Poet letters to the FBI and to psychologists, law enforcement officials, and linguists throughout the Midwest for comparisons and psychological profiles.

When the reports came back, they dismissed the possibility that BTK and Ruth's attacker were the same person.

As for the profiles, the most respected of the linguistics experts, Dr. Murray Miron, a psycholinguist at Syracuse University who had helped crack the Son of Sam case in New York City, wrote that Ruth Finley's attacker was "severely psychotic" and dangerous.

"The volume of his productions, the regressive infantilism, narcissism, and word plays are all characteristically definitive of schizophrenic psychosis," Miron's report said. "In my opinion, this subject should be considered extremely dangerous."

Considering all possibilities, Miron dismissed the idea that Ruth had written the letters. "I do not detect any evidence for such interpretation and do find considerable positive indicators to the contrary," he wrote. Miron also believed it was highly likely that the subject would attack Ruth again.

Drowatzky, an old-school cop who had little faith in the ability of psychologists to solve crimes, was unwilling to let go of the possibility that BTK and the Poet were the same man. But he was relieved that experts had confirmed his conviction that Ruth was telling the truth. Her assailant had tried to kill her once, and he would try to kill her again. Unless Drowatzky and his team found the man and stopped him.

The key, Drowatzky thought, had to be in Fort Scott. There must be a connection between the Poet and the attack on Ruth in 1946. But they would need Ruth's help to uncover it. She knew something—she just didn't *know* that she knew it. But it was there somewhere—in her high school yearbook, in police mug shots, in her old friends, in her relatives . . . somewhere.

And so, on a sunny but cold November day, Drowatzky and Anderson drove Ruth and Ed Finley back to Fort Scott.

7

THE BOARDINGHOUSE

Visits home always filled Ruth with bittersweet memories. As she rode with Ed and the two officers through the Flint Hills of southeastern Kansas and its vast sea of undulating, fall-green tallgrass, she shifted in her seat, knowing that she was expected to delve back into her trauma.

The countryside had made for an ideal childhood. If you had to be a kid during the Depression, she reflected, you couldn't beat growing up on a farm.

In those days, Richards had a population of 250 people. Two railroads, the Southern and Missouri Pacific, ran along the town's southern edge. The train station provided most of the town's employment. Richards also had a bank, a hotel, a hardware store, a general store, the telephone office, and five churches. Over time, however, both railroads lengthened the sections of track between stations, and when they no longer stopped in Richards, the town began to die. By 1979 it had shrunk to a village of 105 people, with only a post office, a grain elevator, and one church. The main street was lined with worn, empty buildings and littered with rusted farm implements. A sign on one of the storefronts summarized the social stance of the community: "God help me keep my nose out of other people's business."

The Smocks' former farmhouse still stood on a rise southwest of town. It was a handsome two-story structure that Carl's father, Albert, had built by expanding a two-room log cabin. The farmhouse featured a large front porch with five white columns. Two giant catalpa trees filled the front yard with graceful looping branches.

Behind the house were a big red barn, a smokehouse, a chicken shed, a well, and an outhouse. Railroad tracks bounded the property on the north.

When Ruth was a child, the farm had 165 acres of wheat, corn, milo, and beans, along with grazing land for cattle and horses. There was a peach orchard out back, later converted to apples, and Fay had tended a garden with grapes, rhubarb, and an assortment of vegetables.

Ruth's bedroom was on the second floor. She loved waking up to the sunlight and the sound of birds chirping outside. But the room was freezing in winter. The house was heated by a single coal stove on the first floor. Her parents' bedroom had the only fireplace. Illumination at night came from gas lamps.

Ruth never considered her family poor. Food hadn't been a problem on the farm. Fay loved to cook and always had an assortment of homemade bread and cinnamon rolls on the table. Meat was scarce, but they managed on one ration of meat per person per meal. The only hardship was that Ruth and her siblings couldn't afford to buy the hot meals at school.

Fay stitched nice dresses for Ruth and Jean out of feed sacks; they never looked dowdy. She made Ruth one beautiful dress every year, full of lace and ruffles, that enabled Ruth to be the May Queen at school. The children had new shoes for the start of every school year, although Ruth preferred going barefoot, like many kids at her school.

Unlike Morris, Ruth enjoyed helping her dad with chores around the farm. She loved milking cows so much that Carl even put her on a milk route. Ruth made deliveries twice a day, selling the milk for ten cents a quart. The money was hers to keep. Sometimes Carl gave her a calf or a lamb to care for, and she was allowed to sell those and keep the money, too, although she always cried when she sold them.

Ruth adored her father. Carl stood six feet two and had a thick neck and broad shoulders spreading over a solid torso. He was quiet and patient and loving toward Ruth and Jean, although he was tough on Morris. Carl loved to play croquet with the kids in the front yard and take them in his Model A Ford down the hill to the pond so they could go swimming.

Ruth could get away with just about anything when it came to Carl. She painted his fingernails red while he lay snoozing on the floor one night before he had to attend a school board meeting. When Carl woke up, he was greatly amused by Ruth's prank, even though he had to attend the meeting without removing the polish.

He was so easygoing that when a neighbor's teenage son ran a car through one of his fences, Carl just shrugged and said it was bound to happen because the kids in Richards were a fun-loving bunch.

Carl died of emphysema in 1974. Carl hadn't smoked, nor had Fay. His doctor said the emphysema came from inhaling tractor fumes and dust all his life. Carl also never drank, and Ruth could only remember one time when she heard her father say something bad. He had been mowing the backyard with a team of misbehaving plow horses. When the horses bumped into a tree, he muttered, "You hoodlums!"

That was Carl Smock's idea of swearing.

The Smocks were raised Methodists, but Carl wasn't particularly devout—unlike Fay, who knew the Bible in and out. Her mother didn't push religion on the children, but they knew that if they had a question about God or the devil, Fay had the answer.

Just before Ruth and Ed left for Fort Scott with the police officers, Fay had suggested to Jean that all of Ruth's problems with the man who stabbed her would disappear if Ruth would just turn her life over to God. She and Ed went to a Presbyterian church in Wichita every Sunday, but Ruth attended primarily because she liked the people in the congregation, not because she was devout in her faith.

Looking back now, Ruth saw how naive she must have seemed to other kids when she started school. The first day she joined Morris in the tiny schoolhouse in Richards, she heard a boy announce that he was going to "take a piss." She had no idea what he was talking about.

In high school, Ruth was shocked by some of the books her English teacher assigned, which contained what she thought were vivid sexual passages. But then, the teacher, Mrs. Henderson, a pretty woman with white hair pulled into a bun, was quite sophisticated. She used to work for a publishing house in New York. She had a whole library at her home and assigned most of the class reading from her own shelves, bypassing the school board and infuriating many parents.

Ruth knew better than to tell her parents about the sexy stuff in the novels. She had seen her mother literally jump when somebody started talking about babies and how they were made. Being a farm girl, Ruth knew what animals did, but whenever she tried to talk to her mom about it, Fay Smock would lapse into silence or change the subject.

When it came time to discuss the birds and the bees with Ruth, Fay Smock's advice was brief. "You just behave yourself, or you'll get in trouble," she told Ruth. "And if you get in trouble, don't come to us."

In her sophomore year of high school, Ruth transferred to Fort Scott, twenty miles west of Richards. Her hometown school, which was geared toward boys' education, didn't provide the sort of classes Ruth wished to take, such as typing and home economics.

Her parents had moved her to Fort Scott in their Model A and placed her with a family for whom she worked as a babysitter in exchange for room and board. Eventually Ruth began working at the phone company there, and so she moved into the boardinghouse to be closer to work.

The boardinghouse was a two-story, green-gray house on National Street, the main street in town, with fifteen rooms and a vast front porch. Surrounded by elms, the house felt isolated to her, even though it was in the middle of town.

Situated at the junction of two major highways, Fort Scott featured a large population of transients, and it was full of beer joints, pool halls, and brothels to service the drifters and the returning GIs. As a telephone operator, Ruth had a ringside seat on some of the coarser action. Men on the way to town would phone ahead, collect, to make appointments at the brothels, and Ruth and her coworkers occasionally listened to the conversations after making the connections.

Perhaps it had been one of the men she talked to on the phone who had found her in the boardinghouse that night, she thought afterward. Screened by trees, the house must have seemed inviting to some lowlife who had followed her home from work.

Ruth still could not get over the humiliation she had felt sitting on a sofa in her bedroom that night in 1946, listening to the police question her version of the attack. "Where's the handkerchief now?" they kept asking. Ruth could still taste the handkerchief, but she had no idea where it was. How could she? She had passed out. Her assailant probably took it with him.

"I don't know," she said.

"Don't be tellin' us stuff," one of the cops said.

She was furious. She finally went quiet on them. Clammed up. Just sat there and cried.

She cried even harder when her parents arrived from Richards to take her home. Ruth couldn't bring herself to tell them what had happened, and they didn't ask her to. She got the feeling they wanted to pretend it hadn't happened. "Don't mention it, and you'll forget it," her mother told her.

Ruth remembered what it felt like to be shut up in her parents' bedroom all the next week, remembered the loneliness, fear, shame, and guilt, and the overwhelming sense that nobody cared about her anymore. She wasn't allowed outside the room. She felt like an outcast, a source of scandal for her family. She couldn't talk to anybody about it, not even Morris, who was home on vacation from his job on a wheat farm. All week, she heard the phone ring outside the bedroom door and she had to listen in silence as her mother told callers that nothing had happened to Ruth. She wanted to scream. But she also felt she had put a burden on her mother, and on the whole family, so she kept quiet.

Her parents made her go right back to the boardinghouse when the week was up. It was like falling off a horse, her father explained, you have to get right back on it.

So Ruth moved back. Soon, however, she began to suffer intense vomiting. It got so bad that her mother sent Jean to live temporarily with relatives in Cherryvale, Kansas, and moved into the boardinghouse with Ruth. But that didn't help.

Finally, her mother sent for Doc Cooper, who put her on medication.

Then she started hearing the rumors. They were all over town. The most popular rumor was that she'd made the whole thing up at her father's request because he wanted to cover up a pregnancy.

Classmates began avoiding her at school. When Ruth wasn't in class or at work, she stayed in her room, fighting back nausea. Only one person, Marie Friend, stuck by her. Marie, who worked with her at the phone company, even moved in with her for a while. They hardly slept at night. They just stayed up, frightened, listening to the wind and other noises of the night.

"Branded," the newspaper had said. No kidding. But in ways the paper couldn't imagine. A few weeks after she returned to class, a counselor called her into the office and accused her of missing a day of school that week. Ruth never skipped classes and she knew she had been present that day, but the counselor insisted. "We don't have you marked absent, but you were," the woman told her. They even knew where she had been, the counselor said. "You went with some boys to a cabin by a lake. We even have a picture to prove it." And the counselor produced a photograph of a girl who looked like Ruth standing in the middle of a group of boys. A mother of one of the boys had found the picture and showed it to her bridge club, the counselor said.

Ruth felt as if she was trapped in a nightmare. She recognized the girl in the picture as a classmate—oddly enough, another girl named Ruth—but the counselor refused to believe her.

"If you miss one more day of school, you'll be expelled," the counselor said.

Ruth broke into sobs.

Months later, Ruth was standing at her locker when the counselor came by to clean out the locker of the other Ruth, who was leaving school after becoming pregnant by one of the boys who had been at the lake.

"I guess people have been getting the two of you mixed up all year," the counselor said, smiling at Ruth casually. Then she walked away.

She never apologized.

A short time after that, a man Ruth knew drove alongside her in his car as she walked home from work and offered her a ride. She knew the man had a family and a reputation as a flirt, but she climbed in anyway. He drove straight past her boardinghouse and headed for the lake.

He told her he had a blanket in the back seat, and that he wanted to show her that not all men were mean and cruel, like the man who had branded her.

"I will treat you very nice," he said.

When she started crying, he changed his mind and took her home.

Ruth became afraid of men. She had been shy around the boys in Richards, but she had never felt afraid of them.

—⁓—

Ruth spent the afternoon with Ed, Drowatzky, and Anderson going through a box of mug shots in the Fort Scott police department, but she saw no familiar faces. Anderson and Drowatzky started tracking down people who went to the high school with Ruth, showing the sketch of her attacker around town, and checking with building contractors to see if they could recall any employees who looked like the suspect.

The officers were escorted around by Elvin Cox, an investigator for the Western Insurance companies in Fort Scott, and the husband of one of Ruth's cousins, Mary Best Cox. Elvin Cox knew nearly everybody in town.

Like so many, Mary Cox had idolized Ruth as a kid, and she admired her as an adult. The Bests lived on a farm five miles from the Smocks, and Mary spent a lot of time with Ruth, riding horses, playing hide-and-seek, walking the railroad tracks. She always felt Ruth had something special. Ruth was bright without flaunting her intelligence, quiet, and very ladylike. Whenever Mary's mother wondered aloud why Mary couldn't be more like Ruth, which she often did, Mary seldom resented it. She wondered the same thing.

She didn't know how Ruth could handle everything that had happened to her with such poise. She had come to Wichita to stay with Ruth at Jean's house for a few days after the stabbing. When Ruth made casual jokes about it, Mary had once again marveled at her cousin's inner strength. She doubted she could cope as well. But Ruth never took her burdens to others. Not even after the branding incident. Mary, like all of Ruth's relatives, had been asked by Fay not to mention the incident to Ruth.

The night it happened, Mary's mother came home after visiting the Smocks and burned the family Bible. There couldn't possibly be a God, she thought, if something like this could happen to a sweet girl like Ruth.

—∞—

Anderson and Drowatzky were having zero luck in Fort Scott. Nobody could identify the man in the sketch, no contractors knew him, no friends or relatives could think of a link between the troubles of Ruth's past and those of her present.

When Ruth finished looking at mug shots, she and Mary went downtown to shop while Ed, Elvin, and the officers continued the hunt.

As the two women strolled past the stores in downtown Fort Scott, they spoke about the case. At one point, Ruth began to giggle.

"The poems are so silly," she said to Mary. "I can't make any sense out of them. I think *I* could do better than that."

Mary managed a nervous giggle of her own. But she couldn't help feeling like a man with a knife might be waiting in any doorway.

8

HYPNOTIZED

The next letter was mailed on November 16 to a newspaper reporter at the *Wichita Eagle and Beacon* named Fred Mann. The Poet wanted his help.

Mann's byline had appeared over one of the stories that followed up on the Finley stabbing. The Poet wanted him to take out two personal ads in the classified section of the paper. The Poet had included a five-dollar bill to pay for the ads.

"To RSF—The price of my service to stay alive can now be settled at 5," read the first.

"To Lt.—Study my message & you will see, the meeting with me calls for 3. Day told later, time midnight. Easy to see how many cars by lights. Go E. on 54 to 1st airport you see. Turn S. & go on to Pawnee. I'll wait on a bridge by a bend in the road. Stop yur car here & I'll count yur load. This will be called Big Game 3. The winner of this one will be me."

Then the Poet warned Mann, "I am beginning to dislike the Lt. as much as some bitches & I don't want to do that. Man should not turn on man. There are mongrels after the little guy.

"I don't want to hate the Lt. as much as bitches. You agree with that. I told her not to tell the pigs. All bitches are dum & shuld be desexualized for punishment. This is man to man."

The police wanted to exploit the situation and establish Mann as a link to the Poet through the newspaper's personal ads. They saw a chance to communicate with the man, draw him out, and perhaps eventually establish a trust between the Poet and Mann. That might allow them to find out something personal about the Poet, some small piece of information that could lead to his identity.

The police and the media generally eye each other with suspicion and mistrust. The nature of their jobs automatically creates an adverse relationship: The media must find out what's going on in an investigation to keep the public informed, and the police must release only as much information about an investigation as they think the public should know. But to the Wichita officers in charge of protecting Ruth, the Poet's new letter had just erased that line.

Drowatzky, Zortman, and Chief LaMunyon gathered in the office of the newspaper's executive editor, Davis Merritt, to make their pitch. The meeting also featured the new officer in charge of the Criminal Investigations Bureau, Captain Mike Hill, who had recently replaced Thimmesch. Mann and a few of the newspaper's top editors joined in as well.

"This is the first chance we've had to communicate with the Poet," LaMunyon said after the officers briefed Merritt on the history of the case. "We believe he might be reaching out [to find] a friend."

The officers wanted the paper to print the Poet's ads as they were written, deleting only the specific directions to the meeting site to keep curious readers from flooding the area. The bridge the Poet chose was the same one he had mentioned to Ruth before he stabbed her. Police scouted the area and devised a stakeout plan.

Below the Poet's ads, the reporter was asked to place an ad of his own asking the Poet to contact him if he needed any other assistance.

Of course, the police made it clear that the paper could not report on any of this.

"What's in it for us?" Merritt wanted to know.

"You will be given all the letters and kept up-to-date on the investigation," LaMunyon said.

Merritt turned to Mann. "What do you think?"

Mann wanted to cooperate. A woman's life might be at stake; there seemed little choice. On top of that, BTK had given up on the paper after it failed to print one of his letters. BTK had sent his next letter to a TV station, thereby handing the station a scoop.

"I think we should go along with it just to keep this guy writing to us and nobody else," Mann told Merritt.

Merritt paused. "We just want to be sure that if we climb into bed with you, it's not a one-night stand," he told LaMunyon.

"We're in it all the way," LaMunyon replied.

The Poet's ads ran the next three days. Mann's ad ran between them. On the advice of the police, Mann's ad was written in verse. They wanted him to establish rapport by aping the Poet's preferred form of expression.

> *Have done what you ask*
> *as you can see*
> *Directions deleted, but will get message to he & she*
> *Anything else, feel free*
> *to get in touch with me.*

The lines weren't Shakespeare, but the tactic worked.

"I like you," the Poet responded by letter on December 7. "I am glad you joined up with me. Do you like females?"

A poem for Ruth was enclosed.

> *Twas the night before Christmas & all through yur house,*
> *Ruth wasn't stirring, yur as quiet as a mouse. Yur stocking*
> *was tight around her neck with care. I hoped the Lt. wuld*
> *not soon be there. You couldn't nestle, a female might be dead,*
> *while visions of yur ignominy danced in my head. Her mouth*

shut by a kerchief, a knife in yur lap. No air makes it easy for a permanent nap. When out on the street there arose such a clatter, I had to escape to see what was the matter. Away to the window I flew like a flash. Tore open the shutter, knifes make for a slash. The moon on 2 breasts in the new fallen snow gave me a great cephalic glow. When what to my victorious eyes should appear, a Police Lt. too late to rescue you, dear. But watching the drivers so lively and quick, I knew in a minute it was pigs with guns & sticks. Faster than anything the necrology came & they whistled & shouted & called out the name. So up to the house all the pigs flew, a trunk full of female & the lt. too. As I drew in my head & was turning around, down the chimney yur lt. came with a bound. But as you lay in yur state of decompose, no one can find you to send you a rose.

There was no mention of the meeting by the bridge.

Mann placed another ad letting the Poet know his poem had been forwarded to Ruth.

"I knew I culd count on you to assist," the Poet replied a week later. "I have this all worked out. No more correspondence to her for plans. She & her lt. would conjure retaliation."

So much for the meeting. But a dialogue had been established. The Poet included a few poems about Ruth he hoped Mann would admire. They were all written in the familiar Mother Goose style and had Christmas themes.

"It's Xmas eve with tinsel on the tree," said one. "No one will relate a thought to me."

"It's Xmas eve, a time dubbed divine, with expensive cogitation on vexations of mind."

"It's Xmas eve, with wind & snow. A mystic advantage for a way to go."

A system was devised for turning the letters sent to Mann over to the police. Mann would take them unopened to the police station, where he would be escorted to the lab. There, the envelope would be sliced open on three sides by a letter opener. The sheets of paper would be removed with forceps and placed on a piece of black backing paper, then put in a folder of clear plastic.

Saliva tests were performed on the envelopes just below the gummy strip on the flaps; the pages of the letters were treated with ninhydrin acid to raise prints.

All of the letters were fingerprint-free.

Two days before Christmas, Ruth opened the drapes over her back-door window and saw a piece of paper wedged between the slats of the back porch. It was rolled up and tied with a red string.

Ed took the paper to the police. "All the females butchered, some of them dead. Blood flowing from wounds in crimson Xmas red. My penance will be a just, greedy lust. Why into a world of penurious females are we thrust?"

Zortman planned to stay in the Finleys' house on Christmas Eve. He would arrive at 11:00 p.m., after the Finleys finished their family celebration. Until then, the house would be bustling with activity because Brent and Bruce, the Finley boys, would be home. The boys knew almost nothing about the Poet's violent campaign against their mother.

Ruth regretted that Zortman had to spend the night with them, although she supposed it was necessary, considering how much the Poet had written lately about doing something to her on Christmas. She had spent the day cleaning the house from top to bottom and baking pies; she relished the chance to feel like a mother again.

Ruth thought back to a Christmas Eve several years earlier when her son, Bruce, had finally phoned home.

—◊◊◊—

Bruce had always been the son Ruth and Ed worried about. When his high school experimented with not taking attendance, Bruce had taken full advantage. He'd walk in the front door, walk out the back door, and go play pool at the Golden Cue, a local hall. When Ruth confronted him one night, Bruce refused to promise to stop. The very next day, Ruth found him back at the Golden Cue.

Bruce would flash his mom a winning grin and bat his blue eyes. Ruth couldn't resist his charm and forgave him easily. He wasn't lazy—he worked hard at construction jobs in the summers—he just didn't want to live his life on anyone else's terms.

When Bruce's risk-taking led him to drugs later in high school, his charm disappeared. He started lying to Ruth and Ed. Little things, like denying responsibility for parking tickets, or telling them he had renewed his driver's license when he hadn't. He became lethargic, a shell of his formerly energetic self.

One night, Bruce was involved in a shooting outside a movie theater. He escaped, but most of the crew he ran with wound up in jail. When Ruth read about the incident in the paper the following day and saw Bruce's friends' names, she felt sick.

She and Ed began to suspect Bruce was dealing drugs. When Ruth found a white powdery substance in his room, she phoned the police. She could think of no other way to stop him. The police, however, were not interested. They told Ruth that even if it was cocaine, the amount was too small to be of any significance.

Without other recourse, Ruth told Bruce what she had done. "Either you stop it, or I will," she warned.

At the time, Bruce seemed contrite. But he didn't stop.

One day Ed came home unexpectedly during a workday, surprising Bruce and a couple of his friends, who were getting high.

The boys bolted from the house, and neither Ed nor Ruth heard from Bruce for an entire year.

Finally, on Christmas Eve, Bruce had phoned his parents. He had moved to Haysville, he explained, to live with a girlfriend and work construction. He had stopped using drugs. He loved Ruth and Ed, he said, through tears, and he wanted to come home. What had started as another sad holiday without their youngest son had ended with hope and connection.

After that festive Christmas, things worked out for Bruce, but since the year he'd disappeared, Ruth always felt additional pressure. He moved to Denver to build houses and to take classes in computing. He worked a steady job for a Denver computer firm, and he visited his parents more often than Brent did, even though he lived farther away. He was also much more interested in the Poet's activities than Brent was. He was furious about what was happening to his mother, but also fascinated by the case. He couldn't talk about it enough.

Brent always changed the subject.

—◊◊—

While they waited for Zortman to arrive, the Finleys enjoyed Christmas Eve dinner, filled with conviviality and the warmth of family. After dinner, the family exchanged gifts, the lights of the Christmas tree glittering in the windows.

Later, somebody would remember hearing a car start up outside the house shortly after 8:30 p.m. Thirty minutes later, when Brent picked up the receiver of the basement phone to call his girlfriend in Kansas City, the line was dead.

He went upstairs to use the kitchen phone, but that one didn't work, either.

Ed went to the back porch to inspect the phone lines that climbed up the house.

They had been cleanly cut.

—◊◊—

"You are floating in clouds, Ruth. Floating, floating, floating, going back, back, back. The pages of the calendar are turning back, now, turning back, back."

The voice of Dr. Donald Schrag issued softly from the headphones on Ruth's head, riding a wave of mellow music. Ruth lay on a gently vibrating leather chair in Schrag's office. The interview room was carpeted and contained a closed-circuit camera mounted in the ceiling. Ruth, covered by a blanket, listened to the voice in the headphones and felt herself floating on the clouds while she envisioned calendar pages peeling away.

"Would you like flowers?" the voice asked.

"Yes," Ruth said.

"What kind of flowers would you like?"

"Roses."

Schrag, a trim man in his mid-forties, watched Ruth in a monitor from another office down the hall. "Back," he said into a microphone. "Back, back, back."

Hypnosis, Schrag had told Ruth, could help her see things as she had not seen them before. He would guide her through the kidnapping and stabbing incidents, and Ruth would be able to relive them with greater clarity and perhaps remember details that had slipped from her conscious mind. Perhaps she'd even recall something like a license plate number.

Schrag was the first private psychologist in Tuscaloosa, Alabama, and he had been a believer in hypnosis since the late 1960s, when he'd attended a seminar on the procedure. He became convinced of its merits after one of his toughest patients, a chronically depressed woman, had been transformed. Her experience with hypnosis helped her to remember that she had been raped as a child by her father. Discovering why she was depressed had enabled Schrag's patient to begin the healing process.

Schrag believed in hypnosis enough to offer his services free of charge to the Oklahoma City police. In one case, he'd hypnotized the victims of a serial rapist and extracted from them enough similar details that a police artist was able to draw a highly detailed composite. The rapist was identified and captured. He pled guilty to the crimes.

When Schrag moved to Wichita, he again volunteered his services to the police department. He had worked on the BTK case, drawing up a psychological profile and also publishing an editorial in the *Wichita Eagle and Beacon*. The editorial described BTK in more-sympathetic psychological terms than other experts had used. Schrag's underlying purpose in writing it, of course, was to encourage BTK to get in touch with him. The strategy had not yet worked.

Zortman sat with Schrag in the office, down the hall from Ruth. The detective had worked with Schrag before and seen for himself how witnesses could open up under hypnosis.

Still upset that he had not been at the Finleys' house when the phone lines were cut on Christmas Eve, five days earlier, he diligently supplied Schrag with all the information the police had gathered on the case. Such an oversight would not happen again, Zortman and the other detectives vowed. After the last incident, the Poet was the top priority in the CIB. They were willing to try anything.

Schrag flipped the calendar in Ruth's head all the way back to 1946. He asked her to picture the boardinghouse where she was branded by the flatiron. He had her walk around it, finally had her walk inside. Ruth, bundled in a blanket on the leather chair, felt more relaxed than she had in years.

"Do you see the man?" Schrag asked.

"Yes."

"Can you describe him?"

"Oh, big, kind of ugly."

"Is that the same man who stabbed you, Ruth?"

"No."

Schrag turned the calendar forward, to the night Ruth had received the first phone call about the brand on her thighs. Ruth could recall no new details about the conversation.

Then Schrag led her through her two downtown confrontations with the man, but she was again unable to recall anything new.

Schrag stopped the calendar again on November 21, 1978, the date of the kidnapping. Ruth saw the car immediately. "Do you see a license plate?" Schrag asked.

Ruth went silent. "No," she said at last.

As Schrag led Ruth through the entire incident, she remembered a new detail: the Poet had pulled a knife out of one of his boots after spotting a police car. The knife had a red-and-white-striped handle with an inlaid star.

The sight of the squad car had enraged the Poet, Ruth said. "He told me no fucked-up whore or no goddam police lieutenant would ever get him again, and that if they came to our car, I wouldn't say a word. So I shut my eyes. Then the driver said it was all clear and he made up another poem."

"What's the poem?" Schrag asked.

"'Creatures in mighty arms are snatched / Females against man are mismatched,'" Ruth said.

She also remembered seeing a red handkerchief on the floor of the back seat. She said she picked it up when the Poet wasn't looking and put it in her purse.

Schrag asked her if she had picked up the handkerchief in an unconscious desire to keep the Poet from shoving it in her mouth, the way the man in Fort Scott had in 1946.

Ruth said, "No. It just seemed like the thing to do."

But then she remembered the police in Fort Scott had not found a handkerchief at the scene, and so they assumed Ruth was lying about having one stuffed into her mouth.

Maybe she had taken the one in the car so she would have proof that the kidnapping was real, she told Schrag.

Schrag flipped the calendar to August 13, and led her step-by-step through the stabbing at Towne East, but Ruth was unable to supply any new details.

After the session, Schrag and Ruth were disappointed.

"I guess I wasn't very helpful," she said, shaking hands with Schrag as she exited his office. "I'm puzzled why I can't remember more, but I guess I was in such a state."

Schrag watched her walk down the hall to the reception area. He was struck that she had not shown much emotion as she relived the events.

One possibility, he reasoned, was that Ruth Finley wasn't a good subject for hypnosis. Some people simply were not.

The second possibility was that Ruth wasn't very bright. She was impervious to the surrounding world. Unobservant. Dumb.

But Schrag had trouble with that one. He couldn't square it with the fact that she had raised a son bright enough to become a doctor.

9

POETRY IS HARD WORK

Soon after, the Poet wrote to Drowatzky. "Execution not carried out on schedule. Am working on new time and am going to let someone no when plan complete. She can't keep her mouth shut."

Five days later, the Poet wrote again to Drowatzky. "I missed carrying out this execution by about 15 seconds. I will have timing better next attempt."

Drowatzky did not see this letter. A few days earlier, he had been promoted to captain and placed in charge of the vice division. Much to his frustration, the Poet case was no longer his.

The next day, the phone lines at the Finley house were cut again. There was no way to determine precisely when this had happened, however, because the cut lines were fake. The phone company had run new lines underground after the Christmas Eve incident, putting the dummy lines on the house so the Poet would not notice.

That wasn't the only new security measure. A video camera had been installed in an old cement fountain in the backyard, its cables concealed in a garden hose. The back gate had been rigged with an alarm system. A still camera had been mounted beneath an eave overhanging the back porch; its shutter would be tripped if the telephone lines were cut.

"Ring, ring, yur phone don't ring," the Poet wrote to Ruth in mid-January. "Can't call yur Lt and tell him a thing. You have been a real sorry ass whiner and for that and other things I will see you in hell."

The Poet's recent binge of activity signaled to Dr. Schrag that he was agitated, on the verge of coming into the open. He encouraged police to have Fred Mann, the reporter, put another ad in the newspaper. The Poet had not written to Mann for several weeks, so Mann placed an ad in which he complained that the Poet had forgotten him.

The ad was answered almost immediately.

"I wunder if you talked to Lt. Drowatzky with me, but I think he listens to females and wuld try to get me in trouble. Poetry is hard work. I am going to try a new approach."

At 1:45 p.m. on Friday, January 25, the phone on Ruth's office desk rang.

She would later tell police she had recognized the voice on the other end instantly. The man told her to come down to the lobby; he had a package for her. Ruth said no, but she offered to think it over and call him back. "No," the voice said, "you'll just call your fucking lieutenant." Then he hung up, and she phoned Zortman.

The police had installed an automatic tracing device in the phone, which showed that the call had been made from the pay phone in the phone company lobby. Zortman sped to the scene. On the phone booth's counter, he found a twelve-inch butcher knife wrapped in white butcher paper and old newspaper and bound with a red bandanna.

He radioed for backup.

The Poet had picked a risky place and time to strike. The lobby had been busy all afternoon with people coming in to pay bills, buy telephones, or establish accounts. The police had plenty of potential witnesses.

A few customers remembered a commotion near the booth around the time the call to Ruth was placed. Somebody had been using the phone and wouldn't get out of the booth. When Zortman showed the interviewees the police rendering of the Poet's face, two women positively identified it.

"He was in the booth," said one of the women. "He was turned away, but that's the same hair and glasses."

The other woman agreed.

Zortman and the other cops felt relief. For the first time, they had witnesses who had actually seen the man who had been terrorizing Ruth.

The lab found no prints on the knife, the butcher paper, the newspaper, nor the bandanna. Lab officers X-rayed the knife, to see if it contained some sort of explosive device, but found nothing. There was no note, no poem, no letter in the package.

They studied the newspaper for a message scrawled in the margins, or anything else relevant. Nothing.

However, when Ruth arrived home that night, a new letter was waiting.

Think in yur mind that you are dead
You no in yur brain my soul is quieted.
Think of going around being a tramp
Yur under the ground where it's cold & damp.
Dream of me and obey my commands
Think of me with a knife in my hands.

—⁓—

Detective Richard Vinroe, a nine-year veteran of the force, was stunned by the volume of material the department had amassed on the Poet case. It surrounded him on his new desk in the Criminal Investigations Bureau, where he had recently been transferred from the forgery and fraud division. He felt swamped, but he knew he had to push forward; the case was all his now. Zortman was in the hospital for a back operation that would take him out of commission for weeks. George Anderson had been promoted to lieutenant and reassigned. The sandy-haired, boyishly handsome Vinroe had heard a great deal about the case, but he had no idea where to begin.

Vinroe prided himself on his common sense. It was, he thought, his greatest asset. He had an ability to put himself in other people's shoes, to understand both the motives of criminals and the feelings of their victims. When he first joined the department, Vinroe had volunteered for the northeast beat because he thought it was where the action was. He was right: his very first day on the job, he'd worked a homicide.

Vinroe had reported to work every day with a sunny attitude. Eventually, life on the beat had grown smooth.

But in the Poet Vinroe faced an adversary he did not understand, a crazy person whose shoes were difficult to slip into, somebody who confounded common sense.

Vinroe studied the massive paperwork the case had generated. The police had investigated more than three hundred suspects. Records and backgrounds had been checked on most, mug shots taken of all, a card catalog system established to keep track of them.

Calls continued to come in. Some were from other states, people reporting uncles and cousins they hadn't seen in twenty years who bore scant resemblance to the sketch of the Poet. Every name had to be checked, every suspect photographed. It had been eighteen months since Ruth had received the first phone call, and the case had become both embarrassing and costly for the department.

Vinroe was confused by the reports. He talked to the officers who had spent time with Ruth, and they all spoke fondly of her. Vinroe himself had returned Ruth's purse to her in the hospital after she was stabbed. He had liked her, too. But he couldn't make sense of the timeline and events.

One thing Vinroe wanted to do was reinforce the link between the Poet and Fred Mann, the reporter. Letters from the Poet to Ruth and the police contained only rambling poems. They needed hard information. The more letters the Poet composed to Mann, the greater the chance he would slip up.

Vinroe urged Mann to place another ad.

"I like your poetry," Mann wrote, coming as close as he dared to lying. "Send more."

The Poet's answer came one week later.

The Poet's opening line was a grabber: "I decided to tell you my plans." But the rest was merely a list of items the Poet had taken from Ruth's purse during the abduction: matchbooks, buttons, a handkerchief, a grocery list, and a one-hundred-dollar bond.

Three days later, the Poet wrote a letter to Ruth saying he planned to tell the public that she had willingly given him the items he had mentioned in the previous letter. "They will no I haven't been bothering you," he wrote. "You think about that. It won't sound too good for you when I start talking."

When he read the letter, Captain Mike Hill was furious. He wasn't about to let the Poet get away with a lie like that. Hill was fed up with the case, anyway. It was taking time away from other cases and draining his men and his budget.

Hill, a large, beefy man, six feet two and 230 pounds, suffered frustration poorly. Hill was a man in a hurry.

Hill possessed a feverish desire to rise to the top of the law enforcement business. In June, it had been decided that he would succeed Thimmesch as head of the CIB that autumn. There was some irony in his appointment—he had previously been a vocal critic of the CIB because he did not see the point of having a separate unit to investigate major crimes.

His goal was to be chief or sheriff. Soon after his appointment, Hill had traveled to the University of Louisville to attend a six-month course in police administration. Hill had been in Louisville when Ruth was stabbed, and he was still catching up on the case.

Hill lay in bed at night thinking about the Poet. And now the guy was boldly declaring his intention to lie about stealing from Ruth's purse.

Hill had had enough. He decided to go to the media.

The course in Louisville had included classes on media engagement. Taking the course material to heart, Hill called a news conference, with the goal of beating the Poet to the punch.

At the conference, Hill released the contents of Ruth's letter, and then, right there in front of the TV cameras, he called the Poet a liar.

Hill knew it was risky to anger the Poet and potentially place Ruth in greater danger, but he thought the time had come to take risks. They weren't going to catch their culprit by sitting around reading poems. Those had been analyzed to death by experts, read upside down and backward, studied for anagrams and other word games that might reveal hidden messages—all without luck.

"The only way we'll get him is to bring the son of a bitch into the open," Hill told his men.

That meant the police would have to bring Ruth into the open as well. She had not left the phone company building by herself since her abduction more than twelve months before.

Detectives had ruled out the possibility that the Poet would try to pick Ruth off with a rifle. Striking from a distance wasn't his style. He liked to get close to Ruth and taunt her; it was part of the game. So, on selected days, the police put Ruth in a bulletproof vest and had her walk to lunch downtown during the busy noon hour, accompanied by a policewoman in plain clothes and watched by undercover officers stationed along a preplanned route. The police were trolling, and Ruth was the bait.

Just about everybody in the CIB was called in for these walks. In addition to the policewoman at Ruth's side, six to eight detectives were planted on the streets, while several more cruised the area in unmarked cars.

The walks started in February, in bitter winter winds. The Poet, they believed, would watch Ruth carefully, calculating his moves, waiting for the right moment to strike. In the meantime, the officers on the streets were looking for the Poet in the crowd, peering into windows of restaurants, trying to spot his thin face and haunted eyes. He had to be there somewhere. He was always there somewhere.

Ruth hated the walks. For one thing, she never knew when they would occur until just before her lunchtime, so she couldn't plan ahead. The detectives would wait until 11:30 a.m. to phone her.

Ruth was embarrassed by all the fuss. The bulletproof vest was uncomfortable. But the worst part was that she had to eat lunch by herself. The policewoman who walked beside her took a seat at another table in whichever restaurant had been selected. Even surrounded by officers, sitting by herself at a table in a downtown restaurant made Ruth feel lonely.

Ruth started to have a recurring dream about the walks. In the dream, she was walking past the large windows of a downtown bank when she noticed the Poet inside, staring out. He dashed out of the building and started after her. Ruth noticed he was carrying a book under his arm. She tried to read the title but could only make out the words "Poems by . . ." The Poet's hand covered the rest.

In the dream, Ruth ran. The police were all around her, but she couldn't get their attention. She ran faster, but the Poet kept gaining on her. She knew she couldn't outrun him, but she still kept running. Soon the Poet was right behind her, reaching for her. She darted into the middle of the street, right into the path of an oncoming bus. Then she woke up.

Ruth hated the walks.

—⁂—

The Poet began harassing local Wichita businesses, sending out more than fifty letters in a six-month period. He told a local mortuary to contact Ruth about its services, saying she would be requiring them soon. He told the gas and electric company to turn off the Finleys' utilities. He informed the health department that Ruth was spreading venereal disease. He sent a construction company to cover the Finleys' driveway with dirt, and he asked the DMV to confiscate Ruth's license because of her "hazardous" and "dangerous" driving habits. He wrote to Ruth's bank to say it should transfer all her money. He mailed a five-dollar bill to a local florist with the request that one black flower be sent to Ruth.

Most of the businesses recognized the handwriting and turned the letters over to police. Only the construction company followed through on the Poet's request, dispatching a truck loaded with dirt to the Finleys' house. The truck was about to dump the dirt in the driveway when a host of police officers—summoned by a neighbor—arrived at the house and told the truck driver to leave.

Vinroe investigated each business that received a letter. None of the businesses, except the electric and phone companies, were the biggest or most prominent in their field, nor were they widely advertised. Why, he wondered, did the Poet pick those particular places? He interviewed employees and owners to see if the Poet might be a regular customer. He even made a list of the organizations the employees and owners belonged to, searching for one in common, an organization that might include the Poet as a member.

With Vinroe performing the grunt work, Hill called again on the media. He wanted to appeal to "Buddy," the man who had driven the car during Ruth's abduction.

"I, or any of my detectives, will meet to talk with Buddy anytime, at any hour of the day he wants," Hill announced at a press conference on February 21. "If he didn't know the intentions of the Poet at that time, he didn't commit any crimes." Hill also noted that the three-thousand-dollar reward offered by Ed's boss still stood.

Two weeks later, a man identifying himself as "Buddy" phoned KAKE-TV. He asked the station to contact the police; he would call the following day to talk with an officer.

Hill was exultant. "Tell him I'll kiss his ass in the middle of Douglas and Market!" he whooped.

Recording equipment was hooked to the station's switchboard, and a detective was stationed at the phones all the next day, waiting.

Buddy never called.

—⁂—

On March 18, more than one month after Ruth embarked on her police-escorted walks, the Poet wrote Mann a tantalizing message: "I saw her Friday but she was with some other female at the tele. ofs. I think she went to eat early because she went back at 12:35."

The police checked their records. They had indeed walked Ruth to lunch that Friday. And they had returned at exactly 12:35.

Where had the Poet been? Why hadn't they spotted him? They had blanketed the goddam area.

It was time for Ruth to walk alone, without the female officer at her side.

On March 21 at noon, a nervous Ruth stepped out of the phone company building truly by herself for the first time since her abduction. The day was cold and damp. Ruth walked through the bustling crowd of lunchgoers along a prearranged route, ate alone in a restaurant, and then returned to work along the same route.

Nothing happened.

—⁂—

Later that week, Ruth returned to the office of Dr. Donald Schrag accompanied by a police artist. Hill wanted her to describe the Poet under hypnosis for an updated, more detailed sketch. The session lasted two hours. The new drawing, sketched in colored chalk, showed a man with shorter hair and a deeply furrowed forehead. He possessed a sad, worried look in his brown eyes, and his mouth was slightly open. He seemed on the verge of tears.

Detectives were only slightly bothered that this picture was different than the others. Under hypnosis, Ruth was bound to give more details that would alter the sketch. When the session was finished, Ruth told Vinroe that it was the most accurate sketch yet.

Zortman had recovered from his back operation and returned to duty. Privately, he and Vinroe began to doubt that Ruth really remembered what the Poet looked like. She hadn't seen him since the stabbing, and the police had shown her hundreds of mug shots since then. All those faces were bound to cloud her memory. They decided not to release the new sketch to the media right away.

Schrag said the Poet "is obviously a bright individual, which makes it so difficult to catch him. He's not ignorant enough to do something so impulsive that he's going to get caught. On the other hand, the content of his letters and the associations he expresses exhibit mental confusion. He's aware all is not right in his mind, but the emotional conflicts are such that he can't help himself from doing what he's doing. Anyone else who comments about him in public becomes the enemy, and the whole community becomes an extension of Ruth Finley. He's become part of her. She's become part of his emotional needs in some way.

"I think he's getting sicker," Schrag concluded, "and eventually his judgment will become so impaired he'll do something people are going to pick up on."

Two days later, Hill decided to release the sketch, along with Schrag's observations.

The Poet wasted no time in responding.

Dr., smart doctor, tell me true
What harm has this slut done to bring ridicule from you?

After that the Poet stopped writing.

10

WATCHING AND WAITING

Instead of sitting in their basement and engaging in their hobbies like before, Ruth and Ed now watched the monitor every night—a black-and-white still life of their back door. A leaf floating across the screen, or a neighbor's cat, would send a jolt of fear through them. Ed sometimes bolted off the sofa at the smallest flicker of motion.

He and Ruth were alone again—the police had long since moved out of the house—and Ed was beginning to question his sanity. He was frightened by his own actions. One night wind blew open the back gate, triggering the alarm, and he had raced outside and down the street, ancient rifle in hand, ready to kill someone.

He had become foolhardy. Ed had taken few risks in his life. He went to college because that's what men coming out of the service did. His passion was art, but when counselors at the junior college in Fort Scott advised him to go into the more stable business track, he followed their advice. He drank beer at the Land Inn because that's where his classmates went.

The biggest jolt of his life had come in 1941 when his parents moved from Kansas City to Bronson, Missouri. A city kid, Ed felt out of place in the country. When he was forced to skip the eighth grade and start high school one year younger than the other freshman boys, he became withdrawn, making no close friends.

High school was a depressing time for Ed. The war was on and there were no sports or art courses to take. He drew and painted by himself, concentrating on war themes and projecting his own fantasies of heroism onto paper.

But adventure was confined to Ed's imagination. In real life, the only risk he had taken was lying about his age to get into the military. When he graduated from high school in 1945, he wanted to fight for his country, but he was only seventeen. Elmer Finley signed the papers for Ed to join the navy. Elmer himself had been too young to join the Spanish-American War, but he had done so anyway.

Ed entered the navy as an aerial gunner, stationed in San Diego, but within a few months, his dreams of combat had ended along with the war. He wound up typing, filing, and keeping records. When he enlisted for two years, he'd hoped to go on to photography school, but was instead assigned to gunnery school in San Diego, where he learned how to strip and reassemble a .50-caliber machine gun. This, he often reflected dismally, was not the best preparation for a return to civilian society.

The familiar feeling of being out of place was now returning, just at the point he had hoped would be the best time of married life, with his children raised and building lives of their own. The Poet had shoved him into a role he was poorly prepared to play. Preferring a quiet life with Ruth, he was now the husband of a woman being pursued by some sort of sexual deviant. He loved the clean definition of his art and his bookkeeping, but he was forced to live in uncertainty and fear, confronting the frayed edges of his own nerves.

He hated the Poet with a depth of passion that alarmed him. He brooded about it constantly, especially after those times when the gate alarm had sounded and he had dashed outside, gun in hand, heart pounding, fear and hatred pumping through his arteries, running down the street after . . . what? A ghost.

He didn't know what he would do if he ever caught the Poet. But he was beginning to realize he could easily kill the man, and that scared him. Often at night, watching the monitor, Ruth at his side on the sofa, the night alive with its peculiar noises and shadows, Ed prayed the police would catch the Poet before he did.

Friends who used to stop by the house now seldom came to visit. Those who did, Ed and Ruth noticed, began backing their cars into the driveway so the Poet wouldn't see their license plates. One policewoman even removed her plate before coming over in her own car.

The Finleys understood what these people were feeling.

"You know we're there if you need us," their friends told them, and the Finleys would nod.

At work, Ruth felt the eyes of her coworkers on her whenever she left her secluded office. She knew they were thinking that the Poet might be in the building. He might be one of them. He could get her any minute. They didn't avoid her, and they were quite sympathetic, but she could sense their discomfort. They knew she couldn't leave the building, but sometimes friends would start to ask her to join them for lunch, then catch themselves and apologize, and Ruth would have to laugh about it to set them at ease.

Her stomach was bothering her constantly, ever since the stabbing. She would come home from work and be unable to do anything except go to her bedroom and lie down.

Among the few regular guests at the Finley home were Bernie Drowatzky and his wife, Dorann. Drowatzky, now captain of the vice squad, had grown attached to the Finleys when he was in CIB. He and Dorann shared their church and the same conservative beliefs as Ruth and Ed, so the Finleys enjoyed and valued their company. Often their talk turned to the Poet, a subject Ruth never minded. The police gave Ed copies of every letter the Poet wrote, and Ruth typed them up in the evenings on clean white typing paper and kept them in a notebook. They were difficult to read in their original, poorly scrawled form, and typing them helped her make sense out of them, although she had to stop to look up the meanings of some of the words he used.

Ruth was not sleeping well. She'd fall asleep without much trouble, but then she'd awake in the wee hours with her mind racing. Staring at the clock on the nightstand, she'd think about how much like a prison her house had become to her.

The electronic surveillance gear, meant to protect her, she knew, only reminded her of the danger she was in. Ed felt the same way. There was no reason for them to be living like this, he often told her. They'd done nothing to deserve it.

Alone, they watched. And waited. And heard only silence.

Nobody had heard from the Poet for a month. The case had evaporated, leaving the police with nothing but a pile of rambling letters and a woman to protect.

—∞—

By now the police had more than four hundred names of suspects in the card catalog. Even with no new Poet stories appearing in the media, the police received two or three phone calls every day reporting everyone from friends and neighbors to city officials, a sportswriter for the Wichita newspaper, and a police officer or two.

Detective Richard Vinroe focused on names that appeared more than once, but this led him to very few likely suspects. Ninety-nine percent of the men worked every day, and Vinroe doubted the Poet had a job. More likely, Vinroe thought, the man subsisted on some sort of unemployment or disability insurance, or worked temporary jobs.

Everybody on the force was caught up in the search. Officers who had no direct involvement in the case trailed Poet look-alikes in their off-duty hours, sometimes bringing these men in for questioning. Mug shots were snapped of each suspect; invariably, they were rejected by Ruth.

Vinroe went undercover as a homeless person. He let his beard grow, donned a stained army jacket, faded Levis, and soiled running shoes, tucked a cheap bottle of wine in a jacket pocket, and went in search of men who wore their hair just so and sported wire-rimmed glasses.

He was astounded at how many men matched the Poet's description. They were all over—inside the Koma Lounge and the Blue Lounge, two dives on the east edge of downtown; in alleys and behind the dilapidated old buildings on East Douglas, where men shared bottles and huddled against the cold; inside the lobby of the Eaton Hotel, a stately old building on Douglas, once a posh hotel where presidents spent the night. Poet doppelgangers drifted in and out of liquor stores, leaned against storefronts, slept on benches, lounged in the vast, glassed-in lobby of the Fourth Financial Center on Douglas, idly thumbed through books and magazines at Rector's Bookstore, nursed coffee at the Coney Island hot dog stand, and read newspapers or drifted off to sleep in the lounge of the public library on Main Street.

Vinroe's days started at 7:00 a.m. He would watch Ed drop Ruth off for work at the phone company, and then walk an average of twelve miles per day before returning to the phone company at 5:00 p.m. for Ruth's pickup. Vinroe cased the buildings that possessed a good view of the phone company, thinking the Poet was using one of them as a vantage point. Every day he went home exhausted, counting his new blisters, but with no new leads.

On days when he stayed in the office to work on other cases, colleagues would drift to his desk, sipping coffee from Styrofoam cups, to talk about the Poet. There wasn't a cop who didn't have his own theory.

Most of the speculation centered on the Finley family. The Poet had been too lucky so far. He seemed to know a lot about Ruth and her activities, and a lot about what was going on at the Finley house. His timing on Christmas Eve had been impeccable, cutting the phone lines just before Zortman was due to arrive, with the house full of people. And he had managed to leave letters at the house with nobody in the neighborhood seeing him, even though the houses were closely bunched. He had to have inside information.

The police knew of Bruce Finley's past drug problems and his yearlong disappearance. They were no Freudian experts, but they knew the mother-son relationship offered a host of possible psychological problems.

Her brother, Morris, was another possibility. Detectives knew he had a quick temper from his performance at the hospital the night Ruth was stabbed, and he bore an eerie resemblance to Ruth's description of the Poet, although he was significantly taller. Motive was a problem, but the brother-sister relationship could be another source of turmoil. Maybe Ruth was covering up for him.

Morris—they also noted—had been home that night in 1946 when Ruth was attacked in the boardinghouse in Fort Scott, only twenty miles from the Finley farmhouse. In fact, Ruth had told police that when the man grabbed her from behind, she'd thought it was him.

But, even to the police who discussed them, these theories seemed far-fetched. More likely, the Poet was a friend of a friend of the Finleys, perhaps a coworker of Ruth or Ed whom the cops had missed in their background checks of employees at both businesses.

Unless it was Ed. Or both Ed and Ruth, because it seemed unlikely that one could be doing it without the other's knowledge; they were inseparable. At no time during private conversations with either of the Finleys had any cop picked up the slightest hint of marital discord. Ed was always attentive and loving toward Ruth, and Ruth was the same toward Ed.

But you never knew what tensions lurked below the surface of a relationship. An affair would explain so much. Ruth was attractive and might very well inspire an affair. Maybe Ed was trying to pay Ruth back for some transgression. Or maybe Ed had had the affair and he'd hired somebody to terrorize Ruth, hoping she'd go away.

Maybe the two of them had concocted the whole thing to derive some sort of kinky thrill out of writing dirty letters and gaining public attention for it.

Or maybe Ed had some perverse predilections and Ruth was covering up for him. They had seen many cases where women were being mistreated by their husbands but remained quiet or hid the truth. Maybe Ed had stabbed Ruth with one of her own kitchen knives, and Ruth had made up the story about Towne East to mislead the police. If so, it had worked; they had not investigated at the Finleys' house that night, which now struck some officers as a gross oversight.

But their speculation usually collapsed under the weight of everything the police knew about Ruth and Ed.

The first word that came to anyone's mind when describing Ruth was "nice." Nice and friendly. Polite. Stoic. A good mother, and a good worker. Soft-spoken and shy, she wasn't the type who sought attention. In fact, she decided not to talk to reporters, and she always politely declined requests for interviews.

Her shyness was almost girlish; she tended to speak in short sentences and end them with a giggle, sometimes even covering her mouth with her hand. She never used bad language, so it was impossible to imagine her writing anything as vile and profane as the Poet's letters. And when would she have had the time to write them all?

The officers who had spent time with Ruth admired her courage. She seemed remarkably composed for a woman being stalked by a man who wanted to kill her. She never cried; she never even spoke of being afraid.

Ruth could talk about the case, but she never seemed obsessed with it, either.

During their investigation, they had found no evidence of mental illness in Ruth, past or present. She did not seem suicidal.

And then there was Ed. He was the salt of the earth. An accountant. A former scoutmaster. A church elder, loving husband, and father.

A couple of things did bother the police about Ed, however. He was left-handed, and the stab wounds in the lower left side of Ruth's back indicated a left-handed assailant.

Another was that he had been an adopted child. The amateur shrinks on the force knew that adopted children sometimes grow up with a host of emotional problems.

The police had also learned that when Ed had been a scoutmaster, he sometimes led camping trips into the area near the airport east of town where the Poet wanted to take Ruth on the night of her stabbing. But that was a pretty slim connection.

Even the most skeptical officer had to admit that Ed seemed an unlikely suspect. When talking to him about the case, they could sense his helpless rage.

"I know you're doing all you can," Ed would tell them, "and we're mighty thankful. I just hope you get him before I do."

11

DEAD AND DEAD INDEED

"I have found work in Oklahoma & just get here some weekends," Detective Vinroe read. His heart sank.

The letter, postmarked from Wichita, was sent to reporter Fred Mann on May 5, more than a month after the Poet's last communication. The line was scribbled as a note below yet another rambling poem, copies of which the Poet had sent to Mike Hill, Ruth, and two television stations. However, the line about finding work in Oklahoma appeared only on the copy sent to Mann, the Poet's new pal, which made Vinroe think it was true.

And if it was true, that was bad news. The police would have to widen the investigation by notifying Oklahoma authorities about the case, which meant more time, more travel, more money, more manpower. There was no indication of where in Oklahoma the Poet had moved. Worse, if the Poet now spent most of his time out of town, officers would have fewer chances to catch him. Walking Ruth to lunch on weekdays would be futile.

If the Poet was only in Wichita on weekends, that meant working more overtime hours, and Vinroe was drained. His boyish face was haggard and pale from spending twelve hours a day on the case already. Even though the Poet had been quiet, a day had not passed in the last month without Vinroe doing something on the case—prowling the streets, running down names, doing background checks. He had thrown himself into the case with energy and enthusiasm, but now he was tired and frustrated, losing sleep and weight. The thought of expanding the search to another state filled him with dread.

On the other hand, it might open new avenues of investigation. The police didn't believe that the Poet drove a car. If the Poet traveled to Wichita on weekends, the police could check the bus schedule and stake out the station downtown. If he hitchhiked, somebody would identify him sooner or later. If he rode up with a friend, the friend might turn him in some day.

"He must have people in town," Vinroe told Mann.

Whatever the Poet had been doing since his last communication had not diminished his anger. His latest poem read:

> Bitches & whores marked with burning brands
> Gored & traduced by warriors' strong & fiery hands.
> Drowned & frozen & forever dead
> Blood stained the snow & the water is red.

Vinroe and Hill had been looking for a way to reestablish communication between the Poet and Mann, and another note from the Poet gave them an idea. "Culd you find out who was with her at 12:35 on Friday and report her to the chief?" the Poet wrote. "I don't think he will listen to me."

"We want you to tell him she was with a cop," Hill told Mann.

Mann wasn't sure he had heard Hill correctly. "Why?" he asked.

"It'll make him trust you more. He's probably smart enough to figure it out anyway, and he wouldn't believe you if you said she was with a friend. Besides, she's walking alone now. Let's get him stirred up a little."

Mann's response to the Poet appeared in the personals the following day: "Poet: Inquired as you requested and think you should be wary. Not sure, but think she was with constabulary."

The Poet responded to the newspaperman's ad by writing to KAKE-TV: "Something yur female reporters shuld check into. The Wichita police spend our tax payer's money on bitches to walk the downtown streets with whores. I have inside help to find this out . . . Call the chief or Capt. Mike Hill or Lt. Drowatzky & tell them you are on to them. I can't reveal my source."

The Poet also wrote to the Sedgwick County Mental Health Department advising them that a woman named Ruth Finley was spreading venereal disease.

Two weeks later, on May 20, Ed Finley discovered that the lock on the back gate of their house had been stolen.

The first week in June, Ruth and Ed drove to Colorado for their annual wedding anniversary vacation in Estes Park. That week, the Poet flooded Wichita with letters. All were postmarked from Oklahoma City.

The police were riveted by two verses the Poet included that contained BTK references:

> *There once was a female who curled her locks*
> *had to be taken away in a box*
> *So she'd know it was there put her petticoat on a chair*
> *the snorting beast gored by a restless fox.*

And:

> *Curly locks, curly locks, fox of mine*
> *pushed and squealed, but culd not tell the swine.*

To the police who had read BTK's 1977 poem that began "Shirley locks, shirley locks," these lines contained a frightening echo.

The letter concluded,

> *A man of words & not of deeds*
> *Is like a garden full of weeds.*

& when the weeds begin to grow
Like a garden full of snow
& when the snow begins to fall
Like a bird against a wall
& when the bird away does fly
Like a vulcher in the sky
& when the sky begins to roar
Like a lion at the door
& when the door begins to crack
Like a stick across yur back
& when yur back begins to smart
Like a knife in yur heart
& when yur heart begins to bleed
Yur dead & dead & dead indeed.

Three days after receiving the first letter postmarked from Oklahoma City, Vinroe, Hill, and assistant Sedgwick County attorney Paul Clark traveled there. The trio checked in with the Oklahoma City police, left copies of the composite sketch, and went to visit the Veterans Administration Hospital, one of the largest in the country, to look for patients who had recently moved there from Wichita. They suspected the Poet suffered from some sort of disability, and he had used stamps commemorating Vietnam War veterans on his letters from Oklahoma City.

They also left the police in Oklahoma City a warrant, filled in with the name "John Doe," for the arrest of the Poet. The warrant was Clark's idea. He realized that the two-year statute of limitations was about to expire on Ruth's kidnapping. The warrant would allow Oklahoma authorities to hold a suspect should they find one.

Now all they had to do was find one.

That same day, Detective Doyle Dyer received a phone call. "I know the man you want," the voice on the other end said.

Dyer was not impressed. As a member of the CIB, he had taken many such phone calls.

"I worked with him," the man on the phone said. "He's a dead ringer for the picture." Dyer toyed with a pen.

"I saw in the papers that the guy is writing from Oklahoma. Well, about the first of the year, this guy lost his job in Wichita and moved on down there. Fired. Now he makes trips back and forth all the time."

Dyer began taking notes, his interest growing keener.

"He lives out by a reservoir, Foss, out west of Oklahoma City. Lives out there all alone. This guy has never been married. And he's also had some trouble with the phone company. Had his phone pulled out, or something."

"Do you know when this was?"

"No, but I thought you might like to check him out. I'll tell you something—the biggest thing is that picture. If that isn't him, it's his twin, and he ain't got no twin."

"What's his name?"

There was a pause on the other end. "Well, I don't want to get into names," the caller said. Dyer had to stifle a moan. "But I will tell you that he worked for a water supply distributor up here."

The line went dead.

Water supply distributor. Good. There weren't too many of those around, Dyer thought. If they acted quickly, they could come up with a name and phone it down to Hill and Vinroe, who had left for Oklahoma City that morning.

Bill Hoch had been fired in December from a local water supply company. Resemblance to the sketch was uncanny. Handwriting on an invoice he had filled out was similar to the Poet's.

And there was a bonus: Hoch had once worked at the same aircraft company as Ruth's brother, Morris Smock.

—∞—

Hill and Vinroe were still going through printouts at the VA hospital when they heard the news. A quick check revealed that the hospital did not have a patient named William Hoch. But Oklahoma City police found a friend of his in the hospital, a paraplegic named Doc who told them Hoch drove him to the VA hospital once a month.

That afternoon, Hill, Vinroe, and Clark drove west out of Oklahoma City over dry, rolling prairie toward Foss Reservoir, in Custer County. They stopped at the Custer County sheriff's office in Clinton, explained what they were doing there, picked up a Custer County detective, and headed for the reservoir.

The lake, protected by hills and a windbreak of pine trees, was still when they arrived. A dozen houses and trailers belonging to Foss Lake Estates dotted the shore. The sun was low.

They drove to a small general store near the dam and approached the tiny, weathered woman behind the counter. Vinroe identified himself and held out the color sketch of the Poet. "You have any idea who that is?" he said.

The woman didn't hesitate.

"It's Bill," she said. "Bill Hoch."

He lived in a pale green trailer on the northeast side of the lake, she said.

"What do you want with Bill? He's a nice guy. What you ought to do is bust that whorehouse up on the hill. We don't go for that stuff around here."

The officers drove across the dam and down a stretch of dirt road. They spotted the trailer in a clearing of Chinese elms. The sight made their hearts race. From the outside, the trailer conformed perfectly to the residence they thought the Poet would inhabit: old, worn, dilapidated. They could almost imagine the walls inside plastered with pictures of Ruth and newspaper clippings of the Poet's escapades. They envisioned piles of notebooks, red bandannas, and books of poetry all over the floor. They couldn't wait to get inside. Vinroe and Hill walked to the trailer, and Hill knocked on the door.

Nobody was home.

—m—

Twenty-six miles away, in Elk City, three men sat at the bar of the Grenada Motel, sipping whiskey and listening to country music on the jukebox. One was a tool pusher on an oil drilling rig, another the manager of an oil supply outfit, and the third, a newcomer to the area, an oil field supply salesman. The newcomer was a slender man in blue jeans, boots, and a checkered short-sleeved shirt. He wore wire-rimmed glasses and had black hair that was graying on the sides. He didn't usually stop for a drink after work because he preferred to get home to take care of his two poodles, Napoleon Bonaparte and Princess. But after forking out $120 for a new air conditioner for his 1971 Oldsmobile that afternoon, he had felt like a drink. It was his first night out since he had moved south from Wichita.

Wichita had been too large for him. He was a small-town boy at heart. He'd had enough of Wichita by the time he was fired, although he would still see plenty of the city on weekend visits to his sister, Dolores, who lived on the west side.

Everything in his life was fine until he came down with a mystery illness in 1971. He just started shaking and sweating like crazy. He finally saw a doctor who put him in a hospital, where the doctors informed him that he had emphysema, with pneumonia on top. When he got out of the hospital and went back to work, he started to feel nervous all the time.

One day he just went nuts. He blew up. He didn't know what all he did; he was crazy.

Doctors gave him pills that were supposed to calm him down, but he didn't know what they were, and he also didn't know that he wasn't supposed to drink any alcohol while he was taking them. One day after work he took a pill, forgot that he took it, took another one, and then belted down some whiskey. Pretty soon he started sweating and hallucinating. When he drove home, he drove his car right through a neighbor's yard.

His sister, who lived just up the street, came over and told him the pills were a type of dope called Valium. Hoch flushed the pills down the toilet and vowed never to take this Valium stuff again. He didn't tolerate dope.

Doctors later discovered that his nervous problem stemmed from an overactive thyroid.

The man didn't tolerate a lot of things, dope and bad language being at the top of his list. His real passions were current events and dogs. Sitting at the motel bar, Hoch began to miss his dogs. He checked his watch. It was 8:00 p.m. Napoleon Bonaparte and Princess must be wondering where he was. They needed food and water. He looked around. The action at the Grenada was slow. Not many women out tonight. It looked like he would have to wait for another night to find a wife.

Bill "Coyote" Hoch excused himself from his two buddies and headed for his car.

A sliver of moon winked at him as he made the thirty-minute drive home to the reservoir. His head still buzzed from whiskey as he drove down the dirt road toward his trailer. His mind was on his two dogs, so he didn't notice the sheriff's car that pulled in behind him, its headlights off. He stopped the Olds in front of the trailer, switched off the engine, and opened the door.

Suddenly, flashlights beamed in his eyes and he felt hands grabbing him, yanking him out of the car. Then he was spun around and thrown against it. Hands swept his body; then his own hands were jerked behind him and he felt handcuffs being snapped on his wrists.

"What the hell?" he stammered. "Who are you guys?"

"We'll ask the questions," came the response.

As Hoch's eyes adjusted to the night, he picked out a couple of familiar faces. One belonged to Jim West, a detective from the Custer

County sheriff's office. The other was Tom Silas, a detective on the Clinton police force who lived near Hoch.

"Tom, what's this all about?" Hoch asked, but Tom didn't respond.

Hoch didn't recognize the other men. Hoch couldn't think of any reason why they would want to get inside the trailer. It was a junkyard in there. Nobody had lived in it for five years, not since a couple of women had sold it. All of a sudden, Hoch was glad he'd taken the mirrors off the ceiling. He knew what kind of women put mirrors on ceilings. "Go on in," Hoch told the big officer. "That one right there is the key."

Captain Mike Hill unlocked the door and entered the trailer with Vinroe. The moment they had seen Bill Hoch in the flashlight beams, they had grown hopeful. It was as if the color sketch of the Poet had come to life.

But they were disappointed when Hoch didn't object to letting them in the trailer. They were even more disappointed when they went inside. The place was a mess, all right—ashes and thick piles of dirt littered the floor, the rugs were worn, the furniture was losing its stuffing, and soiled dishes were piled in the sink. They found no notebooks, no bandannas, no newspaper clippings, no pictures of Ruth Finley, no physical evidence at all to connect Hoch to the case.

They searched Hoch's car and found nothing.

Then they took Hoch into Clinton for a long talk in the sheriff's office.

They listened to the life story of Bill Hoch from his birth in California in 1931 to his firing from Pumpco in Wichita in December. Then they asked him about a knife he was known to carry. Sure, he told them, it was true he got a jackknife for Christmas, but he never carried it around with him.

Didn't he have an old car? One with smashed-in doors and tape all over it?

Nope. Never had a car like that.

They showed him a one-page letter from the Poet and had him read it into a tape recorder. They would play the recording for Ruth when they returned to Wichita to see if she could identify the voice.

Then they asked him to print the same letter on another sheet of paper, first with his right hand, then his left.

Hill and Vinroe watched Hoch closely as he worked on the letter. Vinroe's heart sank. He had worked extensively in forgery, and he saw few similarities between Hoch's printing and the Poet's. Hill, too, was discouraged. Hoch was too cooperative. The Poet, he figured, probably was hardened to law enforcement officials. He wouldn't be this nice. He'd be reluctant to talk to them. He'd probably be screaming for an attorney.

And yet, the timing of his move to Oklahoma, his sketchy work history, and his uncanny resemblance to the composite still made him the best suspect they had located so far.

Clark advised them to put Hoch in a lineup. This was too important a development, and the case was too sensitive, to rely on merely showing Ruth a photograph.

"Let's bring her down here and see what she says," Clark told Hill.

But holding the lineup in Oklahoma would be impractical. It would take too long to find enough people who looked like the Poet. Meanwhile, they already knew a bushel of look-alikes in Wichita. They would have to extradite Hoch to Wichita, and that meant driving back to town to get a judge to sign the papers.

It was 5:00 a.m. when Hill, Clark, and Vinroe finished the three-hour drive back to Wichita.

They had left Bill Hoch in the Clinton city jail for the night.

Tom Silas had promised Hoch he would look after Napoleon Bonaparte and Princess.

At noon, Ed and Ruth arrived back in Wichita from the Colorado mountains. They were exhausted.

Ruth, tanned by the mountain sun, was the first to reach the front door and find the note taped to it. Fearing another letter from the Poet, she was relieved to see the note was from Vinroe. He wanted her to call him as soon as possible.

"Don't get your hopes too high, but we have a suspect in Oklahoma we'd like you to take a look at," Vinroe told her on the phone. He filled Ruth in on Hoch.

Ruth covered the receiver and whispered the news to Ed.

Ed was thrilled. If they've gone to this much trouble, he thought, they must have a pretty good suspect.

Ruth removed her hand from the receiver and told Vinroe she was ready anytime.

—m—

Bill Hoch hadn't slept much that night, either. He was still wearing the clothes he had been in when the police picked him up at his trailer. He felt like a mess as he waited in his cell in the Clinton jail for something to happen.

At 2:00 p.m. Hoch was moved to the jail in Arapaho, the Custer County seat. Then he was fingerprinted, photographed, and hauled into a courtroom, where a judge stunned him by informing him that his bond had been set at $501,000. Hill and Vinroe had flown back to Oklahoma after obtaining the extradition papers and made it to the courtroom.

Hoch declined to waive extradition. Within the hour he was airborne in a Piper Scenic, which landed at a small airfield in northeast Wichita. Hoch was driven to the Sedgwick County Courthouse and placed in a small holding cell on the second floor. A sheriff's deputy offered him cigarettes. Hoch sat in his cell, puffing nervously, listening to two officers talking outside.

"Where'd they catch him?"

"Oklahoma somewhere."

"Boy, I'd hate to be him. He'll never see the light of day again."

Ruth and Ed were escorted into the courthouse through an underground walkway to avoid reporters. Tipped off that the Poet had been caught, KAKE-TV and multiple newspapers had journalists waiting outside. KAKE had already broken into its regular programming to announce "a major break" in the case.

Ruth was led into the lineup room while Ed waited in an adjoining office. She stood with Hill and Vinroe behind a one-way window.

Suddenly, lights came on and flooded a small stage on the other side of the window. Five men entered the room and walked single file across the stage—a banker, a grocer, an attorney, a sheriff's deputy, and an oil supply salesman.

Ruth's eyes quickly focused on the oil supply salesman, number four in the lineup, a slender man, unshaven, with unkempt black hair and rumpled blue jeans.

She didn't say anything, but she knew instantly.

Hill called the men to step forward one by one. He asked each to take quarter turns to the right and left. Then he asked each to repeat two phrases: "Ruth, get back here, you stupid bitch," and "Ruth, I didn't know you'd make this so easy."

The fourth man felt weak in the legs. The harsh lights blinded him, and he could only dimly perceive the mirrored window before him. Racing through Bill Hoch's mind was an old movie he'd seen on TV not too long ago about a guy who'd been locked up for twenty-five years for an armed robbery he did not commit. Hoch thought of his dogs.

When he was asked to repeat the two phrases, his mouth was dry and his heart pounded in his throat.

After the ordeal, he was led back to the holding cell, where he collapsed on the cot. He didn't think he would ever be able to stand up again.

Hill and Vinroe took Ruth back to the office, where Ed and Paul Clark waited. She sat in a chair, and as the group settled around her, her composure began to dissolve. She could feel herself trembling, could feel tears forming in her eyes.

"I know which one you're talking about," she said in a wavering voice. "It's number four."

They waited.

"It looked like him," Ruth continued. "It sounded like him. But it wasn't him." Then she broke down.

The men stared at their shoes.

"Can you tell us what was different?" Clark asked, breaking a long silence.

"Well, it's hard to describe a difference," Ruth said between sobs. "It just wasn't him."

"Nose? Eyes?"

"I don't know." More silence.

"Ruth, you're positive this isn't the man?" Clark said finally.

"Yes."

Lying in his cell, drained, Hoch heard the voices again. "I guess they're letting him go."

"That right?"

Then a man appeared at the door. "It's over," Vinroe told him. "She couldn't identify you."

You could pick cotton out of my mouth right now, Hoch thought.

Supported by deputies because his legs still hadn't recovered their strength, Hoch was given a cigarette lighter that didn't belong to him and fifty dollars in cash for a bus ticket back to Clinton. His sister, Dolores, volunteered to drive him home instead.

Twenty-four hours after he'd been picked up at the lake, Bill "Coyote" Hoch was on his way back to the trailer, where, he supposed, Napoleon Bonaparte and Princess were waiting to give him a piece of their minds.

Clark broke the news of the failed lineup to reporters in the hallway outside the county jail. As the questions faded and the TV cameramen packed up their gear, Fred Mann, leaning against a wall, thought about a phrase from the Poet's last note to him. The phrase began repeating itself in his mind; it became almost a chant.

"I am not where you think I am," the voice said, "but they will think I am there, and this will make it easy."

12

SNAKES TWINE IN YOUR BRAIN

The Poet was furious.

The lineup touched off a barrage of angry letters throughout July. And Paul Clark was at the top of his mailing list.

"Now just cool yur interest in my game," the Poet wrote to Clark soon after Clark had appeared in the media discussing the failed lineup. "I have done nothing against you, so let's keep it that way."

Ten days after the lineup, Ruth received the following note:

> *This simple quibble was just between us*
> *Til you broadcast yur mouth & raised a fuss.*
> *I can't drop it now. You no in yur mind*
> *Will I get you from yur front, or yur behind?*
> *Thoughts like snakes twine in yur brain*
> *I won't stop till yur dead or insane.*
> *Think every time you go to yur mailbox*
> *A letter from me, or dead like a fox.*

Letters poured in at an unprecedented rate, most postmarked from Wichita, some from Oklahoma City. The thought that the Poet was still spending time in Wichita kept police taking Ruth for walks during the noon hour, hoping to lure him out. She was still walking alone, watched closely by detectives.

One letter to Ruth included a xeroxed photo of the emaciated face of a female corpse. "View with sublime expectation yur face after poetic execution," the Poet taunted.

Another to Ruth included a photo of a woman's corpse, with a picture of a knife displayed prominently in the foreground.

On July 25, Ruth opened the front door of her house and found a glass jar on the porch. It contained a liquid she couldn't identify. A red bandanna tied to the bottle's mouth marked it as the work of the Poet, so the Finleys took it to the police, who identified the liquid in the jar as human urine, with a trace of ammonia.

Still interested in Bill Hoch, police found out from postal authorities that Hoch's mail could be postmarked either in Oklahoma City or Wichita, depending on which direction he drove from the reservoir to mail it.

"If that isn't the Poet, it's his clone," an officer would say.

"I think it's him, too," another would say. "There's more to this fella than meets the eye."

"I think Ruth knows it was him and she was just covering up for him. Probably an old boyfriend."

"Yeah, did you hear how shook up she was after the lineup? When's anybody seen her fall apart like that?"

"But she was so certain," somebody else would chime in. "Didn't hesitate a bit."

On August 9, Mann, the reporter, heard again from the Poet.

I'd like to bring you up to date on my plans. I tried a mind control approach to get her to shoot herself, but I have to work on it some more. She was walking on Aug. 1. I watch & then I saw a pig across the street with green coat & curly hair. I watch for my chance. May have to wait til cold weather & less people.

Photography is my past time.
She wuld not have got away in Nov. if I had my own car. I
had to dump Blackwater & I wanted to wait until dark. But
it won't happen again.

Police jumped on the reference to Blackwater. Did the Poet finally make a mistake and give out a person's name? Was Blackwater the guy who drove the car used in the kidnapping?

Officers flipped through telephone books and city directories. They found nobody named Blackwater. But maybe he lived somewhere else, like Oklahoma.

The Poet's supposed new interest in photography opened another line of investigation: They could start checking with camera supply stores to see if they had a customer who matched the Poet's description.

Potentially, a valuable letter. These were just bits and pieces, as tangible as the wind, as substantive as cotton candy, but most difficult cases were solved by tracking down tidbits like these.

—⁓—

Sun sparkled in the office windows of downtown Wichita. To Detective Doyle Dyer, standing in the shade of the recessed entrance to a jeweler's store, the throngs of lunchgoers appeared to be floating in the ripples of a late August heat wave. But at a towering six feet eight, Dyer had no trouble seeing Ruth as she walked south on Broadway toward the intersection with Douglas. Nor did he fail to notice a small man who was coming toward him down the sidewalk with short, quick steps. The man was moving toward the same intersection.

The man wore blue jeans, a blue denim shirt, and boots. His brown hair fell in bangs over a pair of wire-rimmed glasses. He stopped occasionally to look back over his shoulder.

Dyer had seen him before, when he had been cruising downtown in an unmarked police car a week earlier, and he'd been following him on foot for the last three days. Each day, the man had walked the same route: east along the south side of Douglas past the Eaton Hotel to a railroad overpass, across the street, back west to Broadway, north on Broadway past the telephone company to First Street, west across Broadway, and back south to Douglas. Dyer had stood beside the jeweler's store for two hours one day and seen the man walk the same loop over and over.

Dyer had taken a black-and-white photo of the man and shown it to Ruth, who said she wasn't sure if he could be the Poet. Then he had brought the man into the station, where Ruth rejected him because his eyes were blue; the Poet's eyes were dark brown, she had said. But with Ruth's ability to give an absolute identification compromised by time, he wanted to keep a close eye.

Dyer wondered about Ruth in general. Fifteen minutes after he'd first taken a seat in her living room, just days after her stabbing, Ruth had asked if he wanted any magazines, then brought him several *Playboys*. Then she'd asked him if he wanted to see her wounds. Startled, Dyer hadn't had a chance to respond before she turned her back and raised her sweater for him.

From his post in the jewelry store entrance, Dyer now saw Ruth directly across from him, following the preplanned route. He swung his head around and saw the man still moving toward him on the south side of Douglas. The man stopped for a moment and stared across the street in Ruth's direction, then resumed walking at a quicker pace. When he walked past Dyer, the big detective fell in behind him.

The man continued walking fast on the south side of the street, Ruth walking more slowly on the other side. One block later, he was ahead of Ruth.

Then he changed his normal route. Rather than continue to the railroad overpass, he crossed the street and turned back west. He was heading straight for Ruth.

Dyer ran across the street, dodging traffic and reaching for the gun in his shoulder-holster, his pulse racing.

The man moved to the left side of the sidewalk into the path of oncoming pedestrians, picking up steam. Dyer, running as fast as he could, one hand on his gun butt, dodging oncoming people, realized he was too far behind to catch up.

The man bore straight down on Ruth, moving through the crowd like a bowling ball until all the bodies had parted to reveal her. He walked up to her. She stepped aside to let him pass. And the man kept walking.

Dyer, panting, pulled up short and yanked his coat over his holster.

As Ruth walked past him, he stood squinting under the sun, watching the man disappear into the crowd.

—w—

The drawing haunted the room.

Slack-jawed, the Poet gazed from the bulletin board of the CIB office on the fifth floor of city hall, his sad eyes following detectives as they moved back and forth.

Mann, seated at one of the desks, felt as if the drawing was watching him as he read a copy of the Poet's latest letter, which had just been processed in the lab, futilely, for fingerprints.

"I have this neat plan & I need yur help," it said. "Noon is the only possibility. She is always around too many people & I need someone to distract her so I can get her in the car. You culd talk to her & I culd drive up & then you culd just go on & you wuld not be involved. When I pick the day & see her leave, I will just come to the Eagle & ask for you & they won't know me as I mostly wear a blond wig & have a mustache. I will try to get you a picture."

Mann stared up at the sketch.

"What do you think?" Detective Mike Jones asked.

"I think I don't want to kill Ruth Finley," Mann replied.

"Glad to hear it," Jones said. "At least we don't have you to worry about."

"You think he'll show up?"

"Nope."

Jones, twenty-eight, stocky, with a shock of short red hair, was the fifth detective assigned full-time to the case, taking over in late August for Richard Vinroe, who had been transferred to run the department's new Crimestoppers program. Vinroe felt both disappointed that he hadn't solved it and relieved to be off the case.

Jones was excited to be assigned to the case. He wanted action. He couldn't understand cops who shied away from danger.

For his first four years on the force, Jones had worked the high-action northeast Wichita beat. He loved how he never felt alone up there because every officer responded to a call for help. Superiors practically had to force them to take a weekend off because nobody wanted to miss a chance to help a buddy out when one of the nightclubs or party houses erupted.

When Jones made detective, he discovered that all you did was follow up on events that had already happened. The guy on the street got there first. That's where the fun was.

When he had joined the CIB in June, he'd started out working cases about bad checks, which quickly bored him. How tough was it to track down somebody who had written his name on a check? He was eager to work on the Poet. He'd heard about the case. He knew it could be solved. The Poet was too active. The busier a bad guy is, the more chances you have to catch him, he thought.

He was not discouraged by the volume of material sitting on Vinroe's desk, nor by the frustrations the other detectives felt. He was eager to succeed where they had failed.

Jones wanted to keep the Poet riled up, and that meant continuing to exploit the link with Mann. This letter provided the perfect ammunition.

"Should we tell him you're willing to help him?" Jones asked Mann, who was sitting on the other side of his desk.

"Why not? Let's tell him I'll even bring the knife."

"Keep it simple. You can't sound too eager."

Mann scribbled in a notebook. "How's this: 'Poet: Will do what you request. Am available at your behest'?"

"Not bad. You have a gift for poetry. Maybe you're writing all this stuff."

"Could be," said Mann, flipping his notebook shut. "It'd make a great story."

Jones stretched and yawned. He picked up the letter and started scanning it again. The tip about the blond wig was helpful, if true. He would start showing the sketch around at wig stores.

More helpful, potentially, was a reference the Poet made to being hassled by pigs in a park. For the past few weeks, the police had been cracking down on homosexual activity in the city's parks. Maybe Jones could find an officer who remembered "hassling" a guy in a blond wig who otherwise resembled the Poet.

—⁊⁊—

While Jones and Mann were meeting at city hall, Ruth received a phone call at the phone company. The voice on the other end told her to come down to the lobby to pick up a package for Captain Mike Hill. Ruth, meanwhile, used a different line to call the police; the Poet had hung up by the time she returned to his line.

The call was traced to a phone booth at the intersection of Broadway and Douglas. Jones raced down there and found a swatch of red bandanna in the booth.

—⁊⁊—

It was an unseasonably warm October. Mann's note in the newspaper had failed to lead to an in-person meeting with the Poet, but the two men continued to communicate via the personals. The two-line ads were becoming more stressful to write than Mann's regular stories. The wrong approach, even the wrong word, Mann sometimes thought in his more melodramatic moods, could end up costing Ruth her life. And then he would receive a letter, tote it back to city hall, and again be faced with the chore of thinking up a couplet that might elicit some clue without also elevating Ruth's danger.

He opened his notebook. "Poet," he wrote, "the day you ask about is fine. Await your bidding when you pick the time."

On Thursday, October 16, the day the Poet had agreed to meet with Mann, Ruth, dressed in blue, took another walk at noon as plainclothes detectives followed along.

Nothing happened.

Four days later, the Poet wrote to Mann. "I'm still working on the car. I have been needing to go to Okla. soon. My head has been aching & I got a dr. there & may go soon if it keeps on. Sure as hell won't go here. Hope to see you soon."

Several verses were enclosed that referenced Nancy Jo Fox, the BTK victim, and also hinted that evidence connected to the case might be found in a box buried near a river.

The following Saturday morning, eight officers, determined to find the Poet's box of treasures, drove to the Augusta airport east of Wichita and turned down the dirt road toward the bridge where the Poet had tried to lure Ruth the day of the stabbing. It seemed a likely location for him to plant his box.

They combed the riverbank looking for freshly turned earth. They dug beneath trees, peered under rocks, pushed aside heavy underbrush, dug many holes.

Eight hours later, they returned to Wichita with sore backs and blisters, but no box.

The Poet was not the only person who read the personal ads in the newspaper. Many readers wondered what was going on with all the messages to the Poet. Each new ad from Mann, who signed with his initials, brought a flurry of calls to police from people wanting to tip them off that somebody out there was trying to help this joker.

Reporters from other media badgered police for information about the messages. Jones was upset that so many people were in a position to know what was happening with the investigation. It was becoming difficult to maintain any degree of secrecy.

As far as Jones knew, nobody had leaked word that Mann was being used as a tool by police, but it was only a matter of time. And if that information ever got out, the Poet, who seemed to have an uncanny sixth sense about what was going on in the case, might stop writing. Worse, the Poet might be furious enough at Mann's betrayal to do him harm. Then the police would have to protect two people instead of just one.

They had to risk changing a rule in the Poet's own game and stop addressing the ads to the Poet; they had to find a new code name for him.

At Jones's urging, Mann placed an ad requesting that the Poet come up with a new name for himself.

"It's OK with me," the Poet replied a few days later.

> *This [the name "Poet"] is not a self-proclaimed honor. I first was aware of it in a restaurant when I heard some men talking about RF wondering how much she owed me. It was their talk she shuldn't have to pay. I got the paper & found out what they were reading. I have never used it, as well as I can recall. I don't even like it.*
> *This is not ejaculatory ramblings I put down. It is well thought out. I am not a shoddy person. I have necrologist powers with my knowledge.*
> *I don't want to get you in any trouble or lose yur job. But you won't get caught. As soon as I get car I'll come in & get you. Call me "Necrologist" for now.*

A necrologist is a person who compiles lists of dead people. An obituary writer.

The friendly tone of the letter and the ease with which the Poet had accepted the demand to change his code name indicated a high degree of trust in Mann. Jones therefore wanted Mann to start asking the Poet questions, beginning with what his connection to Ruth was. Jones wanted to find the link between this man and the Fort Scott spark that had ignited his war on Ruth.

"Necrologist," Mann wrote. "Yes, it's well thought out by one not shoddy. What is the truth about the past that compels one to seek freedom?"

"A little clumsy," Jones said after he read it, "but I guess it makes the point."

A week passed without a response.

Had they lost him?

"Necrologist: Why no answer?" Mann wrote.

Another week.

Finally, on November 7, a reply:

"I am just in town to get my check. I got yur paper in Okla. & have to go back. I saw yur answer & really thank you & I want to come in & talk to you when I get back. In my blond wig I think it will be OK."

He had ignored Mann's question, but he had not been scared off by it.

Another series of poems was enclosed, as usual, but one of them introduced a new element:

There once was a fat ass'd bitch named Sharron
The king is now lean
But not so the fucked-up queen.
Bitches pictures in papers are bold, flagrant and darin'.

It took a while to figure out. Then an officer remembered: Police Chief Richard LaMunyon and his wife Sharron had been featured in a story in the Lifestyle section of the Wichita newspaper recently. The story was about people who had tried a fashionable new rice diet. LaMunyon had lost fifteen pounds on the diet, Sharron only five. A picture of the couple had run next to the story.

Officers who read the letter were amazed. The Poet had just threatened the chief's wife.

13

A PRIME SUSPECT

Ruth struggled to stay awake. The string section of the Wichita Symphony Orchestra had about lulled her to sleep. She preferred it when the symphony cut loose with trumpets, trombones, cymbals, and kettledrums. It really woke everybody up when they did that, she thought.

She and Ed sat in the rear of the concert hall inside Century II in downtown Wichita, a round structure with a low ceiling that resembled a spaceship and hosted conventions, concerts, sports events, and other cultural activities. As the flutes and strings began the third movement, she noticed that Ed, sitting beside her, seemed lost in reverie. Bless his heart, Ed didn't have a musical bone in his body. Nor, she had to admit, did she. They both liked listening to music, and the radio in the living room of the house was always on when they were upstairs—although it was often tuned to right-wing talk radio, not music—but neither had ever shown a flair for an instrument.

In fact, Ruth didn't really know why she and Ed went to the symphony. They weren't classical-music buffs, nor did they go to socialize. She supposed they just liked attending a cultural event, supporting the arts, that sort of thing. They enjoyed it when the symphony played traditional music with pretty melodies, but they also managed to endure, with gritted teeth, the dissonant, atonal music of modern composers.

When the concert was over, Ruth and Ed filed out with the rest of the crowd, arriving back home at 10:30 p.m. Ed parked the Olds in the garage, and while Ruth went inside through the door to the kitchen, he started his nightly check of the property.

He didn't get far. The first thing Ed saw as he walked along the west side of the house was that the electronically rigged back gate was hanging wide open.

On the back porch he found two beer bottles wrapped in newspaper and filled with liquid. Heart racing, he bent over for a better look and smelled gasoline. He saw a swatch of bandanna material stuffed in the mouth of one of the bottles, an unlit wooden kitchen match resting at the bottom of the other, and several other unlit matches strewn about the porch.

The Poet, Ed realized with shock and a sudden wave of rage, had delivered two Molotov cocktails to their house while they were at the symphony. He had slipped through the gate, walked in front of the camera in the backyard fountain, and passed beneath the camera mounted in the overhanging eave without being detected. The Poet had turned off all the gadgetry while he and Ruth were at the performance.

The Poet had either been lucky, or he had known they would be gone. It was his first visit at the back of the house since Christmas Eve, when he had cut the phone lines. His first since the alarms and cameras had been installed.

Ed cursed with frustration. Then he phoned the police.

To his amazement, he had to call the emergency number twice before they responded.

Eventually, officers swarmed the house and fanned out through the neighborhood to find anyone who might have seen the Poet. By now, the neighbors were exceptionally alert. People kept their eye on the Finleys' house constantly. They looked out their windows every night almost as a reflex. But on the night of Monday, November 10, none of them had seen or heard a thing.

Lab officers dusted the gate, the porch, the two beer bottles, and the matches for prints, but found none.

The next morning, Jones, reading a report of the incident, was overwhelmed with frustration. Only two days before, in his letter to Mann, the Poet had threatened to set the Finleys' house on fire. Jones had wanted to stake the residence out, but it had been a busy week in the CIB. Jones had been assigned to a new homicide, and he was also trying to help locate a missing truck driver, whose cab had been found soaked in blood. Worse, a fellow officer had been shotgunned to death in the northeast part of town and the entire department was in mourning. Nobody was available to perform a stakeout. The Poet had picked the perfect time to strike.

Obviously, he had not seriously tried to set the house on fire. The bandanna stuffed in one of the bottles as a fuse had not been lit, and neither had any of the matches. Jones knew the Poet had instead wanted to deliver a message: He was serious, and he could get Ruth anytime he wanted. He was in control.

But Jones couldn't figure out how the Poet had known the Finleys would be away that night. If the Poet didn't own a car, he must have arranged to get one, and that took planning. He would not have hitchhiked or taken a bus, not with a couple of Molotov cocktails in his hands. No, he had known exactly what he was doing.

Jones was in a difficult position. As lead investigator, he was being second-guessed by officers who had no connection to the case, but who knew what was in the letters and felt compelled to offer him their own opinions. More troubling, some of those officers were picking up on the leads in the notes to Mann and were investigating on their own. Several times, Jones had phoned the Finleys to check on a piece of information, only to be told that another officer had just phoned to ask the same question.

Jones didn't mind so much that everybody was reading the poems, but the letters to Mann were packed with bits of information about wigs, restaurants, dates when the Poet saw Ruth walking downtown, and news of his comings and goings to Oklahoma. True or not, they were the only leads the police had. Each letter had eight copies made, only three of which were for the CIB. Jones had no idea where the others went.

Jones felt as if he had lost control of his own case.

He studied the newspapers that had been wrapped around the bottles, hoping they contained an article or anything else that might be a clue. It was a special section from a twelve-year-old edition of the *Wichita Eagle and Beacon* that listed all the zip codes for every major city in the country. It also contained several advertisements from local businesses. One of the ads was for the company the Poet had asked to send a sewer cleaner to Ruth's house. Another was for a wig store in southwest Wichita. Was this where the Poet had purchased his blond wig?

Jones went to Hill, who said there was no way they could prevent all the Mann letters from being known. Still, there had to be a way they could limit access to the letters.

Jones phoned Mann. From now on, Jones told him, when he received a letter from the Poet, he should phone Jones, and the two would meet at a neutral site. Mann had been on the police beat when the letters started, a daily visitor to the department, but he had since been transferred to a new assignment, so every appearance by him in the CIB sent a signal that he'd received another letter and touched off a scramble to get copies. Furthermore, there was a remote possibility that the Poet would follow him from the newspaper building someday and watch him deliver a letter to the police.

Jones asked Mann to take out an ad that would make the Poet phone him. The detective wanted the Poet's voice on tape, and he also wanted officers to stake out phone booths in the downtown area.

"Necrologist: Need to talk," Mann wrote. "Urgent. Can't print it."

Now all Mann needed was something "urgent" to tell the Poet if he called. Jones decided he should to tell the Poet to change his code name again. It wasn't a phony request. Readers had picked up the "Necrologist" ads and were pestering the department with complaints again. Mann was also going to tell the Poet that he needed to communicate with him in a different part of the newspaper in order to limit the number of people who would find the messages.

The Poet responded to the ad promptly. But not by phone.

"I have self-foiled the attempt to end this game," he wrote. Mann read the letter in a booth at the Pancake House near Kellogg and Main. Jones sat across the Formica table, watching. He had read the letter several times already. Mann had turned it over to him earlier in the day, and Jones had taken it to the lab for print processing, then returned to the restaurant to give Mann a copy. He was living up to the bargain the police had with the newspaper of sharing everything. "I will have to mail this today because I am heading back to Oklahoma City," the letter continued. "I don't think the police listened to her witless accusations because I am sure she found my fire bomb by now. I was going to light it when she got back. You would have liked being with me."

Mann had hooked a tape recorder to his office and home phones, and he hadn't strayed far from either one in the last several days, but the Poet hadn't called.

"I read it twice before I really noticed the bit about Oklahoma City," Jones said. "It's the first time he's given us a specific location."

"If it's true," said Mann. "If it's true."

"I don't know if it was a slip, or if he's intentionally misleading us," Jones said. "But what really bothers me is that he doesn't sound too worried about your urgent message."

"Unless he knows I don't have one."

"Exactly. Or unless he's so sure of himself that he knows he has nothing to worry about. But I doubt that. This guy is supposed to be paranoid. No, I think the guy is still lying to you. He still doesn't trust you.

"And those dogs," he continued. "When our guys talked to the neighbors that night, nobody had heard a thing. There weren't any dogs raising hell."

"So, what do we do now?" Mann asked.

Jones shrugged. "We try it again. Put in the same ad. Only I think we need to make it sound more urgent. Maybe we should just come right out and ask him to phone you."

"He'll know it's a trap."

"Maybe. But we need to keep pushing him. I'm tired of being careful. Besides, he's called Ruth from pay phones before. He knows it's safe. There's no reason for him not to call, unless he knows you're helping us, in which case he *has* to have inside information."

"What about these trips to Oklahoma City to see his doctor? Can't you do some checking down there and maybe come up with the doctor?"

"The problem is, I'm not supposed to know about his doctor, his headaches, or his trips to Oklahoma City. I might burn you. If I go poking around for doctors down there, he might find out. Then he'd know for sure who gave me the tip. I don't know what his sources are, but he always seems one step ahead of us."

Mann opened his notebook. "Need to talk," he wrote. "Won't take long. Call."

He had abandoned the use of rhyming verse to make the message more direct and heighten the sense of urgency.

—✖—

Blackwater. That was the key, thought Bernie Drowatzky. Find out what, or who, this Blackwater was and you could start to unravel the mystery of the Poet. And if anybody was going to unravel it, it was going to be Bernie Drowatzky.

Drowatzky hated being shut out of the case. But ever since he'd been appointed captain of the vice squad, Hill had done his best to keep him away from it. Vice had its offices on the fourth floor of the city building, only one floor below the CIB, but Drowatzky sometimes felt as if he had been exiled to another country.

Drowatzky understood that you didn't mess with another unit's case, but the problem went deeper than that. Hill, he knew, didn't trust him. Drowatzky was close to Ruth, a regular dining companion of the Finleys. He was their primary defender on the force. If there was a leak in the department, Drowatzky was number one on Hill's list of suspects. Drowatzky knew all that, and he resented it. He had been the first one contacted about the case, and the Poet was still taunting him, still mailing him letters.

Drowatzky had done all he could to wrangle copies of the newer letters, but he knew he wasn't seeing all of them, and he was frustrated. He had spent too much time investigating Ruth's case to just let it go.

He had even tried to get the case transferred to vice, which had the manpower and the undercover expertise to investigate it. After all, the vice department, Drowatzky believed, was what you made of it. You could spend all your time busting strip joints, or arresting underage drinkers, or raiding homosexual hangouts in the parks, or breaking up parties in the northeast community. You could channel your time and resources any way you desired. If you made the Poet your top case, you could work it full-time—unlike the CIB, which always had more than it could handle.

Drowatzky's deputy chief, Colonel John Coonrod, had left Ruth's case in Hill's hands. Drowatzky had only been allowed to investigate officially once, back when the Poet was writing to all the businesses in the area, asking them to perform a variety of nasty deeds at the Finleys' house. Vice and narcotics officers had spent four days examining envelopes of the bills sent in by customers of the Kansas Gas & Electric company, searching for handwriting that matched the Poet's. The theory was that even the Poet had to pay his electric bill. But they hadn't found any envelopes with writing that matched the Poet's.

Drowatzky had been investigating the case in secret since then. Friends on the force slipped him copies of the letters when they could, and Drowatzky pored over them for clues. Blackwater seemed like a pretty good one. It sounded like a Native American name. And it probably had something to do with Oklahoma. Drowatzky was glad when the Poet started writing about Oklahoma, which was Drowatzky's home turf.

Drowatzky put in a call. Officers in the area began scouting for Blackwaters in Oklahoma and checking out any other shady characters they encountered.

Drowatzky ran the names these officers passed him against his own department's records. He discovered a Blackwater who had been born in 1931 in a small Oklahoma town, a man who had been arrested in Wichita for drunk driving. He thought instantly of the driver of the kidnap car, Buddy, who had been sipping from a bottle in a brown paper sack the day he drove Ruth and the Poet around town.

Drowatzky arranged to have two pictures of the man sent to Wichita. When he showed the photos to Ruth, she ruled the man out. But then, she never did get a very good look at this Buddy person, Drowatzky remembered.

Blackwater was still the key, he thought.

—◆—

On Friday, November 21, the two-year anniversary of Ruth's kidnapping, the security guard at Southwestern Bell received an early morning phone call in his office. The phone, locked and enclosed in a case, had an unlisted number. When the guard picked up the receiver, a man identified himself as the Poet and declared that he was on his way over to shoot Ruth Finley.

When Ed pulled in front of the building to drop off Ruth for work, he saw several police officers waiting outside. Inside the lobby, watching through the door, were Ruth's coworkers and her sister, Jean.

Ed was outraged when he found out the reason for the welcoming party. Nobody had alerted them to the threat. Nobody had phoned them at home before they left. The police had let him drive Ruth right up to the front door of the building, as if they were using her as bait.

But the police had not believed the caller was serious. Shooting was not the Poet's style. And he certainly wouldn't tip them in advance if he *did* intend to do it.

But Ed seethed over the department's seeming indifference toward Ruth's safety. He was still angry about the lackadaisical response to his call for help the night he found the Molotov cocktails on his back porch.

The police were playing games with his wife's life.

That was going to end right now, Ed decided.

That afternoon, he met with Chief LaMunyon in the chief's fourth-floor office.

"I'm not here to complain about your officers," Ed began quietly, his red face betraying his anger, "but I am here to complain that we're not being told everything."

LaMunyon had been skeptical about the Finleys from the beginning, and he found it curious that one of them had come to him to complain about not knowing enough about the case just when the Poet had started threatening his own wife, Sharron.

The chief watched closely as Ed spoke. Was this guy really just a mild-mannered accountant concerned about his spouse's safety, or was he a deranged and possibly violent husband? Maybe Ed had stabbed Ruth and kept up the parade of letters and acts of vandalism not only to cover it up, but to derive some sort of cheap thrill, or to relieve the pressure of some deeply rooted mental problem.

LaMunyon seldom interfered with his men's cases. A police chief was more politician than investigator. But he had taken a keener interest in the Poet after Sharron's name appeared. And he had noticed, as had others, that the Poet never wrote about Ed. Never mentioned a word about the husband of the woman he intended to kill. Surely, the Poet knew about Ed. The Poet seemed to know everything else about Ruth.

When Ed finished talking, LaMunyon assured him that the department had its methods of dealing with a case like this, that everything they did was designed to protect Ruth, but that he would see what he could do to ease Ed's concerns.

The two men rose and shook hands.

Ed felt better when he left LaMunyon's office. He felt relieved, like a man who had unburdened himself of a heavy weight. He felt lighter, spryer, more optimistic.

He didn't feel at all like what he had just become: the case's prime suspect.

14

PEOPLE EXPLODING OUT OF YOUR HEAD

Christmas lights glowed from the windows and eaves of the houses lining East Indianapolis. The Finley house sported a wreath of white-painted fir, the boughs interwoven in a steel-mesh frame and encircled by a halo of small red bulbs. Ed had constructed the wreath himself and hung it on a wire outside the front window.

Late on December 21, Ed and Ruth were in the basement watching a Christmas variety show when they heard an explosion above them, followed by the tinkle of raining glass fragments. Ed raced up the stairs. An orange glow filled the living room. He threw open the drapes and saw flames licking what was left of the window.

Ruth had followed him up from the basement, and he yelled for her to phone 911, then ran to the door, grabbed a club he kept beside it, and rushed onto the porch.

The wreath was engulfed in flames. It looked like a suspended bonfire. He swatted it down from the window, stamped out the fire, and ran into the street.

"You son of a bitch!" Ed yelled into the night. "I'm going to kill you!"

He stood still, panting, looking up and down the street, his eyes straining to adjust to the night. He saw nothing. He began pacing back and forth in front of the house. Ed felt prehistoric stalking the street like this, club in hand, consumed by animal rage.

He wanted to go after the guy, but he was suddenly afraid.

The Poet might still be near the house. Maybe he had set the fire as a diversion and was waiting for a chance to sneak inside and kill Ruth. Ed started backing up toward his yard.

"I'm going to kill you!" he shouted again into the night. The words bounced down the row of houses.

Ed stood still for a moment, listening for footsteps, hearing only the soft rustle of leaves. He wondered why none of his neighbors had come to their windows.

Slowly, he let the club fall to his side and walked back to the house. A siren wailed in the distance.

Later that night, an arson investigator found burned fragments of waxy paper wrapped around the top and bottom of the wreath.

The next morning, Jones found several pieces of similar paper in the green dumpster on the west side of the Finleys' house.

The paper looked to Jones to be the type you peel off sections of pre-glued tile. He would bet his next paycheck that the Finleys had recently tiled a floor.

Jones removed the pieces of paper from the dumpster and tucked them into his jacket pocket. Then he drove back to the office, wondering why Ed had hung a wreath on the outside of the window rather than the inside, creating such an inviting target.

Jones sent samples of the paper he found in the trash and the paper that was found on the wreath to an independent lab, one that often helped with arson investigations. The lab quickly concluded that both samples were the same kind of paper.

Yes, Ed told Jones on the phone, they had tiled their bathroom floor recently. The same day that the wreath was set on fire, in fact. That was their paper in the dumpster.

"Where were you and Ruth before the fire?" Jones asked.

"Watching television in the basement," Ed answered. "We were both down there together for at least an hour."

The incident made no sense to Jones. It would have taken time to wrap paper around the top and bottom of the wreath, and a guy as squirrelly and paranoid as the Poet would not have wanted to spend that much time being visible in front of the Finleys' house. And he certainly wouldn't have gone through their dumpster to locate the paper. That would have taken too long. He would have brought his own paper, and he would have done the job as quickly as possible.

The police hadn't found any of the Poet's signature items at the scene that night. No red bandanna, no letter. Maybe it was just some kids getting their kicks by committing a Poet-like act of vandalism.

But the Poet had made specific threats to torch the house. These threats hadn't been released to the media. Local kids wouldn't have known to ape him by setting a fire. It was too coincidental.

Which gave Jones a nauseated feeling in his gut. He wasn't sure who the Poet was, but Jones was now almost positive that he knew where the Poet lived.

—m—

"The headaches aren't much better. I took the medication as long as the dr. thought advisable. But he got to asking a lot of dumb ass'd questions about my depressive vs. hyped-up mental condition."

The letter, mailed to Mann, was postmarked December 21, the day of the fire.

I can't call you. I dialed yur paper one day & hung up. That goddam phone co. may have voice pickup devices & I bet that bitch recorded my voice. Think I'd be safer to come in & talk to you & let you see some of my books.

I described to the dr. these blasts. Feel people exploding out of yur head. Must undo accusations of aberration of oneself. This female has negative & remonstrant attitude & one or two successes brings thoughts of her invincibility. I wuld rather take her with me, but I have this ice pick all fixed with my red bandanna, if that's how it is.

The letter went on to threaten Ruth in florid language; it sent Jones to the dictionary to look up "onanistic," "odalisque," and "necropsy." Psychologists and linguists who had studied the letters had determined that whatever else the Poet might be, he was well read, innately bright, and likely well educated.

But Jones found only one bit of information in the letter that interested him—there was a part about dressing up like a painter to get inside the phone company. Ed, he knew, loved to paint. Not only on canvas, but also on his house. For Ed, painting the house was a perpetual task. He would paint one side at a time so slowly that by the time he finished, it was time to paint the other side again.

And Ed had been painting the house again in recent days. Jones noticed the discarded paint gear when he went through the Finleys' dumpster after the wreath-burning incident.

—⁓—

Christmas Eve was clear, but bitterly cold. Jones and Detective Darrel Schneider froze in an unmarked police van parked fifty yards west of the Finleys' house, watching for movement through the exploding puffballs of their own breath. Jones was certain something would happen at the house. Christmas Eve was the Poet's favorite night to strike.

Police had watched the house many times, but this stakeout was different, for two reasons. One, Jones and Schneider were doing it on their own time. The department hadn't authorized it. The department didn't even know about it.

Two, the Finleys didn't know about it, either. Jones and Schneider were way out on a limb.

Jones was happy Schneider had agreed to go along with him. He appreciated the company. Jones hated stakeouts, especially in the winter.

Jones and Schneider shivered in their frigid van. Their limbs were almost numb. But so far, they had not witnessed anything suspicious. Cars and pickups moved up and down the street, but none slowed at the Finley house. Just the normal comings and goings of a quiet residential neighborhood snuggling in for a homey Christmas Eve.

Jones envied the family scenes he imagined taking place inside the houses. He wondered what the Poet was doing. He pictured him hunched over a desk in some cheap, dimly lit, poorly heated hotel room or mobile home, furiously scribbling another poem amid piles of Big Chief notebooks and red bandannas.

Or maybe he was sitting on the sofa in the warm, cozy basement of the house fifty yards away.

Jones and Schneider waited and watched long into the night. Finally, they gave up and drove away, their spirits as chilly as their bones.

"Have a merry Christmas," Jones wished the Poet bitterly.

—∞—

The day after Christmas, Ruth received another poem.

Jones was sick of this stuff. He wanted to hit back at the Poet, and hit back hard. The Poet, if he existed at all, was pure bluff. All he did was write poems. And he could do that for another century if they let him. Jones needed tougher ads from Mann. It was time for the Poet's pal to get mad. Time to push the Poet to take action.

Risky? Jones doubted it. They had pushed the Poet before, and he had only responded with more letters. He hadn't tried to hurt Ruth. Ruth was well protected, anyway.

Maybe they could finally force Ed to make a mistake.

"Make up a new name for him," Jones told Mann on the telephone. "You do it for him. That'll piss him off. Besides, we need one. We still get flak every time people see 'Necrologist.' Pick out something from his last letter, a word he's sure to recognize. Then give him hell."

Mann studied the last letter to Ruth. The Poet had sent him a copy of it, as usual. The Poet, apparently proud of his work, often mailed copies of poems to TV reporters, as well. One word struck the reporter as an appropriate new code name: "scofflaw."

"Scofflaw," he wrote, "I don't believe you're afraid to call. You've called others before without any problems. I'm not stupid."

The message ran in the newspaper the final two days in December and the first two days of the New Year.

15

THE SCOFFLAW

In a duplex in southeast Wichita, a slender, middle-aged man read the ad one more time, then threw the newspaper to the floor and walked to the front window. It was Monday, January 5. A dull gray sky hung over the city like a sheet of aluminum foil. The sky matched his mood. He didn't know what to think about the ad.

He gazed up the street at the rows of matchbox duplexes, their yards littered with campers, motorcycles, and cars mounted on blocks. He looked at the U-Haul truck in his own yard. Soon he would be packing it up and moving away, and he couldn't wait.

Scofflaw? What was the reason for that? He'd been offended when he saw it in the personals three days before. He wasn't any damn scofflaw. He had to straighten that out right away.

He'd brooded about it all weekend before realizing there was only one thing to do. It was a big risk, but nothing else would work.

Standing at the window, he tried to muster his resolve, when suddenly a dog barked to complain about its leash. He took the bark as a cue. It was time. Do it now, he told himself.

He turned from the window and pulled the phone book out from under the telephone on a small table beside the sofa. He sat on the sofa, put the book on his knees, and thumbed through it. Then he lifted the receiver and dialed the *Wichita Eagle and Beacon* newspaper.

The operator patched him through to the classified ad department, and a woman's voice came on the line.

"May I help you?"

His heart was in his throat. He fought to control his breathing. "If I took out an ad in your paper, would I have to give you my real name?" he said.

His voice had trembled badly. No good, he thought. Get a grip.

"Yes, sir," the woman replied. "For billing purposes we'd need your real name and address."

Well, he had half expected that. "Do you give out the name to anyone else?"

"No, sir, we don't give out any names. It's our policy to keep the names confidential. But we need to know it so I can send you the bill."

"Okay," he said after a moment. "I want an ad."

"All right, sir. What would you like it to say?"

He'd written the ad on a scrap of paper, which sat on the table beside the phone. "Okay," he said. "Here's what I want: 'I no scofflaw.'"

"Scofflaw?" the woman said. "How do you spell that?"

"Look it up. It's in the dictionary," he said. "And that's N-O, not K-N-O-W."

There was silence on the other end. "So it's 'I no scofflaw,'" the woman finally said.

"Right."

"Okay. Anything else?"

"Yeah." He checked the scrap of paper again. "'I no scofflaw. Very much want to call, but you tell every Tom, Dick and Harry. Privacy very important to me.'" He paused. "I guess that's it."

The woman repeated the message.

"That's right," he said.

"Okay, now I need your name and address, sir," she said. The man swallowed. Then he gave them to her.

On the other side of town, Jones drove down a large commercial street lined with convenience stores, small shopping squares, fast-food restaurants, and bars. He was returning to the office after checking out a dead lead on another case and was in a lousy mood. Sometimes he wondered if he should have stuck to engineering. He stared vacantly at the traffic.

As he cruised, he spotted a sign in one of the shopping squares for Mr. K's Toupee and Wig Salon. He remembered the newspaper that had been wrapped around the Poet's Molotov cocktails. An ad for the salon had appeared on one of the pages. He hadn't had a chance to check the place out yet.

Might as well keep the streak of bad luck going, he thought.

He turned into the lot and pulled up to the store. He removed a copy of the color sketch of the Poet from his briefcase, entered the shop, walked up to the counter, and set the sketch down on it. He pulled out his badge to identify himself to the clerk, and then said, "Have you ever seen this man in here?"

The clerk, a young man Jones estimated to be in his twenties, didn't hesitate. "Yeah, I sold him a blond wig. I remember because he paid cash for it—forty-nine bucks—and he wouldn't sign a card we keep on all our customers. Said the wig was just a gag, or something. He was in a real hurry to get out of here, too."

Jones was shocked. The public didn't know about the blond wig. And he hadn't asked the clerk about it; the clerk had volunteered that information.

He asked the clerk if the store still had a wig like the one he had sold to the man. The clerk disappeared into a back room and returned with a wig of straight, mid-length blond hair, parted on the left side.

A phone call was waiting for Jones when he arrived at his desk in the CIB. Mann was on the line. He wanted to read Jones an ad that had just been called in to the newspaper.

Jones listened without much enthusiasm as Mann read him the ad. The personals, he figured, had a loyal readership of lunatics, voyeurs, and the sort of lonely people who might respond to the types of messages Mann had been writing. The scofflaw ad had probably just hooked some nut by accident, Jones thought.

Then Mann told him how the caller had spelled the word "no" in the first line, and his blood froze.

"I don't know if he means 'K-N-O-W,' as in, 'I know who the scofflaw is,'" Mann said, "or if he's trying to say, 'I'm no scofflaw.'"

"Well, then why didn't he just say, 'I'm no scofflaw' instead of using baby talk?" Jones said.

"Right," said Mann. "I think he means 'K-N-O-W.' And if he does, guess who else spells it like that."

"Unless it's his buddy," Jones said. "I don't suppose this guy left a name."

"Thought you'd never ask. Got a pencil?"

"You're kidding," Jones said.

"Name's James Nicholl. N-I-C-H-O-L-L. He lives at 1555 South Fircrest."

This was impossible—the Poet would not be dumb enough to give the newspaper his name and address.

That night, Ruth and Ed arrived home from work to find this in their mailbox: "You goddam dum bitch. You did it to me again. You've made my friend pissed at me."

On Tuesday, the Finleys received another poem that repeated all of the Poet's familiar themes. "I have to get you & prove to my friend I will be a great person," it ended.

Mann received a copy of the same letter late that afternoon.

—∞—

By late Tuesday, Jones knew a great deal about James Nicholl. Nicholl had worked as a draftsman at Boeing and been laid off only a few days before placing the ad. He had changed jobs thirteen times in the last twenty years, according to his personnel file. He was five feet six, weighed 150 pounds, wore wire-rimmed glasses, and had brown hair and brown eyes.

Jones found the postman who delivered mail to Nicholl's neighborhood and convinced him to check the letters Nicholl mailed. The next morning he drove to Boeing and picked up a photo of Nicholl. Nicholl's forehead was higher than the Poet's, his jaw was thinner, and he wore a mustache. Still, it was possible he had changed his appearance.

Jones didn't want to rely on a lineup. If Ruth rejected Nicholl and Nicholl was the Poet, they would lose him. Lacking any other evidence, the police wouldn't be able to hold him, and he would flee.

Investigating a citizen whose only crime was responding to an ad in the newspaper placed Jones in a delicate position. He would have to circle Nicholl at a wide distance, keeping the investigation restricted to former employers. Jones needed to find something he could show a judge to obtain a search warrant. Or he needed to find something that would clear Nicholl as a suspect.

Jones half hoped he would clear him, but the more he dug, the more similarities with the Poet he unearthed. Nicholl, he learned, sometimes made weekend trips to Oklahoma City to consult with a psychiatrist at the VA hospital for problems related to stress; he had a habit of hitchhiking and renting cars; he had a son who once worked at Gates Learjet at the same time Ruth's brother-in-law, Bill Jones, worked there; Nicholl was divorced and described as something of a loner.

The bad news was he lived with a daughter. It was hard to imagine the Poet living with anybody, let alone a daughter. It was hard to imagine the Poet having any children at all.

Still, the parallels were remarkable. Jones wanted a stakeout on Nicholl. He also wanted Mann to place another ad, this time to "Necrologist," to see if Nicholl picked up on the change.

"Necrologist," Mann wrote. "Have some important information. Tell me where I can leave it."

The ad would appear below Nicholl's ad, which had one more day to run. If Nicholl was the Poet, maybe the officers staking him out could catch him mailing his response to Mann's ad. If Nicholl was not the Poet, the real Poet would surely be angry that somebody else was horning in on his act. Either way, the new ad would turn up the heat a notch. An angry Poet was an active Poet, Jones knew, and action was what they needed right now.

Jones asked Hill for an around-the-clock stakeout, but his request was denied. Instead, two teams of vice and narcotics officers were assigned to watch Nicholl's house from early in the morning until one hour after the lights were turned off at night.

The stakeout was in place by Wednesday. Shortly after noon, Nicholl left the duplex carrying a guitar case and climbed into a red 1966 Ford Mustang parked in a lot behind the duplex. He drove to a music store, spent seven minutes inside, and then returned to his car and sat there for six minutes, reading something. From there, he drove east to a shopping mall and entered a game room, where he played pinball for a few minutes. When he finished his game, he left the room and walked to a health-food store nearby, where he bought a small item the cops tailing him couldn't identify, before returning to the game room for another try at the pinball machine. Then he left the mall and drove to Towne East.

Nicholl pulled up at the Fourth National Bank branch office in the mall's vast parking lot, parked his car, and entered the bank. He came out twenty minutes later and drove to a liquor store. He emerged carrying a paper sack, got back into his car, and drove to a Town and Country convenience store to put some gas into his Mustang. From there, he drove to a post office.

Nicholl pulled up to the drive-up mailboxes and stopped. And sat still. He did nothing. He made no move to mail anything.

Instead, he pulled into the main lot, parked, and walked inside. Two detectives followed him in and watched him slide a letter into a slot.

Nicholl left, but the detectives stayed and radioed Hill about the letter drop. Hill contacted federal postal authorities and drove to the post office. He turned the detectives loose to resume their surveillance—a police helicopter had been keeping track of Nicholl since he had left the bank—and stayed to wait for the postal inspector. He watched as the inspector removed a manila envelope from the drop box addressed to the court clerk of Oklahoma City.

The handwriting did not match the Poet's, but the Poet, Hill figured, probably disguised his handwriting in his poems.

On Thursday, the police tailed Nicholl to a dentist's office, then to St. Joseph Medical Center. When he entered the hospital, Nicholl was carrying several white envelopes. When he came out, the envelopes were gone.

The officers followed Nicholl to Towne East, where he again parked by the bank and sat in his car, apparently writing something. A few minutes later, he pulled up to a drive-up window, used the pneumatic tube to conduct some sort of transaction, and then pulled away and headed south through the mall's parking lot. He left Towne East, crossed Kellogg, and pulled into the Eastgate mall on the opposite corner. He entered a drugstore, picked up some medicine at the druggist's counter, walked to the magazine rack, flipped through several bodybuilding magazines, picked one out, and paid for the magazine and the medicine. Then he climbed into his Mustang and drove home.

Shortly after 6:00 p.m., Nicholl came back outside dressed in blue jeans and a blue denim jacket. He walked to a blue Oldsmobile in the parking lot behind his duplex. The car was hooked to a U-Haul trailer. He took some tools out of the Olds and began to work on the brakes of his Mustang. When he was done, he tested the brakes several times and returned to the house.

To the officers who were observing him, it appeared as if Nicholl was preparing to make a long trip.

On Friday morning, Nicholl drove his Mustang to a nearby auto center for repairs. He returned home on foot.

That same morning, a new ad from Mann had appeared in the personals. "Scofflaw," the ad said. "Got your message. I understand. Tell me where to leave information."

Later that morning, Nicholl phoned the newspaper to place an ad. "No scofflaw," he dictated to the clerk. "Reply Eagle Box 196F."

Jones regarded Nicholl's new ad with mixed emotions. On one hand, it indicated that the word "no" in his first ad had been meant in the negative sense rather than as an intentional misspelling of the word "know," which was the Poet's trademark. On the other hand, the ad seemed to be chiding Mann for calling him a scofflaw—a Poet-like reaction. And by taking out a box at the newspaper, he might be giving Mann the drop site he had requested.

The newspaper offered two types of boxes—one for people who wished to come to the paper to pick up responses to their ads in person, the other for those who wished to have the responses mailed to their homes. Nicholl had chosen the latter. The Poet most likely would have made the same choice.

Hill had an idea. The captain typed a letter, ostensibly from Mann, and mailed it to Nicholl's box. The letter was a harshly worded message asking Nicholl to send Mann proof that he was the one who wanted to kill Ruth so Mann could be sure he wasn't dealing with a phony.

If Nicholl wasn't the Poet, Hill figured, the letter would scare him off. And if he was, the police were in business.

Officers tailed Nicholl back to the auto shop that afternoon. After chatting with a mechanic, Nicholl climbed into his Mustang and drove to a Montgomery Ward store in the same mall. Carrying a briefcase, Nicholl entered the store, went to the personnel office, made copies on a Xerox machine, and left the store carrying a large manila envelope and no briefcase. He returned to the store, reemerged with the briefcase, and drove home.

At 3:00 p.m., he and his daughter drove to an optometrist's office. They spent nearly an hour inside. The surveillance team wondered if he was being fitted for a new pair of glasses, ones that did not have wire frames. Or maybe for contact lenses.

The following day, Nicholl stayed in his house until evening, then drove to the post office again and mailed two letters. Police found that one of the letters had been addressed to the Kansas Employment Office and the other to a daughter in Texas.

Neither letter featured the Poet's handwriting on its envelope.

Later that night, Nicholl ducked inside his U-Haul with a flashlight for a few minutes and then came back out carrying another briefcase.

Early the next week, having allowed time for Hill's letter to arrive at the newspaper and be forwarded to Nicholl's house, Mann placed another ad to the Necrologist in the personals. It was intended to soften the blow of Hill's letter. "Hope you understand," it said. "I need to be very cautious also."

If Nicholl wasn't the Poet, the real Poet should be thoroughly confused and profoundly agitated by what was happening in the personals. Perhaps he would finally make a mistake.

As soon as Mann's new ad appeared, Nicholl phoned the newspaper. He wanted to place another ad. This one was to be addressed to "Betty." He wanted Betty to phone him. And he wanted to include his telephone number in the ad.

The Poet, Jones believed, would never put his phone number in the newspaper.

Still, Jones phoned Ruth. She said she had never been called "Betty" in her life.

Jones was miserable. He had stuck his neck in the noose, and the trapdoor had just opened beneath his feet.

But he knew he couldn't lay off Nicholl yet. There were still too many coincidences, too many unanswered questions. He and his bosses agreed that the surveillance on Nicholl had to continue.

Jones decided to try one last ploy: Mann would phone Nicholl the night after Nicholl's ad appeared in the newspaper. Without identifying himself, Mann would try to pry relevant information from Nicholl. Nicholl would either be confused by the questions from an unknown caller and hang up, or he would warmly greet his coconspirator. Either way, there was no longer anything to lose.

Mann placed his call to Nicholl at a prearranged time, 7:00 p.m., with a tape recorder hooked to his phone.

A man answered. Mann asked to speak to Scofflaw, but the man said he wasn't home. Scofflaw was a friend of his who was out.

No, the man hadn't received a letter. But he didn't know about his friend. He didn't have any idea what his friend got in the mail.

Who was Betty? Just somebody who called his friend a scofflaw some time back. That's all he knew. It wasn't any big deal, as far as he could tell. But his friend would know more. Try him later. He would be back in about an hour.

Shortly after the phone call, vice and narcotics officers watching Nicholl's house saw him bolt out the front door carrying a box of books. He ran to the U-Haul, fumbled for his keys, dropped them, picked them up, unlocked the back door, and threw the box inside.

More than one detective was convinced they were watching the Poet packing up to blow town.

At 8:00 p.m., Mann phoned Nicholl's number again. There was no answer. He phoned Jones, who was monitoring activities from his home. Jones phoned officers at the scene.

Nicholl wasn't home, they told him. He and his daughter had jumped into the Mustang and taken off.

Trailing them in unmarked police cars, officers were surprised as Nicholl drove through southeast Wichita at ten miles per hour under the speed limit. Usually he drove like a demon. He drove like a man who was afraid of being stopped by the police.

The night was clear and cold, but the pavement was dry. Nicholl drove carefully along the dimly lit residential streets of southeast Wichita, working his way slowly east, avoiding major arterials, preferring to stick to darker, quieter streets.

Soon, some of the officers tailing Nicholl felt their pulses quicken, for they began to suspect where he was going.

At last he pulled into the driveway of a modest, one-level house on the far east side of the city.

The officers were ready to spring.

The home where Nicholl had stopped was on Orme. It was one block north of Ruth's house. Nicholl climbed out of the car and walked to the front door of the house, followed by his daughter. They entered the house and stayed a few moments. Officers could see them in a window, talking to another man. Then they came back outside, walked to their car, climbed in, and left. The officers followed them back to their house.

Mystified but excited, the officers phoned in their report. When he heard where Nicholl had gone, Jones wondered if Nicholl might be the right guy after all. Was the man they visited, the man who lived a block away from the Finleys' house, the Poet's "Buddy"? Is that how the Poet had been able to keep track of Ruth?

The next day, the police moved in. The U-Haul had been bothering them. Nicholl clearly was planning to leave, and soon, so Jones had obtained a search warrant. But a search of Nicholl's duplex and U-Haul turned up nothing to connect him to the case. A stack of crime magazines he had placed in the trailer interested them, but possessing magazines was hardly proof that Nicholl was involved in criminal activity.

Still, the police wanted Ruth to take a look at him, so they took Nicholl into custody and arranged for a lineup.

Ruth failed to identify him, but they weren't deterred.

Hill and Jones took Nicholl aside to question him. Nicholl explained that Betty was a woman he had long admired from afar. She had called a friend of his a scofflaw once, he said. When he saw the first Scofflaw ad, he thought it might be from her, and he saw a chance to get in touch.

Hill and Jones listened to the story with considerable skepticism. They were sure Nicholl was hiding something. But they had no reason to hold him, so they let him go. The next day, Nicholl left town.

Jones felt himself dangling from the rope. He had urged the surveillance on Nicholl, and it had cost the department two weeks of wasted time and manpower.

He wondered what the Poet would say about the whole thing.

A week later, he found out.

"Some son of a bitch is going to get killed if he smarts off," the Poet wrote to the reporter.

—⚂—

By the end of the month, Hill and Jones were desperate enough to have Ruth meet with a psychic. They decided they had nothing to lose. Maybe the psychic could get Ruth to open up. Perhaps the psychic could get Ruth to fall apart completely and confess whatever truth she might be hiding.

The detectives set up the meeting on a Monday night at the First United Methodist Church, only two blocks from the phone company. Ruth thought a Methodist church was an odd place to meet a psychic, but why not? She was willing to try anything to rid herself of the Poet.

Jones and Hill met Ruth at the phone company and walked her to the church. Approaching the church's round sanctuary, she gazed up at a huge swirling mosaic of blue and green clay tesserae over the entrance. A shrouded figure rose from the middle of the mosaic, with several rectangular shapes to the lower right of the figure. The mosaic symbolized the raw forces of nature flowing through God to form the cradle out of which man arose.

Hill and Jones led Ruth through a lengthy network of halls inside the church. They hoped to lose anybody who might be following, partly out of concern for Ruth's safety, partly because they didn't care to have anybody in the media know they had resorted to such a desperate ploy. Using a psychic was one step shy of admitting defeat.

Hill and Jones led Ruth into the pastor's gold-carpeted study on the third floor of the church. Ruth had expected to meet a wizened old woman with gold earrings and a crystal ball. Instead, the psychic was a young woman in a business suit. She was visibly nervous.

The psychic had entered the church by another door, she explained to Ruth, because she was so terrified of the Poet that she hadn't wanted to be seen in Ruth's company. The woman was convinced the Poet was after her, as well. She said she knew precisely where the Poet intended to kill her. Her fear of the Poet had become so severe that visions of him had occasionally forced her to leave her regular job at Cessna and go home. She'd explained the problem to her boss, who knew Ruth's brother, Morris. That was how the police had heard about her. She was willing to do anything she could to help Ruth, she said, because it would be like helping herself. Ruth was immediately put off.

Hill and Jones finally finished setting up the tape recorder and left the room. The psychic began asking Ruth about the kidnapping and stabbing incidents, probing for details about the kidnap car, the Poet, Buddy, anything she could remember. Ruth tried to be patient as she retold the stories, but soon the psychic started asking her to get more emotional, and that irritated and confused her. She didn't know how that would help the psychic pick up auras, or whatever it was psychics picked up. Ruth felt her face flush as she talked about the stabbing, and the psychic grabbed her arm and encouraged her to let herself go. Ruth was astounded. She felt like the woman would not be satisfied until Ruth had completely fallen apart. Ruth didn't know how to oblige her. She had told these stories many times and wasn't about to let them bother her.

The two-hour session ended with Ruth's composure intact.

Hours later, the police found out that the tape recorder had failed to work.

16

THE PARADE

The Poet was not making lab investigator Richard Cook's job easy. Cook, a slender fifty-eight-year-old man with glasses and thinning sandy hair, was meticulous and exacting. He processed every page of every Poet letter with great care. These letters flooded into the lab at such a rapid rate that the job had become a painful, time-consuming chore. Sometimes the letters were eight pages long, and because the Poet never numbered his pages, Cook had difficulty keeping them in order. He had just complained to Ed Finley about the lack of page numbers last week.

Cook's motto was, "A place for everything, and everything in its place"—a motto he had appreciated on navy ships during World War II.

Cook had an analytical mind, and he believed in science rather than speculation when it came to solving crimes. He had spent almost all of his twenty-eight years in the Wichita Police Department working on fingerprints because fingerprints eliminated speculation. Leave just one print on a weapon you had used to kill someone and you might as well have signed your name on it, Cook believed. You could lie all you wanted, but if he could identify enough points of identification in the whorls and ridges of one of your prints, he would nail you every time.

But the Poet had frustrated Cook for two years. He had processed more than 150 of the Poet's letters and several other pieces of physical evidence, and the only print he had raised came from a piece of tape on the flap of one of the Poet's envelopes. It probably belonged to a postal worker who had stuck on the tape to seal the flap.

Cook had recently switched to a more sensitive procedure in which he sprayed ninhydrin acid on the pages, then passed a steam iron over them about one inch from the surface. The iron's heat and moisture combined with the chemical to raise any present prints. Cook was so devoted to the procedure that he had even provided his own iron when the department declined to supply one.

Cook had gone back to the letters he had treated with a less precise method and tried ninhydrin, but he had still come up empty, except for a few indistinguishable blobs where the side of a hand had brushed the paper.

But he was a patient man, and he processed each new letter that came to him as carefully as he had the first. So when Ed showed up on March 6 with yet another letter that had been mailed to Ruth, Cook set about the task without complaint. As usual, he slit the envelope on three sides with a letter opener, then extracted the pages with forceps and spread them out on a table. Ed read the contents over his shoulder.

Cook, however, wasn't paying any attention to the text. He had noticed something else. The letter consisted of three pages. And each page was numbered.

Cook had often wondered about Ed. Ed usually joined him in the lab after bringing letters to the station, and he often talked about how much alike the two of them were because they both were meticulous in their work and demanded neatness and order in their results. Ed even pointed out that they dressed alike. Cook was not offended by Ed's observations, but he didn't think a police lab officer and an accountant had much in common. It seemed strange to him that Ed kept mentioning the comparison.

Cook was staring at a letter with numbered pages only a week after complaining to Ed that the Poet didn't number his pages.

At that moment, Cook would have traded in his steam iron for a set of Ed's fingerprints.

Cook wanted Ed to take a polygraph exam. He argued his case to Colonel Coonrod, but Coonrod, a lanky forty-year-old with angular features and an easygoing manner, put him off.

Privately, Coonrod saw nothing but problems in polygraphing the Finleys. First, even if one of them *was* the Poet, a polygraph might not prove it. Ed or Ruth might be schizophrenic and unaware of the dual personality within, and therefore able to pass the test. In that case, the polygraph results could be used to defend them in court.

Second, if the Poet was real, asking the Finleys to take a lie detector test might alienate them. If the Poet was ever caught, they didn't want the Finleys to be hostile witnesses.

Mike Jones had also asked to polygraph Ruth and Ed. But after more than two years, the case had become a circus. The media was all over it, and newspapers in cities as far away as London were still phoning for updates. At this stage, Jones was told, you couldn't confront the Finleys even indirectly with the suggestion that one or both of them was the Poet unless you had something more solid than suspicions.

The previous month, Jones had phoned Ruth at work one day to ask if she had been to Towne East the weekend before. The reason he was asking, he lied to her, was that an officer had tailed a man who looked like the Poet around the mall before losing him on an escalator.

If, in a future letter, the Poet was to describe a visit to Towne East, Jones would have written proof that the Finleys were involved, because only three people knew about his call to Ruth: Jones, Ruth, and Ed, whom Ruth surely would have told.

But the Poet hadn't yet referred to Towne East in any of the subsequent letters to Ruth or to Mann.

So, Jones came up with a new idea: Mann would complain about the Poet's lack of action and strongly imply that he would take matters into his own hands if the Poet didn't do something fast.

If the Poet was real, Jones was provoking a madman and possibly even putting Mann in danger; the Poet, after all, might choose to keep Mann in line. But Jones doubted the risk of that was very great.

"Necrologist: I will contact her," Mann's first ad said.

A week passed without a reply.

Mann tried another one: "Necrologist: Made contact. She says you're a liar, but I no what to do. Will take care of this myself."

The response was prompt.

> *Dear Fred. I think you're on the right track now but I want to do it, so I hope you haven't made any plans. There must not be too many like you & me. I am surprised she talked to you. She used to hang up a lot but for one time she told me to go to hell. I hate females with foul mouths.*

"Necrologist: You're too slow," Mann replied. "I'm ready. Can give you plan."

> *Dear Fred. I don't like yur goddam attitude now. Can you still be trusted? Not slow, fool, just careful. But to insure my success, not yurs, I will expedite things. Thought it out. Day of fucking KAKE parade [a St. Patrick's Day parade sponsored annually by the television station] perfect for my getaway. I am sure RF wuld not go with me & not raise a stink, so have things ready for her there. Not my way of operation, but you understand. You won't get this in time to outdo me with yur fucking plans.*
> *Go to hell.*

"Necrologist: Glad you have a plan of what to do," Mann responded. "Sounds good to me, still want to work with you. Chrome stallion will be my view. Would like to make contact with you."

At 1:45 p.m. on St. Patrick's Day, Mann made his way through the crowd of parade-goers in downtown Wichita. He walked north on Broadway toward the Southwestern Bell building. He wore a sweater over a bulletproof vest and a sport coat with a white handkerchief in the pocket.

Halfway up the block, Mann stopped at a sculpture of a horse made of chrome car bumpers. The life-size sculpture stood outside an entrance of the Fourth National Bank building just south of the phone company. Reflections of the buildings and the passing parade-goers bounced off the bent chrome bumpers. Behind the sculpture lay an alley that sliced between the bank and the phone company. Mann figured the alley would be the Poet's most likely approach.

Soon he heard faint, sporadic bursts of trumpets in the distance. Mann moved away from the horse and stood in the middle of the sidewalk, in clear view of the eleven officers watching him. He glanced around, but he didn't see anybody he recognized.

High in the Southwestern Bell building, Ruth walked to the cafeteria to meet her sister, Jean, for lunch. She and Ed had been told the day before of the Poet's plan to make his move during the parade, and the news made her ill. She had not wanted to come to work, but Ed and the police had convinced her it was the right thing to do. She had to be inside the building when the Poet made his move, they explained. If she stayed home, he would know she had been tipped off, and that Mann had betrayed him.

Detective Dyer had met Ruth at work first thing in the morning and stayed in her office all morning, so she had felt perfectly safe. But walking to lunch alone, tailed at a distance by Dyer, Ruth was seized by fear.

Down on the street, the parade was in full swing. Mann could see the tops of floats over the heads of the people who lined Douglas.

Standing alone a half block north, he felt conspicuous and a little silly. He noticed the guards at a drive-in bank across the street were watching him with interest.

Few people passed. A friend from the newspaper spotted him and trotted up the street to ask what he was doing there. He told him he was waiting for somebody. He began to feel hot and glanced up at the sky. The rain clouds had parted to expose a bright spring sun. He had dressed for a chilly day, but now he began to perspire heavily in his sweater and bulletproof vest. He fought the temptation to pull out the white handkerchief to mop his forehead, knowing the gesture would bring a horde of cops down on his friend.

After Mann's friend left, the reporter saw detectives walking up the sidewalk on the opposite side of the street. Then another pair strolled down from the north. He wondered if they had spotted something. But they passed each other without a word and continued walking.

Another hour passed before the parade ended. The crowd broke up and people began drifting by him, some giving him curious looks. Within ten minutes, the crowd had dispersed entirely. As the last small group of people walked by, a detective stopped to say that Mann could go back to work.

Suddenly there was a commotion across the street. A fight between two teenagers. One of them pulled a knife and held it against the other's throat. The teen's timing was poor. A group of detectives moved in on him immediately.

One officer remained outside the door of Ruth's office on the twelfth floor of the telephone company. He could hear her typing and answering the phone the rest of the afternoon, safe behind the heavy wood door with its tiny peephole.

One week later, the Poet sent Ruth this letter:

Whores bring on war for their great sins.
Let dictates of the sexual appetites drive them & crime begins.

17

SWORD & GUN

Ruth peered in the window of the Fourth National Bank lobby and saw the Poet standing there, staring back at her.

People, including police officers, surrounded her. She screamed at them, but nobody paid any attention.

She looked again at the Poet. He was holding a book under his arm. She could only see part of the title: *Poems by* . . . The rest of the cover was obscured by his arm.

The Poet smiled at her. Then he moved toward the revolving doors. She started to run, screaming, but nobody noticed her. She ran into the street. A city bus bore down on her. She stopped and stood still, frozen by fear.

Once again, Ruth woke up before the bus hit her. She was lying in bed, her heart racing, Ed asleep beside her. She rolled onto her back. It was still dark outside, but she doubted she would be able to go back to sleep.

Ruth wondered if she was cracking up. The dream would not leave her alone. She'd had it several times in the last two weeks. Ruth lay still, staring at the bedroom ceiling, and thought about another dream she'd been having in which she was climbing the stairs of a building with the Poet directly behind her. When she reached the top, she found a door that would not open. Ruth would struggle with the door and pound on it, yelling for help, but nobody would respond. Then the Poet would grab her and she would wake up.

Ruth felt Ed stir beside her. She wanted to wake him up and tell him about these dreams, but she knew she would keep them to herself, as usual. She had never spoken about them to anyone.

She had been feeling so strange lately—a vague sense of unreality. Sometimes she felt as if she wasn't in her body anymore. Earlier that day, at work, whenever she'd had to walk somewhere, she had felt as if her legs were disconnected. She'd had to look down to see if they were still attached to her. She could see them moving, but they didn't seem to belong to her. Fearing that she might topple over, she had stayed close to the walls whenever she had to walk somewhere.

She'd had the same feeling walking down the basement steps of her home that night. What's more, she'd become dizzy when she looked at Ed's painting of the bridge at the foot of the staircase. Ruth thought about the bridge. She remembered how it rattled when she and her father drove over it in their car. As a child, she'd had nightmares in which the car fell through the bridge into the Marmaton River. She had always awakened, as she had tonight, with her heart pounding.

But no. There was something else about the bridge, Ruth thought. What was it? She couldn't think of it. But something. She stared at the ceiling until the sun came up, feeling as if she was floating.

In the morning, as Ed ate breakfast and she prepared their sack lunches, Ruth told him, "I think this is finally getting to me." She forced a laugh.

Ed asked her if she wanted to visit Dr. Schrag again. The doctor, he said, would be the perfect person to talk with. He knew the situation and would understand the stress Ruth was under. She could see him privately, without the police around.

"Fine," said Ruth.

Ed phoned Dr. Schrag to make an appointment. A few days later, he drove her to Dr. Schrag's office and waited outside while Ruth met with the doctor alone.

Schrag had been intrigued by Ed's phone call. He hadn't seen Ruth since his hypnosis had produced the composite sketch more than a year ago. He had been forced to divorce himself clinically from her situation because he had been acting as an agent of the police. He looked forward to meeting as patient and doctor.

But soon after the meeting began, Schrag began to wonder why Ruth had come to see him. She didn't seem to have anything on her mind. They discussed some of the details of the abduction and the stabbing again, but he had expected more.

Ruth, meanwhile, was disappointed that Schrag wasn't asking her the questions she had hoped he would ask. She wanted to tell him of her dreams and feelings, but she couldn't find the right way to start, and he wasn't asking her anything like that. He was just going back over the case. Then she started to doubt her decision to come. In the past, she had never been able to open up to anyone, and it wasn't likely that she could change in one meeting. The conversation eventually dried up, and Ruth rose to leave.

Schrag was mystified as he led her to the waiting room, but he felt compelled to comment.

"It must be really upsetting to you to be going through this," he said, "knowing he's out there waiting, thinking he could get you any night."

"I guess I don't really worry very much about it," Ruth replied.

Schrag once again was amazed by what he viewed as Ruth's lack of emotional depth. As he and Ruth joined Ed in the waiting room, he felt guilty about charging the Finleys for the session.

"We're just not finding out a great deal more," Schrag told Ed.

"Well, we'll just keep trying," Ed said.

"Honestly, I think it's a waste of your money," Schrag said. "I don't think we'll get anything. But if this starts really getting you down, Ruth, I'll try to help you."

Ruth and Ed left the building. Ruth was depressed. She hadn't said what she had come to say.

That night, she remembered Dr. Schrag's comment about telling the police she had been to see him. She thought they would probably be upset with her for not telling them first. They had not been acting very kindly to her lately.

In the morning, she phoned Schrag and asked him not to tell the police about her visit.

Hanging up, she felt like she was losing her mind.

—⁂—

On April 1, shortly after midnight, Ed found an ice pick wrapped in a red bandanna on the front porch.

Mike Jones found out about the ice pick when Coonrod dropped by his desk that morning. When he finished explaining what had happened, Coonrod leaned over and, without a hint of amusement, told Jones, "If I was a sharp young detective, the one day of the year I'd think the Poet would try something would be April Fool's Day."

Jones seethed. It was true he had not thought to watch the house that night, but there was no way to predict when the Poet would strike. Senior officers never asked him for his opinion about the case. Since the wreath-burning incident, he had become increasingly doubtful that the Poet was real. He'd reported his feelings to his captain, Mike Hill, and he assumed they had been passed up the line of command, but Hill hadn't told him as much. To go over Hill and speak to the senior officers would have been a serious breach of procedure in a department that operated within the strict guidelines of a paramilitary organization. He prayed that Coonrod, or Chief LaMunyon, would come to him just once and ask him what he thought.

But Coonrod's comments that morning convinced Jones that the top brass didn't know or care about his opinion. He was crestfallen. Hill kept demanding that Jones gather proof of the Finleys' involvement, but he was coming up short. He was certain Ruth and Ed were being tipped off about information in the Poet's letters, and about the procedures he was using to investigate. They simply had too many friends in the department. He wanted to establish a motive for their involvement, perhaps find some record of mental instability in their past, but he knew if he questioned family and friends, they would tell Ruth and Ed. He had asked once to get clearance for an investigative trip to Fort Scott, but he'd been denied permission because other officers had already gone. Jones thought another trip was vital. The detectives who had made the earlier trip were looking for a link between the Poet and the 1946 attack on Ruth, but Jones wanted to visit to look into the personal backgrounds of Ruth and Ed.

Still flushed with anger over Coonrod's remark, Jones phoned Mann and asked him to take out another ad. Jones's only recourse was to keep the Poet riled up, to keep him writing letters. And the time was right to turn up the heat. He could put Mann back on the attack since the Poet hadn't followed through on the St. Patrick's Day plot.

"Be tough," he told Mann.

"Necrologist: You don't have a plan," the reporter wrote. "You have lied to me all along. You don't deserve a friend like me."

"The hell you say," the Poet replied. "Just watch. I no when & where & you smart yur goddam mouth off so you have to wait. It is all worked out, but maybe last of April because I may go home & have brain scan. When my headaches are bad I can't wear my wig & that is required."

"Necrologist: If I'm your friend you must confide in me. You have neglected me and my loyalty too long. Trust me now or I tell the other side."

"Goddam, now I am going to be pissed. You will be a real double-crossing bastard if you do this now, Fred. I need a friend & I have not fucking used you. I have shared all this with you & I thought you were with me. Now I will have to ask you to, hell, please give me a little more time."

"Necrologist: Big deal. I don't care if you're mad. I have more to lose if you fail. How can I help if I don't know who I'm dealing with? Tell me or I tell the other side."

There was no response.

Jones phoned Ruth to ask for a meeting. He had talked to her several times since taking over the case, but only briefly, to take reports about the incidents of vandalism at her home. He had never sat down with her one-on-one to review the entire case. He had many questions, but the most nagging ones, about her childhood and her teenage years, could not be asked without arousing suspicion.

Jones wanted to know about Ruth's boyfriends, about whether she had ever considered herself an easy mark as a young girl, and also about any emotions she might still be feeling about the Fort Scott attack. If she or Ed was indeed the Poet, they might become more guarded in their letters, more wary of being tricked. Trapped as he was by the paralyzing restrictions that had formed and hardened around the nearly three-year-old case, he didn't know how he would ever find out the truth about Ruth's past.

But Jones saw no harm in reviewing the entire case with Ruth. He had been rereading all the reports, and each of Ruth's accounts about the stabbing and kidnapping—the ones she had given to police officers and, under hypnosis, to Dr. Schrag—varied in minor ways. Nobody else in the department seemed to consider the variations significant. She had been a confused victim, one who had feared for her life, at the time she gave the reports.

But Jones believed that most victims remember exactly what happened to them and rarely alter their story even in the slightest way. Being stabbed and kidnapped make a definite impression. Victims aren't likely to be confused about details; they are more apt to remember vividly and never forget.

Jones wanted Ruth to tell her story all over again, from Fort Scott to the stabbing to the ice pick, and he wanted to watch her eyes as she told it. He had recently attended an FBI training session and learned that when people lie, their eyes dart away for a brief moment, as if searching for answers. Jones had been laughed at by fellow Wichita detectives when he mentioned that fact, but he wanted to see if it held true with Ruth.

The meeting took place in Ruth's office on the twelfth floor of the Southwestern Bell building. Jones took mental notes as he walked in. Ruth's boss worked in an adjoining room, meaning Ruth had her own room with her own desk. Her boss traveled a great deal, giving Ruth even more independence.

Jones took a chair opposite Ruth's desk and pulled out a notebook. After a few moments of polite small talk, he began the questions. Jones noticed that Ruth's eyes darted to the side after every single question. At first, he was excited, but the more her eyes moved, the more he began to doubt he was reading her properly. As a test, he threw in a question about what kind of hubcaps the Finleys had on their Oldsmobile. When Ruth's eyes moved again, Jones gave up in dismay. Why would she lie about hubcaps?

The questioning produced nothing new until Jones asked about something he had seen in a report from Schrag about the account of the kidnapping that she'd given under hypnosis.

"Is it true you found a red bandanna in the car during the kidnapping?"

"Yes," Ruth said. "I picked it up when he wasn't looking and shoved it in my purse."

"Why?"

"I wanted some proof, I guess, that it was happening. I never did get the feeling that the police in Fort Scott ever believed me. But, you know, I didn't even remember doing it until months later. I think I was watching a police show on television."

"You took it when he wasn't looking?"

"Yeah."

"Do you think he saw you?"

"No. He was leaning forward, with his elbows on the front seat, talking to the driver."

"So he probably didn't know it was gone, then," Jones said.

"No, he couldn't have."

After the interview, Jones and Ruth discussed his collection of Civil War relics. He was a compulsive Civil War addict, and Ruth showed a polite interest in hearing about his extensive collection of rifles, swords, belt buckles, bullets, and artillery shells. Their small talk was pleasant, but Jones left her office thinking about the red bandanna.

The police had been mystified about why the Poet used swatches of bandanna material as his calling card. Then Ruth had told Schrag about stealing one during the kidnapping, and from that point on, they'd believed he had enclosed the swatches in letters and left them at the house with his other handiwork to remind her of how she had humiliated him by stealing it. Each piece, they thought, was intended to reinforce the notion that she had stolen something from him and, therefore, that she was a bad person. But if the Poet hadn't seen her take it, Jones thought, he may not even know it was missing. And if he didn't know it was missing, what possible significance would a red bandanna have for him?

—m—

May arrived and the sky over Kansas convulsed with thunderstorms. The Poet's mind reflected the riotous weather.

"Mind unclear," he wrote to Mann two weeks into the new month. "More mundane psycho barriers removed. Butcher or magician. Scenery on stage with sawdust. Tenuous players. Fucking morbid curiosity. Hell to Capt. & Lt."

The letter was incomprehensible.

"I have to work without Blackwater. He's been shooting off his fucked up . . ."

The Poet apparently was so distraught he couldn't finish the sentence.

A few days later, three eggs, wrapped in newspaper, were thrown onto the Finleys' rear patio, splattering the sliding glass doors. There was no way to tell if it was the work of the Poet or other vandals.

The reference to Blackwater in the letter to the reporter was the first since August, and it inspired Jones to come up with another idea: Jones wanted Mann to write an ad to Blackwater asking for help finding the Poet. He hoped it would widen the rift that apparently existed between them, and if Blackwater was a real person, he might come forward. If he wasn't real, the ad would at least keep the Poet agitated.

"Blackwater: You have information I need," Mann wrote. "Write Eagle Box 422B."

The Poet replied within days.

> *Fred, you are a goddam traitor. I saw the ad & Blackwater won't the fuck tell you a goddam thing or he nos he will hang by his balls. Don't talk or listen to him, he's a mental disorder. This may be the last time I let you hear from me. I will leave the day I do it & I am not the fuck telling you. You are a goddam chicken shit double crosser. I hate you. I hate everyone.*

He enclosed a stamped envelope addressed to Ruth, which the Poet wanted Mann to forward to her, and a threatening headline clipped from one of the tabloids about a person who was living with half a dead body.

Instead, Mann took out another ad to Blackwater: "I didn't do what he said," the ad read. "You don't have anything to worry about. Reply Eagle Box 422B."

The ad first appeared on Monday, June 1. On Tuesday, Mann received a letter from the Poet. It had to have been mailed before the second ad ran. But it was the Poet's most intriguing letter yet.

"This will be straight forward & down to earth. I think I was a little unkind to you & I am sorry. I would never do harm to a male good friend." Then it mentioned that the Poet had seen Ruth with a woman who "was big pregnant & some guy was talking to them & thought about 5 p.m., but hell it was pouring rain. I am glad to say on Wed. I walked right out at noon while about 15 waited on elevator & even joined in conversation. She don't no. Someone was saying they Jean, Ruth, or some shit, & she said & the elevator came they all went down but her & so I went down." He seemed to be saying that he'd joined in a group conversation with Ruth and possibly her sister, Jean.

"Christ, Fred, all I wanted to do to her was talk about this fucking paper [the *Fort Scott Tribune*]. . . . I still thought this bitch was nice & believed her fucking lie about taking a leak [during the kidnapping]. I think I would have killed her that night after she talked, though. I no I would."

—⁂—

Ruth and Ed were in Estes Park, Colorado, on their annual wedding anniversary vacation, so the police reached out to Ruth's sister, Jean, to check the information in the letter. Jean told police she remembered a coworker confusing her and Ruth in the cafeteria that week. He had called Jean "Ruth" and Ruth "Jean." Others at their table had laughed at the mix-up, and a pregnant woman had turned to them and told them she sometimes got the siblings mixed up, too.

Jean remembered only four people being at the table. She couldn't remember anyone sitting at a nearby table who might have overheard the conversation. She hadn't seen anybody who looked like the Poet.

The police told Jean to be careful, in case the Poet also mistook her for Ruth.

When Ruth and Ed returned from Estes Park, Jean phoned to let Ruth know that a police officer had warned Jean to be careful. Ruth was angry that he had upset her sister. She reassured Jean that the Poet wouldn't bother her, and Jean insisted she wasn't worried but that she wished she could remember who else had been in the cafeteria on the day of the mix-up. Neither she nor Ruth could come up with anyone who might have seen them.

On her first day back at work, Ruth phoned Mann to find out what else was in the latest letter. He read it to her over the phone, and she told Mann that the Friday she and Ed had left for Colorado had been gloomy and wet and she had worn her blue dress. She had gone to the cafeteria, and she was returning to the elevator when she encountered a pregnant lady, a friend of hers whom she rarely saw. But she couldn't remember anyone who looked like the Poet standing near the elevator.

The Poet had written that the incident at the elevator had taken place on a Wednesday, but Ruth thought it had happened on a Friday.

A few days after the phone call from Ruth, Mann received another letter from the Poet that threatened Mann and said:

"My occult endeavor may now be thwarted by your fucked up tip today and knowledge that you for some reason informed the female."

Jones and Mann read a copy of the letter together at their usual meeting place, the Pancake House, after the police had processed the original for prints. Jones admitted he was confused by the rant; he had no idea what the Poet was talking about. Then the reporter told him about Ruth's phone call, and the significance hit him. How had the Poet found out about the conversation? Only a few people could have known of it: Mann, Ruth, maybe Ed, and possibly Jean.

On top of that, the Poet had yet to respond to the second Blackwater ad. Jones groaned. The ad had appeared on June 1, the day Ruth and Ed had left town on vacation. It had only run for a few days, so it had been gone by the time they returned. They probably hadn't seen it.

Jones asked Mann to run the ad again, unchanged, to see if there was any response this time.

There was. A week after the ad appeared, a letter from the Poet arrived in Eagle Box 422B. An identical letter arrived at Ruth's house. Among more-explicit threats to Ruth and Mann, it insisted that they "cease this search for my hireling. Blackwater & Frank are insuperable kibitzers in sui generis position."

—⁓—

On Sunday, July 12, Ruth and Ed smelled gunpowder in their house and found firecrackers, cigarette papers, matches, and a red bandanna in their mailbox. Several burnt matches were strewn about on the porch.

"Hickory, dickory dock," the Poet wrote to Ruth two weeks later. "Your time running off the clock."

The poem was not unusual except for two lines that leaped off the page at Jones when he read them:

> *Pigs armed with sword & gun*
> *have away from whores run.*

Police don't carry swords, Jones thought. They don't even carry knives. Using a sword as a policeman's weapon was curious. Unless the Poet knew about a casual, private conversation between Jones and Ruth at her office back in April that revolved around his collection of Civil War artifacts, which included his dazzling array of swords.

18

ENDING THINGS

Ruth and Ed were quietly distressed at the changes each saw in the other. They had put on a brave front for three years, and their buried anxieties had gradually created a poisonous reservoir within them. They were both experiencing sleeplessness, mood swings, and bouts of depression. They had been suppressing their anger with the Poet in order to continue being nice to each other and to family, friends, and coworkers, and that suppression was taking a toll.

Neither Ruth nor Ed thought they could endure the Poet much longer, and each formed their own plan to try to bring the case to an end.

Ruth found herself plagued by odd thoughts: she'd thought about committing suicide, believing it would somehow beat the Poet at his own game. It had started as an idle whim and, over time, had grown into a compulsion. Toward the end of July, when she and Jean went to cash their paychecks at the bank, she secreted $120 in twenty-dollar bills in her purse. Then she prayed for courage.

Ed went to the police station to talk to Captain Hill. He wanted to take out a series of newspaper ads aimed at forcing the Poet to send proof that the Poet and BTK were the same person. Like Drowatzky and a few other officers, Ed was convinced that the Poet and BTK were identical because of the repeated references to Nancy Jo Fox's "petticoat" in the Poet's letters.

If the Poet proved the theory, Ed explained, he believed the police might be able to file more-serious charges against Ruth's tormenter when they finally caught him. Ed wanted the Poet put away for a long time, but the most serious crime he had committed against Ruth was aggravated assault, and a lawyer might be able to get him a minimal jail sentence.

Hill was confused.

"Why would he want to send us that kind of proof?" Hill asked Ed.

"Because I think this guy has always wanted to be taken seriously. He wants respect. He's probably been a nerd all his life."

Hill had been suspicious of Ed for months, but listening to him talk about his desperate plan made Hill wonder even more. And yet, he couldn't think of any reason not to let Ed take out the ads. In fact, Hill believed he might be able to use the ads to his advantage by setting another trap. He could arrange to have someone in the department slip Ed a bit of information about BTK that was unknown to the public. If that information showed up in one of the Poet's future letters, Hill would know where it came from.

The trap was set on the last day of July, when Ed brought in another letter from the Poet for processing. Before examining it, lab investigator Richard Cook reached into a bottom desk drawer and handed Ed a copy of BTK's last letter, a sheet of single-spaced typing. At the bottom of the sheet was a symbol that BTK used as his signature. Police had kept the symbol a closely guarded secret, to distinguish BTK from imitators. Cook stole glances as Ed scanned the page.

"You think that was written by the same guy?" Cook asked after a while, attempting to sound casual.

"Yeah, it could be," Ed replied.

"Of course, you notice he doesn't use all the profanity and doesn't have the same word phrasing."

"Well," said Ed, "this isn't written to a woman he's trying to terrorize. It's written to the police."

Ed handed the letter back to Cook, his eyes settling briefly on the symbol at the bottom of the page.

Cook knew Ed was taken by the symbol, which was formed by an interlocking of the strangler's three initials. To Ed, it looked very much like a brand.

—⁂—

The following Monday, August 3, Ed phoned Mann to dictate his first ad. He employed Latin phrases because he'd noticed the Poet had used Latin in recent letters.

"Onus probandi [the burden of proof] for heptad [seven, meaning the seven victims of BTK] is on you. We do not believe. Mr. F."

The ad appeared in the paper for three days running. On the third day, August 7, the Finleys and Drowatzky received a letter from the Poet written entirely in Latin. In Drowatzky's envelope was a piece of lace—presumably intending to represent the "petticoat" of Nancy Jo Fox—and a metal rendering of the letter *F*. A tracing of an ice pick slashed through the letter, and drawings of the Greek symbols for male and female were at the top and bottom of the page, respectively.

Police asked Mann to insert his own ad in response.

"Necrologist: I saw what you sent. It proves nothing. Nice try, fallax [a false or deceptive person]."

Two days after the ad appeared, Ruth opened the front door of her house to get the newspaper and took a step right onto an envelope that had been placed on the porch. Her shoes were sullied with a dark substance that later turned out to be human feces.

At the end of the week, the Poet mailed two letters, one to Ruth and the other to the television station KAKE. On the top of Ruth's were the words "fox" and "lace ribbon & chain." On the top of KAKE's, the words were replaced by photocopied pictures of a fox, a small chain, and lace material.

The letter consisted of several verses divided into what the Poet called "chapters," beginning with chapter 7, which referred to Nancy Jo Fox:

> *A day in December [Fox died December 9, 1977] with no*
> *one she knew*
> *kiss the bare breast & bid her adieu.*

Chapter 8 concerned the death of Ruth Finley:

> *He pierced her heart & caused her blood to flow*
> *Then into her grave he did her throw*
> *Lie dead & soaked in her own blood*
> *deep in gore as anger floods.*

Chapter 9 referred to Sharron LaMunyon:

> *Silence the tongues of all fat bawds*
> *Whores in taffeta, all men were awed.*

At the top of the second page of Ruth's letter were the words "The End." In the same spot on the copy of KAKE-TV's letter was a photocopied picture of a bridge.

This note was appended at the bottom of the copy to the TV station: "Everyone is against me, I think. She—Chapter 9—is a fat asshole & pushes men around. Can't contact her until rid of Chapter 8, which is soon I hope."

The Poet's "proof" of a link to BTK was easy for Hill and Jones to dismiss. They were more interested in the fact that the Poet seemed to be trying very hard to establish a link, and that one of the letters hinting at such a link had been sent to a TV station at the same time that Ed Finley was pressing police for action.

They were even more interested in Ed's response to the Poet's letters. He wanted to take out another ad, this one complaining that the "proof" was inadequate.

They saw no reason to stop him.

"Subveria non corpus delicti," Ed's second ad said, meaning the souvenirs sent by the Poet in his letters weren't enough to prove any crime had been committed.

Ed signed the ad "Mister F." He explained to Hill that he wanted to spell out the "mister" because the Poet probably thought Ruth had taken out the first ad, somehow mistaking "Mr." for "Mrs."

"I want him to know I'm around, whether he likes it or not," Ed said.

While Ed's plan was in full swing, Ruth hadn't taken any further steps since hiding the $120 in her purse in July. Every day she sat in her office thinking about ending things.

She'd envisioned walking out of the phone company in the middle of the day.

She would walk to the bus station, a few blocks south of the telephone company on Broadway. She'd be unprotected by the police, vulnerable to another attack by the Poet.

Ruth knew that if she could somehow manage to get out of the building unnoticed and make it safely to the bus station, the rest would go smoothly. She'd buy a ticket to Oklahoma City, and it would be a pleasant three-hour ride on an air-conditioned bus. Once there, she would check into a motel, where she would spend the night under an assumed name.

The following morning, she would find a store that sold knives.

Having never been to Oklahoma City before—she didn't know why she had picked Oklahoma City—she would have to inquire about rivers and lakes. But that wouldn't be a big problem.

All she would have to do then was tie some heavy rocks to her body, wade into the water, stab herself, and vanish beneath the surface.

She would beat the Poet to the punch. As many times as she'd gone over the plan in her mind during the past few weeks, she still didn't know whether she would be brave enough to leave work and walk to the bus station by herself.

Ruth envied the Poet his courage.

19

THE CHIEF

Police Chief Richard LaMunyon wondered if he was crazy. After spending the better part of the last week examining all the evidence in the Poet case, he had found enough holes to make even the weakest investigator suspicious that the whole thing was a fraud.

LaMunyon rarely interfered in his officers' cases. But this case had dragged on too long, and the Poet had gone too far when he'd linked his wife, Sharron, with the victims of the BTK serial killer. LaMunyon had asked Hill to have copies of all the letters, reports, and pieces of physical evidence sent to his office on the fourth floor of city hall so he could see what the case was all about and why his people hadn't solved it yet.

LaMunyon had never believed in the case, although he couldn't explain Ruth's stabbing two years earlier. He still remembered the look in Bernie Drowatzky's eyes after the incident, when the lieutenant, whom LaMunyon respected highly as an investigator, had insisted that somebody was after Ruth. But LaMunyon thought then, and still thought, that if somebody really wanted to kill Ruth Finley, she would be dead.

He hadn't believed that the Poet's threats against his wife were serious, although the idea that Ruth or Ed, or somebody close to them, was using Sharron to get attention made him angry. It bothered him even more that the ploy had worked. Because the Poet now had his undivided attention. Linking a loved one to somebody as vicious as BTK was a good way to get anybody's attention.

A picture of Sharron and his two sons, Slade and Blake, stood on the table behind LaMunyon's desk. Sharron was a slender brunette—the Poet's insults had no basis in truth.

Sharron was on LaMunyon's mind as he studied the case of the person who was threatening to kill her. He had been at it for more than a week, a pale, September sun staring over his shoulder through the blinds behind him, and had not found anything helpful. Lab investigators had turned up no prints on any of the physical evidence—not on the butcher knife, the knife used to stab Ruth, the ice pick, the paper used to burn the Finleys' Christmas wreath, the swatches of red bandanna material, or the hundreds of letters. They had not even found a partial print with fragmented ridges, smudges, or smears on any of the letters, which now numbered more than two hundred. A few partials had been found on the envelopes, but his men believed—accurately, LaMunyon assumed—that they belonged to a postal worker.

Lab tests for saliva on the envelopes to determine blood type were negative. Tests performed by the FBI and the Kansas Bureau of Investigation on the urine that had been left in a jar on the Finleys' front porch had not produced definitive results. Comparisons of Ruth's and Ed's handwriting to that of the Poet had been inconclusive. The FBI and KBI had searched their anonymous letter files to find one that matched the Poet's writing, but that had failed as well.

LaMunyon reread the psychological and linguistic profiles. All of them discounted the possibility that the victim and the perpetrator were the same person.

The department's chaplain, Robert Ely, had a background in psychology and literature, so he had studied each of the Poet's letters and cataloged the types of words and phrases. He found sixty-five words of a literary nature, twenty-three psychological terms, eleven philosophical terms, five theological terms, and four words that were so archaic they hadn't been used for at least half a century. In all, Ely found 107 words that were so technical or arcane they were unlikely to be used correctly in common speech or writing, and yet they had been correctly used by the Poet, who couldn't spell "know" properly. He was an enigma, but to Ely, this indicated a level of literacy on the part of the author that ruled out the Finleys, who lacked the necessary literary training.

Ely also noted a progression in the vocabulary in the letters. The early poems were crude and simplistic, but the latter ones revealed a broader vocabulary. The author, he wrote, "seems to take special pleasure in working these sophisticated terms into the meter and phraseology of his poetry."

Ely found the poetry generally awkward in rhyme and meter, but some of the less awkward poetry reminded him of Milton's *Paradise Lost* or Dante's *Inferno*, suggesting classical training.

The author, Ely declared, "is a male with a deep-seated sense of hatred and rejection where all females are concerned and with a particular fixation on Ruth Finley. Although he may not be exclusively homosexual, I believe that his social contacts will be found to be primarily in the homosexual community."

Ely also noted that the Poet's obsession with Ruth had undergone a transition from mere blackmail to threats of murder to threats of murder after inflicting great mental suffering. Ely concluded his report by saying he had little doubt that the Poet's mental condition was deteriorating rapidly and that he would soon make another overt attempt on Ruth's life.

LaMunyon found Ely's report interesting, but what did it mean?

All the objective and scientific evidence in the case led LaMunyon nowhere.

He pored over the transcripts of Ruth's accounts of the kidnapping and the stabbing, and that fueled his skepticism.

Ruth had been snatched off a major street in the middle of downtown, and yet nobody saw it happen. She had driven around for four hours with two men in a suspicious vehicle and had even sat in the parking lot of a busy shopping mall; yet no one had noticed Ruth, and she had never shouted for help. She and the Poet were in the back seat of the car, and the floor was littered with gas cans, chains, slabs of concrete, boards, and other trash. How could they have both fit back there?

LaMunyon reviewed the reports of the follow-up investigation and saw that his men had covered all the bases, but he wished they had been tougher when they'd questioned her that night. They had just treated her as a victim.

Everything hinged on the stabbing, LaMunyon thought. That had wiped out all the doubts about Ruth's story within the department. Yet even with the stabbing, Ruth's version of what had happened parted company with logic in several details. The first thing that leaped out at LaMunyon was Ruth's statement that she had rolled up the window when the Poet stuck his hand in after she had freed herself from his grasp. That meant the window must have been rolled down until then. But the door had been locked. Why would she lock the door and leave the window rolled down? Ruth's explanation that the window had rolled down when the Poet banged her head against it did not seem credible.

After Ruth escaped, she stopped to use the pay phone in a nearby service station, but instead of calling the emergency number and getting help, she called the CIB. That was not a normal response to a clear and present threat.

In the hospital, a nurse had recorded that Ruth had been courageously calm.

LaMunyon found that curious in someone who had just fought for her life and still had a knife sticking out of her back.

He couldn't believe Ruth would have been able to fight off the man as she had described. If the Poet had wanted to kill her, LaMunyon thought, he would have.

LaMunyon also studied the hospital reports. He'd had to subpoena them himself in the last week. His men had never obtained them. He found it incredible that nobody had thought to review them in the last two years.

He didn't know what all the medical notations meant, so LaMunyon had taken the reports to his own doctor, who had determined that the wound to Ruth's kidney was so severe that she would not have been able to inflict it herself. LaMunyon had explained his doubts about Ruth, and his doctor had concluded that Ed was likely the one who had stabbed her.

LaMunyon's policy about not interfering in his men's cases was a firm one. He had two hundred men under his command, working on thousands of cases, so he had no choice but to trust them and let them do their jobs. Meddling in cases could hurt their morale. LaMunyon believed that if he showed up at a crime scene, he would, in effect, be taking over that particular case. This would imply he didn't trust the officers who normally would have handled it. He was an administrator, an idea man, a motivator—not a detail man.

And he'd always considered himself a good judge of people. LaMunyon felt that Drowatzky, the first man to take charge of Ruth's case, was an excellent officer and a fine investigator with a proven record of success. Nearly everyone else on the case believed Ruth, too, including psychologists, doctors, linguists, and other experts.

Hill was one of his best people, and all the detectives who had worked the case were the cream of the crop. In recent weeks, he had pulled some of his men aside discreetly to sound them out. He had heard from those who doubted Ruth's story and from those who believed her. But one thing they all had in common was a true fondness for Ruth. They all seemed disarmed by her warmth and sweetness, by her air of innocence.

LaMunyon had never met Ruth, and knowing the effect her charm had on his men, he vowed he never would. He had to remain objective about Ruth.

The answer to the riddle of the Poet would be gleaned from reports. And perhaps from his men.

It was time to officially sit down with them.

—⁓—

LaMunyon and his men met on the afternoon of Friday, September 11, in the Civil Preparedness Room of the Sedgwick County courthouse—sixteen officers, including everyone who had ever worked on the case in any major capacity. The only one absent was George Anderson, one of the first, who was busy working the late shift. LaMunyon had chosen the location, across the street from city hall and in the basement of the courthouse, to avoid detection. He was aware of the leaks that had sprung up during the case, and he wanted the meeting to be secret. He wanted to foster a complete and honest evaluation of the case by every officer in the room. He didn't want the Finleys finding out what they discussed.

The room, used as a disaster control center during storms, suited the occasion. The mood of the men, who sat in a circle facing each other, was somber, and the weather outside—hot and muggy, with a sickly sky and revolving winds—threatened to spawn tornadoes.

LaMunyon rose from his chair to begin the meeting. "First, I want to thank you for everything you've done on the case," he said. "But as you know, it's become a personal thing with me, so I want to tell you that, as of today, I'm assuming command of the investigation. I'm doing that because I have the total resources of the department at my command, and this will be a total, concentrated effort to determine who the Poet is.

"I want to go around the room and listen to all of your opinions. We have to figure out what needs to be done, what we can do. I want you to be honest with me."

There was a pause. The officers cleared their throats and shifted in their chairs.

Mike Jones was the first to speak. He had been relieved to hear of the meeting; he had many doubts about Ruth and Ed, and he was anxious to get them off his chest. He decided to start with the stabbing.

"There isn't any doubt in my mind that it didn't happen the way Ruth said it happened," Jones told the room.

He went through Ruth's account of the incident, listing each point that didn't hold up under examination, and concluded by saying he was sure Ruth or Ed was involved, or both. "I'm suspicious of these two, but then, I'm suspicious of a lot of things," Jones said.

Next, Doyle Dyer uncoiled his burly frame. "It's either her or him, or both," Dyer said. He told the room of the time Ruth had identified a black-and-white photo of a suspect, only to change her mind later when she found out the suspect's eyes were blue instead of brown. He also mentioned the time Ruth had, unprompted, raised her sweater to show him the wounds on her back.

The next speaker was Richard Vinroe, who had spent nearly a year on the case and had become more emotionally involved in it than most of the others. Vinroe still felt guilty about not solving the case, and he still felt as if he had abandoned the Finleys. His guilt had been reinforced the past Christmas when they sent him a Christmas card on which Ruth had written "Vinroe—wherever did you go?"

Vinroe had believed in the case from the beginning, and more so the closer he had become to Ruth. But now that his involvement had receded in time, he honestly didn't know what to believe, he told the room.

"I suppose anyone coming into the case now might suspect Ruth or Ed," he said, "but Zee [Richard Zortman] was one of the few people on it longer than me, and we felt it was real. Whether you believe Ruth or Ed are involved or not, they have never been eliminated, so you're always going to have questions."

Zortman backed Vinroe up. "If you have doubts about them," he added, "the first thing we have to do is eliminate them."

The discussion gathered momentum, and the room quickly divided into those who still believed the Finleys and those who didn't.

Those who believed the Finleys argued that Ruth and Ed were not the kind of people who would make it all up. They were normal, churchgoing, salt-of-the-earth types who both held solid jobs in the community. They did not crave attention, and they sure as hell didn't seem to be enjoying it.

Then there were all those doctors and other experts who said the Finleys couldn't be involved.

Two witnesses had seen the Poet in the phone company building on the day he had left the butcher knife in the lobby.

As for the stabbing, maybe it hadn't happened exactly the way Ruth said it did, but she had been scared and confused. It wasn't unusual for victims of violent crime to get some details wrong. She had been stabbed three times, and one of the wounds was extremely serious. Why would she do that to herself? Suicide? Nobody commits suicide by stabbing themselves in the lower back with a kitchen knife. A desperate ploy for attention? Not Ruth. She didn't want attention. She hated it.

And why would Ed stab her? He loved her. Everybody could see that.

No, it didn't make sense that Ruth or Ed was the Poet.

If they were, what was the motive?

Indeed, the motive stumped even those who were convinced that Ruth or Ed *was* the Poet, but they tended to set the subject of motive aside and accept the fact that the Poet was caused by some mental disorder in Ruth or Ed that was beyond the power of the police to understand. What mattered was the objective evidence, they believed, and all of it pointed at Ruth or Ed, if only by virtue of the fact that it failed to point at anyone else.

Nobody in the Finleys' neighborhood had ever seen a man who resembled the Poet lurking about, even though he had been doing nasty deeds at the house for three years. That kind of luck simply defied the odds.

And the Poet had perfect timing. He always seemed to know just when to make a move. His visits always seemed to occur when the camera hidden in the backyard fountain and the alarm on the back gate had been turned off. The phone lines on the back of the house had been cut one Christmas Eve just before Zortman was due to arrive. In fact, the phone lines had been cut twice, but once the hidden camera was installed and trained on the rear of the house, they hadn't been cut again.

Cook told the room about how the Poet had thoughtfully begun numbering the pages of the letters shortly after he had mentioned to Ed how nice that would be.

Jones mentioned the line about "pigs armed with sword & gun" that had appeared in one of the Poet's letters, pointing out that it was written soon after he had spoken with Ruth about his collection of Civil War relics. He also reminded the room that the paper used to set the Christmas wreath on fire had come from the Finleys' own dumpster. And he told them about how the Blackwater ad that had appeared in the newspaper on the day the Finleys left town on vacation had remained unanswered until it had run again when the Finleys were back in Wichita.

The talk continued to swirl like the stormy winds outside for a full two hours before LaMunyon stepped back in. He had said little since his opening statement. He did not want to influence the discussion. But over two hours, he had heard nothing from his men that had changed his mind about Ruth. It was time to let them know how he felt.

"I've gone through all the files," LaMunyon said, "and as each of you will recall, I've talked privately with you alone. In my opinion, Ruth Finley is the Poet. If it's not her, it's Ed, and they're both in on it. I say we start with them, and we either prove it's them, or we prove it's not them."

After letting that sink in, he called for ideas about how to investigate the Finleys. Eventually, an extreme plan evolved. Beginning the following Monday, Ruth and Ed would be placed under an ongoing, twenty-four-hour surveillance led by Captain Richard Granger, the head of the narcotics division. The surveillance would require fifteen officers from vice and narcotics working twelve-hour shifts, and would employ ten cars, a van that would serve as the command center, and air support in the form of a helicopter.

Granger and Lieutenant Gary Stokes, of the vice division, would contact postal authorities to set up a system to monitor the Finleys' incoming and outgoing mail.

Meanwhile, Drowatzky, the Finleys' closest friend on the force, would invite himself to their house for dinner in order to ask veiled questions and plant seeds that might bear fruit in future Poet letters. He would also do a personal history check on the Finleys.

Detectives in Hill's department would track down any leads developed during the investigation.

In short, nearly the entire investigative resources of the Wichita Police Department would be focused for days, possibly weeks, on a middle-aged secretary and her accountant husband.

LaMunyon closed the meeting by swearing everyone in the room to secrecy. To further prevent leaks, LaMunyon decided that only he, his top assistant, Colonel John Coonrod, and Hill would be kept informed on all phases of the investigation.

"If word of this gets out," LaMunyon told his men as the meeting broke up, "you will feel the wrath of the chief's office."

20

SURVEILLANCE

On the morning of Monday, September 14, Ed Finley backed his black Oldsmobile out of the garage and headed down East Indianapolis with Ruth in the passenger seat. He was unaware of the blue car parked east of the house; a police officer, watching through binoculars, was radioing the rest of the team that the Finleys were on the move.

Nor did Ed hear the helicopter circling high overhead. And when he drove past the Eastgate shopping mall, he did not notice the van parked at a service station on the mall's west side, which contained two officers with binoculars and still cameras outfitted with 200-millimeter lenses and infrared nightscopes.

Nor did he see the cars that trailed him from the mall to the phone company to drop off Ruth. Nor did he see the cars that came and went from the lot across the street from Halsey-Tevis all day long.

But then, none of the officers tailing Ed were aware that, on the same day, the Poet mailed another letter to Ruth:

> *The game is over, the players are dead*
> *I play any part coming out of my head.*

On Tuesday, the police tailed Ed and Ruth into town again and sat on them all day. Meanwhile, Stokes was given approval by postal authorities to monitor the mail from ten drop boxes located in areas where the Finleys worked and lived. The monitoring would start the following day. Also on Tuesday, Hill turned over all 220 Poet letters to LaMunyon, who assigned one of his men to the grueling task of recording the dates that each had been mailed and received in order to determine if the Poet wrote according to any pattern.

Ruth and Ed continued to go about their daily lives unaware of the surveillance. The officers were struck by the inflexibility of the couple's daily routine. They left the house precisely at 7:35 each morning and followed the same route to work. Ed rarely left his office, and Ruth never left hers. Ed would pick Ruth up at exactly 5:00 p.m. and take her home, where the lights would burn late into the night.

After three days of this, the police were bored and restless. The Finleys had done nothing suspicious, nor had they mailed any letters. Spirits wilted among the officers who were spending their days and nights following the couple.

On Thursday, September 17, things changed. Officers sitting in the car east of the house saw Ed and Ruth leave in the Olds at 7:40 a.m., five minutes later than normal. They radioed the other cars, which were waiting for the Olds to emerge on Rock Road. It never did.

Suddenly, the voice of Lieutenant Gary Burgat, who was airborne in the helicopter, crackled over their radios.

"I got 'em moving through the parking lot," Burgat said. The officers figured it out: Ed had turned up the first street west of his home and dipped into the back entrance of the Eastgate mall.

"He's stopped," Burgat said.

There was a pause. The other cars tried to maneuver through traffic to get to the mall.

"Okay, now he's going back east through the lot," Burgat reported.

Officers converged on the mall, but they couldn't find the Olds.

Then they heard Burgat utter an oath.

"I lost them," he said.

Ed and Ruth had disappeared.

—⁓—

The black Oldsmobile rose and dipped through the Flint Hills as it glided northbound along Interstate 35. Gazing out the window, Ruth watched the fields of tall bluestem grass, speckled with cattle, float by. She was mesmerized by the whirring wheels of the car and the endless horizon.

It had been Ed's idea that she join him on his business trip to Topeka, and she was pleased to go. It meant she would be free of her claustrophobic office for a day, and from the high-ceilinged hallways outside that had become a nightmare.

Ed had begun to comment on her anxiety. He had noticed she'd been biting her lip constantly in the last couple of weeks.

"Well, I just need a little exercise," Ruth had told him, at once believing it true, yet also knowing it wouldn't really cure anything.

She had started having stomachaches reading the Poet's letters, but lately the aches had intensified. Sometimes, she dashed to a bathroom expecting to vomit, but nothing happened.

One night the previous week, standing in front of the bathroom mirror at home, brushing her teeth, she had felt dizzy. Then the room spun, and she collapsed. She landed on the tile floor on her tailbone, and it still ached.

The bouts of nausea reminded Ruth of those she had suffered after the attack in Fort Scott. They had ultimately required medication and forced her mother to come stay with her in that awful boardinghouse. Ruth was determined not to go through that again; she would not be a burden to Ed, like she had been to her parents. Why couldn't she find the courage to go to the bus station and end things? she wondered. She was determined to try when she returned to work the next day.

ut a day in Topeka would provide a welcome break from these problems. And Ed seemed pleased to have her with him. Ruth felt better than she had in months as she watched the hills sweep by.

—⁓—

When he found out the Finleys had eluded the surveillance team, Hill phoned Halsey-Tevis and learned that Ed had gone to Topeka on business. Then Hill phoned Southwestern Bell and found out Ruth had joined her husband on the trip. Hill passed the word to his men.

Forty-five minutes after Hill called Halsey-Tevis, Ed phoned Hill from Topeka to let him know where he was.

To take advantage of the unexpected lull in the surveillance, Captain Richard Granger went aloft in the helicopter with Burgat that afternoon to take photos of the area. He was looking for other ways Ed might inadvertently elude police, places where Granger might have to station more men. As Burgat guided the chopper over the mall where Ed had disappeared, Granger thought of a question.

"What did they do when they came in here?" he shouted at Burgat over the clattering rotor blades.

"They drove up to those mailboxes," Burgat shouted back, pointing down at two drive-up boxes on the west side of the mall's parking lot, "then they stopped a minute, came around, and went east."

Like most officers involved in the surveillance, Burgat had been told only to follow the Finleys, not about other aspects of the investigation. As a helicopter pilot, he hadn't been involved in the case at all until now. So he did not share the excitement that flushed Granger's face.

"Which side of the car was at the box?" Granger hollered at him.

"Passenger side."

Granger grabbed the radio and phoned the news back to headquarters. It galvanized the entire operation. Three detectives—Craig Stansberry, Kim Brewer, and Gary Olson—drove to the mailboxes while Lieutenant

Gary Stokes phoned the postal inspector and asked him to meet them there. It was 1:30 p.m.

Stansberry saw when they arrived at the box that the first pickup was scheduled for 2:00 p.m. Whatever the Finleys had dropped into the box that morning would still be inside. The three detectives guarded the box for the next thirty minutes.

At almost exactly 2:00 p.m., a postal carrier pulled up to the box to make the pickup. Brewer approached him, identified himself, and told him that an inspector was on the way to check the mail. Then all of them, the detectives and the mail carrier, stood there, waiting.

Ten minutes later, the inspector, Willie Thurman, arrived. He opened the box and removed a white canvas sack filled with mail. Thurman put the sack in the back seat of his car and drove to the nearest post office with the officers following.

Once inside, Brewer emptied the sack onto a table in a back room and began sorting through the mail with Olson's help. Stansberry stood next to them, returning the sorted mail to the sack.

Within minutes, they found the Finleys' mail, five envelopes still clumped together in a pile. Three bore their return address, 8125 E. Indianapolis. Two of those were bill payments, one a personal letter.

The other two had no return addresses. They were addressed in the familiar, childish printing of the Poet. One was addressed to Ruth at her home, the other to a reporter at KAKE-TV.

The detectives' excitement about the discovery was quickly tempered when they found themselves confronted by the red tape of the US postal system. Federal postal regulations are stringent. The post office takes its motto, "The mail must go through," seriously. The officers were not allowed to open or remove the Poet letters, or even to photograph them. The letters had to be put back in the sack and delivered with the rest of the mail.

Lieutenant Gary Stokes, who arrived at the scene with a lab officer, asked Thurman for approval to take pictures of the Finleys' mail, but Thurman turned him down. That launched a series of negotiations between Thurman, Stokes, LaMunyon, and Thurman's boss at the regional postal headquarters in St. Louis. Paperwork would be required before the police could tamper with the mail in any fashion.

But they worked out a short-term compromise to deal with the immediate situation: The letter to KAKE was removed from the mail and hand-delivered to Mann by Thurman. Mann then handed it to Hill, who had accompanied Thurman to the station.

It was laughable, but at least the detectives were able to get their hands on a brand-new Poet letter.

The letter addressed to Ruth was sent through the mail, as usual.

Hill took the KAKE letter to the police lab for processing. Still no prints.

But the detectives' excitement over their discovery was hard to suppress. Hill and LaMunyon tried to keep a lid on what had happened, but it was tempting to shout the news from the top of city hall.

LaMunyon injected a sobering observation at a meeting with his senior officers that afternoon. He pointed out that the Finleys had mailed their letters at 8:15 in the morning, but the mail had not been picked up until 2:00 p.m. "What if somebody came along after them and mailed those two letters?" he asked rhetorically. "I mean, I know it's a hundred-to-one shot, but we've got to be sure."

On Friday, the police borrowed an old, gray Chevy van from the Drug Enforcement Administration and parked it by a gas station on the mall's west side, just thirty-five feet from the two drive-up mailboxes. The parked van faced Rock Road, which the Finleys would pass on their way to work. From the rear of the van, police had a clear view of the mailboxes. Two officers were stationed inside with cameras equipped with 10-millimeter lenses. Their orders were to take pictures of any cars that pulled up to the boxes.

Ed and Ruth had returned to Wichita late on Thursday. Shortly before 11:00 p.m., police saw a blue Oldsmobile pull into their driveway. A middle-aged man got out and went to the door. The door opened, and he disappeared inside. He did not come back out until just after one o'clock in the morning.

Three unmarked police cars followed him to a house on the northeast side of town, but the man seemed to be spooked and drove off without stopping. He wound aimlessly through the area, as if aware he was being tailed. The officers decided to pull back so the driver would relax. Eventually, he returned to his own house. The police ran a check on his license plate and found out the next day that he was the Finleys' attorney, Orval Kaufman. It struck them as more than a little odd that their attorney would visit them so late at night.

Friday morning, Ed and Ruth followed their normal routine. Hill phoned Ed at work later that morning and told him that KAKE had received a letter from the Poet the previous day. It appeared to be a copy of a poem to Ruth, Hill told him. Hill wondered if Ed could swing by the house after the mail came that afternoon to check. And if he did find a Poet letter, could he please bring it to the lab that afternoon?

Ed said he would, though he privately found it strange that he was being asked to make a special trip to pick up the letter, rather than simply waiting for the next day.

The surveillance team followed Ed as he drove home to check the mail, then followed him to city hall. Ed rode the elevator up to the police station and handed Hill the letter addressed to Ruth that police had seen in the post office the day before.

As usual, Ed went to the lab to watch it being processed for prints and to receive his copy of its contents. Then he left city hall, picked Ruth up at the phone company, and drove home.

The whore scraped the dirt away from her womb.
I came out to play.
Little girls should give it away.
Hickory dickory dock
The name on this face is Smock.

Ruth read the lines with her usual detachment. Sometimes she had admired the Poet's work, but she thought this one was below par. The mention of the little girl made her faintly uneasy, however. It reminded her of a little girl with blond hair she had known when she herself was a little girl on the farm in Richards.

For an instant, she had a vision of the girl lying on a bed. The girl was naked except for a pair of shoes. She was crying. Then Ruth saw a wagon and heard a dog bark. There was a man in bib overalls there, too. Tobacco juice dribbled from the corner of his mouth.

All these images spun kaleidoscopically in Ruth's mind for a brief moment and then disappeared. She didn't know what to make of them. She thought of telling Ed, but she didn't know what to say. She had no idea what the images meant.

She felt ill again.

—m—

On Saturday, police followed Ed and Ruth to a Sears in south Wichita, where Ed bought a lawn mower. Then the Finleys returned home, and Ed worked on the house. Later, they drove to the Eastgate mall to buy groceries. They did not stop at the mailboxes.

Sunday, they went to church, then to Fay's house just east of the downtown area. After a short visit with Ruth's mother, they drove to the Towne East mall and then to a Mr. Steak restaurant for dinner. They were home by 7:00 p.m.

Ruth dreamed that night of the little girl and the man in bib overalls. The man laughed horribly, a deep and throaty sound, like thunder. Stubby, her dog, barked. Then Morris appeared, saying, "He couldn't keep his hands off of you. I think he wants to put you in his pocket and take you home."

Then a woman was holding the little girl on her lap, wiping her clean with a damp sponge and comforting her. The scene changed abruptly, and the man was standing beside her by a cave near a river next to a large wooden box filled with jewelry and petticoats. The little girl held in one arm a book of nursery rhymes with her picture on the back cover. She was waiting to destroy the book because it said bad things about her. The little girl started reciting the verses to her own picture:

There was an old woman who lived in a shoe
Got rid of bad girls like you.
One, two, three, four, five, six, seven
Little girls like you won't go to heaven.
Patty cake, patty cake, baker's man
Killed by a great big man.

The man picked up the girl suddenly and held her high over the river, and the girl sobbed and screamed. Dreaming of this, Ruth felt a burning hatred for the little girl and wanted to destroy her.

Then the girl fell, and kept falling, down into a dark pit and a still pool of black water, where she disappeared.

—⁂—

On Monday, the police were stunned when letters from the Poet arrived at KAKE-TV and the *Wichita Eagle and Beacon*. Both had been postmarked on Friday, but the Finleys hadn't been seen mailing anything on Friday.

On Tuesday, Ruth received a copy of the same letter, postmarked on the same day as the others. And on Wednesday, KAKE received another letter from the Poet, postmarked on Tuesday, although the surveillance crew hadn't seen the Finleys mail any letters on Tuesday, either.

Just before noon on Wednesday, Ruth phoned Hill with more bad news. She had received an ice pick in the mail at her office. The ice pick was wrapped in three red bandannas, and it had her initials, "R.S.F.," crudely etched on one side of its handle and the letters "F.A.T."

etched on the other side. Hill sent Zortman to pick it up for processing in the lab.

Clearly, there was a serious hole somewhere. They had been sitting on Ed twenty-four hours a day, so they knew he could not have mailed the letters or the ice pick. Ruth obviously couldn't be watched in her secluded office in the Southwestern Bell building, but they didn't know how she could mail anything from there. Hill cursed with frustration.

At 7:30 that evening, Drowatzky and his wife, Dorann, arrived at the Finleys' house for dinner. After ten minutes of conversation between the two couples in the living room, Ed excused himself to go set the alarm on the back gate and fix drinks. When he returned with the drinks, he smiled at Drowatzky and said, "It sure would be nice if we had a visitor while you're here."

Drowatzky was flooded with mixed emotions. He had been the Finleys' most staunch defender throughout the case, but the discovery of the Poet's letters in their private mail the previous week had converted him. He should be angry, he thought.

Three years ago, the Finleys had come to him with a lie, and he had believed them. Since then, he and Dorann had become close to the Finleys, and he had spent much of his personal time hunting for a man who apparently didn't exist. And yet, he didn't feel angry. He just felt sad. And tonight, he felt deeply uncomfortable. He was in an awkward position—a friend who had come to their house to probe for information that could help put one or both of the Finleys in jail.

Drowatzky's job that evening was to stir the Poet up, whether the culprit was Ruth or Ed. After more small talk, Drowatzky began by mentioning that he didn't think LaMunyon was taking the threats against Ruth seriously anymore.

"Well, it is serious," Ed said.

Ruth jumped in to tell a story about something that had happened at work that day. She said she had left her office and seen a man in the hall struggling to open the door to a stairway. He was bent over and had a piece of paper in his mouth, she said. He wore a white shirt with a yellow tie and had blond hair.

The man asked her if she would hold the door for him so he could get his box through it, Ruth said. Then an elevator rang down the hallway and he said, "Oh, shit," and left. When she looked in the stairway, she didn't see any box.

Drowatzky asked Ruth if she had reported the incident to Hill, and she said nobody had answered when she'd phoned. She would try again in the morning. Drowatzky didn't know what to make of her story, so he decided to move on. He wanted to know if the Finleys had any idea how the Poet had found Ruth in the first place—how he knew that Ruth Smock was now Ruth Finley and was living in Wichita. Ed said it would be easy for anyone to ask around Fort Scott and find out about her.

Then Drowatzky asked what Ruth and Ed thought of the BTK references. Drowatzky, who had headed the BTK hunt and who had shared information about the case with the Finleys, had often puzzled about why the Poet only mentioned one of the strangler's victims, Nancy Jo Fox, in his letters. Ed shared that he thought it was because Fox was his last victim, and he had moved on to Ruth and the chief's wife since then.

The Finleys mentioned that nobody came to visit them anymore because of the Poet. Their attorney came by sometimes, Ed said, but on a recent visit he had felt sure that somebody was tailing him. He had visited them since without noticing anything, however.

Drowatzky tried to keep his expression neutral. He knew that surveillance on the attorney had been ongoing since the first visit.

As Drowatzky and Dorann prepared to leave for the evening, Ed told Drowatzky that he was sure the police would receive more letters from the Poet in the following days.

—⁓—

On Thursday and Friday, the Finleys followed their normal routine. Although detectives were 99 percent certain that Ruth had mailed those letters the previous Thursday, they had no proof she had written them. Maybe Ed was the culprit. There was also the problem LaMunyon had mentioned: nearly six hours had passed between the time the Finleys had mailed the letters and the time the mail had been picked up, allowing for the tiny possibility that somebody else had dropped the letters in the box right after the Finleys.

The police needed more—hard, physical evidence. Not only to be certain that one or both of the Finleys was the Poet, but to get them convicted in court for it.

Saturday started on a typically boring note for the surveillance team. The Finleys didn't move from the house all morning. The noon hour approached, and still nothing.

The officers assigned to watch them would have felt encouraged if they had known what was happening at the Southwestern Bell building downtown just then.

Joe Horvat, Ruth's boss, had gone to the office that morning and noticed the trash was full. Horvat had spent several restless nights in the last week wondering about Ruth. She had been a dependable secretary for two years. He had never questioned her about the case in all that time; he had believed in her and trusted her. But Hill had told him what the police had found in the Finleys' mail the previous week, and Horvat had been plagued with doubts since then. He knew he was frequently away from the office and that Ruth would have plenty of time to write letters. He also remembered he had been out of town the day the butcher knife had been found in the lobby, and on other occasions when the Poet had allegedly called her at work.

Horvat was not the type to meddle in the personal lives of his employees, let alone sift through their trash. But as he eyed the trash can by her desk that morning, he felt compelled to take a look. He found, at the bottom, an interoffice envelope that appeared to contain a book. Curious, he opened the envelope. Inside was a book of poetry by Byron. Flipping through it, he read snatches of poems whose structures reminded him of some of the Poet's work that Ruth had shared with him.

Horvat phoned the police station and spoke to Coonrod, who rushed over immediately. In another can in Ruth's office, the two men found wadded-up paper towels. Inside one of the towels, they found a used yellow Kleenex, and inside that, they discovered a swatch of red bandanna, tied in a knot.

Then they found torn pieces of carbon paper. They unfolded the paper and saw words that were written in the unmistakable style of the Poet.

Horvat and Coonrod turned to Ruth's desk. In the lower right drawer, they found more carbon paper that contained printing in the Poet's style.

Coonrod phoned Hill at home, and the two men whooped with joy. Then they quickly sobered up. They weren't sure if the search of the desk had been legal.

Hill called an assistant district attorney to check. He was asked to describe the layout of the office. Ruth and Horvat had separate offices, Hill said, and there was a storage room off Ruth's office. All the rooms were secured behind a solid wood door that was locked from the inside by a dead bolt. Horvat and Ruth were the only ones who had keys. But the whole area was, in effect, Horvat's office. Horvat even had access to Ruth's desk, where he often went to get pencils and other office supplies.

In that case, the attorney told Hill, the police didn't need a search warrant to go through the desk. All they needed was a signed waiver from Horvat.

Hill brought one with him when he joined Coonrod and Horvat at the phone company, which Horvat quickly signed. A lab investigator soon arrived to collect the evidence.

At 3:45 p.m., Hill held a routine meeting with his surveillance crew at the Hilton Inn. A suite on the top floor of the hotel had been converted into the operation's command center. The suite offered a sweeping view of the Finleys' neighborhood, including a glimpse of their house. Hill did not tell his men about what had happened at the telephone company; that information was too sensitive. He had them review the day's activities and the upcoming schedule.

Meanwhile, down on the street, a few of his men were still waiting for the Finleys to make a move. They had not left the house all day. Lunchtime had come and gone without any action. The afternoon ticked by, and still nothing.

Finally, at ten minutes before 4:00 p.m., the two were on the move. "Here they go," said one of the officers stationed across the creek east of the house.

The black Oldsmobile, with Ed at the wheel and Ruth in the passenger seat, backed out of the driveway and headed for Rock Road. It turned right and drove north past the DEA van stationed in the Eastgate mall parking lot. It continued north on Rock Road to Central, where it pulled into the parking lot of a closed bank. It paused, then turned around and returned south, continuing past the van.

Trailing the Olds in two separate cars, four officers were trying frantically to contact their superiors by radio to let them know what was happening. They knew two cars wasn't enough to tail the Finleys. But the meeting in the Hilton was still underway, and Hill and Coonrod could not be reached by radio.

In the van, Officer Richard Oliverson heard the plight of his colleagues who were tailing the Finleys. He jumped out of the van, ran across the street to the Hilton, and barged in on the meeting, which instantly broke up. The detectives raced for the elevator to join the pursuit.

The Finleys' car continued south on Rock Road, then pulled into a bank a few blocks south of the Hilton. Ed left the car, used the automatic teller in the lobby, and then started driving back up Rock Road toward home. Officers who were racing south from the Hilton spun their steering wheels around as the Finleys drove past them in the opposite direction.

Oliverson had returned to the van when his partner, Detective Roy Rains, climbed in and told him the Finleys were entering the mall through the southwest corner. Oliverson felt a rush of adrenaline.

Rains positioned himself at the camera that had been mounted in the rear of the van. The lens was trained on the mailboxes one hundred feet away. Oliverson picked up the other camera. Within seconds, the two men saw the black Olds circle the mailboxes and pull to a stop.

Rains squinted through the lens and took a deep breath. He watched as Ruth extended her hand, which clutched several white envelopes, out the window. As Ruth reached toward the slot, Rains snapped the shutter.

"I've got it!" he shouted into his radio. "They just made a drop!"

It was 4:15 p.m.

As the Olds drove away from the mailbox, Lieutenant John Garrison and Detective David Andree pulled up in an unmarked car. Garrison popped the hood to fake car trouble and jumped out so that nobody else could use the box. Officers were not taking any chances this time.

Inside the Oldsmobile, Ruth caught a flash of metal in the rearview mirror and turned to look out the back window. She saw a car with its hood up next to the mailbox. Funny, she thought. She had a feeling the car had something to do with her.

One of the unmarked police cars stayed with the Olds as it continued through the mall's parking lot and pulled up to the Dillons supermarket. Ruth and Ed climbed out of the Olds and walked past the Dillons to Hancock Fabrics. Two officers tailed them on foot. Ten minutes later, the Finleys left the fabric shop and walked into the Dillons. After thirty minutes, they emerged with a shopping cart full of groceries. Ed loaded the sacks into the trunk of the Olds, while Ruth turned to look in the direction of the mailboxes again. Then they got in the car and left the mall through the south entrance.

Had they exited through the southwest entrance, the Finleys would have seen several men standing by the mailboxes Ruth had used earlier.

They would have seen one of these men hauling a large white sack out of the box.

Willie Thurman, the postal inspector, opened the sack by the box as Garrison, joined by Hill and Stokes, who had raced over from the Hilton, watched. The Finleys' mail was easy to spot, lying on top of the pile. It included four envelopes. One was a gas credit card payment to the Amoco Oil Company in Des Moines, Iowa; one was a payment to the JC Penney's regional credit office in Shawnee Mission, Kansas; one was a letter to their son, Bruce, in Colorado; and one was addressed to Ruth.

Ruth's letter was from the Poet.

Thurman closed the sack and hauled it to the post office on Harry Street.

The envelopes would be delivered through the postal system, as usual.

—∞—

On Monday morning, Stokes phoned Thurman and asked to begin monitoring the mailbox in the lobby of Southwestern Bell. That afternoon, the police found a letter from the Poet to Cathy Boyer-Shesol, assistant director of the Wichita Rape Center. They also found one addressed to Detective Jan McCloud, who was formerly in charge of sexual assault cases.

The letter to Boyer-Shesol presented a tricky problem: She would have to be informed of the letter, but her husband was a television news reporter, and the last thing the police needed was for the media to discover what they were up to.

Hill called Boyer-Shesol that night. Boyer-Shesol said she understood Hill's predicament and vowed to keep the letter a secret from her husband, who happened to be sitting in the room with her.

Hill picked up the letter on Tuesday afternoon. In it, the Poet offered some twisted opinions on rape.

That morning, Ed Finley had brought Hill the letter to Ruth that Hill's men had seen her mail on Saturday.

As usual, Ed had gone with Hill to the lab to watch the letter being processed for prints. While Ed was at city hall, detectives Doyle Dyer and Kim Brewer were at JC Penney's regional office in Shawnee Mission, Kansas, hunting for the Finleys' payment. At the same time, officers from the Des Moines, Iowa, police department were hunting for the Finleys' payment to Amoco Oil.

These officers needed to find the envelopes because they needed the stamps, which could provide conclusive proof that the Finleys had mailed the Poet's letter. Detective Rains's photograph was a good start—it clearly showed four envelopes in Ruth's hand, the same number of envelopes the police had discovered in the mail sack. But the photograph alone would not be enough physical evidence to prove that the four letters had been mailed by the Finleys.

The stamps could provide that proof if it could be determined that all four had come from the same stamp book. Ruth's letter from the Poet bore a stamp with a picture of a ram's head. Detectives had been told by postal authorities that it came from a book of stamps featuring outdoor animals. When the officers had looked into the sack on Saturday, they had noticed the other three envelopes also bore stamps with pictures of outdoor animals. By analyzing the tears on the serrated edges of each stamp, the lab could prove conclusively that the Poet's stamp had come from the same book as the stamps on the Finleys' personal mail.

But first, they had to find those stamps, which was proving to be difficult. Dyer and Brewer had left Wichita at 3:00 a.m. on Monday for the three-and-a-half-hour drive to Shawnee Mission. By 5:00 p.m., after searching through forty thousand envelopes in the JC Penney regional credit office, they still hadn't found the Finleys' bill. Exhausted and discouraged, the two men drove back to Wichita. Tuesday, they returned to Shawnee Mission, but they still couldn't find the bill. When Dyer and Brewer returned to Wichita Tuesday evening, Hill emphasized the importance of their mission. Two hours later—after just enough time to shower and change clothes—they hit the road back to Shawnee Mission again, arriving at midnight.

Wednesday morning they were still digging through the mail at JC Penney when the Shawnee Mission post office, which had been alerted about the situation, phoned a JC Penney official to report that the Finleys' payment had been sent to a Montgomery Ward's department store by mistake. The store was returning the payment to the post office, where the officers could pick it up that evening.

Dyer and Brewer drove to the post office, got the envelope, and took it to the JC Penney's credit office, where they let a company official open it and remove the Finleys' payment. Then they brought the envelope, with its ram's head stamp, back to Wichita.

That morning, Hill and Stokes had met with assistant district attorney Hank Blaise to update him on the investigation. Blaise started working on a search warrant for the Finleys' house and garbage cans.

The same morning, police in Des Moines phoned to say they had found the Finleys' payment to Amoco. At 1:30 p.m., Hill and Coonrod flew in a private jet to Des Moines to pick up the envelope. They arrived back in Wichita that evening.

LaMunyon and his wife, Sharron, returned that afternoon from New Orleans, where the chief had been attending a policing conference. When they arrived at their house, Sharron found an envelope addressed to her in crude printing. Inside was the following poem:

> *Twinkle twinkle, fat ass star.*
> *Follow the leader to where you are. Sit in the grass not*
> *eating your pie.*
> *Stalk the prey, I am a spy.*

Sharron was confused, then alarmed. Her husband had never informed her of the Poet's threats. This was the first time the Poet had written to her directly. The letter had been mailed on Friday, apparently in the box in the lobby of the telephone company before the monitoring system was in place.

On Wednesday afternoon, Willie Thurman removed another sack of mail from the same box for police to examine. Inside the sack, mixed in with two other pieces of mail bearing the Finleys' return address, were two envelopes addressed by the Poet. One was to Hill, the other to Ruth. Hill's was taken to the police lab, while Ruth's was put back in the sack to be delivered as usual.

Hill's letter turned out to be a copy of the one to Ruth. No doubt the original was in the other envelope.

The letter said, "This succinctly prepared message is to destroy any perceptual expectations you may have been rendered that my hostility will subside. My self-revelation complete, I do intend to kill you."

21

ED'S INTERROGATION

Thursday morning, the phone on Ed's office desk rang. He instantly recognized the voice of Mike Hill.

"You probably got a letter waiting at home," Hill told him. "I got one in here this morning."

Ed knew Hill was probably right. The Poet often mailed Drowatzky or Hill copies of what he sent to Ruth, and both letters usually arrived on the same day.

"Well, I'll be sure to bring it in," Ed said.

"Why don't you go get it today?" Hill asked. "Could you do that?"

He glanced at his watch. It was 10:30 a.m.

"I guess," he told Hill. "Got my lunch hour coming up. I can go get it then. That all right?"

"Okay. I'll just hang loose here," Hill said.

"Right. I'll call you if there isn't one."

Ed hung up, wondering if the request had anything to do with the van he and Ruth had seen in the neighborhood the day they went to Topeka. By now, he and Ruth were experts at spotting police vehicles, Ed thought. Ruth had even wanted to wave to the van, but he had stopped her.

—m—

Mike Hill hung up wondering if he had sounded casual enough. He knew perfectly well Ed would find a letter from the Poet at home. Hill even knew who mailed it, and where it had been mailed. And when Ed brought the letter in that afternoon, Hill was going to sit down and have a long chat with him. Because only a few minutes before Hill had placed the call, the police lab had nailed the case shut.

Fracture analysis, whereby lab investigators are able to match torn pieces of paper, had established that a torn edge of carbon paper found in Ruth's office trash matched a tear at the bottom of the letter to Sharron LaMunyon. It also had established that the stamp on that letter, a puma's head, had been torn from the ram's head stamp that had been found on the Finleys' credit payment to JC Penney.

Shoe leather and science had finally ended the case, Hill reflected. Obviously there was some sort of psychological problem involved that they didn't have the background to recognize, and they hadn't had too much help from the so-called experts. But good old police work had finally done the job.

Hill was giddy from exhilaration, exhaustion, and anticipation. The case was almost over. A warrant to search the Finleys' house would soon be signed by a judge, and that afternoon, Hill would interrogate Ed and Ruth separately.

He would find out once and for all what Ed knew about Ruth, and if he was helping her. Hill, LaMunyon, and a lot of other officers struggled to imagine how a husband who was as close as Ed was to Ruth could not know. He had to be a part of it.

After Hill was through with Ed, he would talk to Ruth. Ruth's boss at the phone company had been told to leave the office in the afternoon to give Ruth a chance to mail another letter in the lobby. If she did, she would be caught in the act by an officer Hill had stationed there. Not that they needed more proof; they had plenty. But it would make it tough for her to deny her guilt. If she didn't mail anything, they would bring her in anyway.

Ed first, then Ruth. And nobody was leaving this building until it was over.

Ruth would go to jail today, be committed, or choose to get help. And Ed would go with her if he was part of it.

If Ruth went to jail, she wouldn't be there long. Talking it over with the district attorney's office earlier that morning, they had realized the most serious crime she could be charged with was falsely reporting a crime, which was a misdemeanor.

Three years to crack a misdemeanor case, Hill thought. It almost made him laugh.

Hill looked at the paperwork on his desk. It included letters, photographs, reams of case jackets that had been cut on the vandalism incidents at the Finleys' house, psychiatric reports, and interview transcripts. Hill hadn't slept well since the surveillance operation had begun two weeks earlier, and the hurried flight to and from Des Moines the previous day had added to his stress. But he had to be alert and sharp today. He had reviewed all the material on his desk quickly and thoroughly, to prepare for Ed and Ruth.

Hill considered himself a strong interrogator. He always felt he could tell if someone was lying or shooting straight with him. His size and his brusque manner were imposing, but he never tried to intimidate people when he interrogated them. Hill preferred the scalpel to the sledgehammer, preferred to probe gently and carefully for details that might trip people up rather than bully them.

But then, he had never interrogated Ruth. Maybe she would need bullying. The question was, Did she know she was the Poet, or was she too sick to understand? Maybe she was suffering from a split personality, where one half of her brain didn't know what the other half was doing. She might very well be shocked and outraged that he was accusing her of being the Poet. She might throw all the physical evidence in his face and deny everything. She might go crazy and become dangerous.

Hill didn't know what to expect.

He prayed she would confess.

All morning, Detective Jack Leon sat at his desk in the CIB office trying to concentrate on the murder investigation he was conducting, but it was difficult. Something was up. He felt it. Doors to offices were opening and closing nonstop, and the top brass was all over the place.

At 11:00 a.m., Hill called Leon into his office. LaMunyon, Coonrod, the district attorney, and an assistant district attorney were in the office with Hill when Leon walked in.

But when LaMunyon and Hill began talking about the Poet case, Leon wondered what he was doing there. He had never worked on the case. He was new to the bureau and hadn't even been involved in the recent surveillance of the Finleys. He had been spending most of his time trying to track down a murder suspect.

As a friend of Mike Jones, the thirty-four-year-old Leon, who sported curly black hair and a black mustache, had heard a lot about the Poet and had listened to his friend's doubts about the Finleys. He had even been to the Finleys' house with Jones once, but that was the extent of his involvement.

But Hill and LaMunyon were laying it all out for him now for some reason. And what the bosses were telling Leon made his head swim: they had found evidence proving that either Ruth or Ed, or both, was the Poet. They were bringing the Finleys in for questioning that afternoon, and they needed one of the detectives in CIB to join Hill in the interrogation.

"You're it," LaMunyon told him.

Leon was stunned. He had never read any of the paperwork on the case, he told the men in the room. He had never studied a single report or transcript. He was a total novice on the case.

Perfect, they told him. He would bring a new dimension to the interrogation: total objectivity.

Besides, the detectives who were most familiar with the case were unavailable. Jones was away on vacation, Dyer was getting the warrants, and Zortman was retiring that day, so he wouldn't be around to do any follow-up investigating that might be required.

Zortman also believed—and the brass agreed—that Ruth and Ed were more likely to confess to an officer they didn't know than to one who had become a friend. Leon smiled and accepted the assignment.

Dr. Donald Schrag entered the room. He would be waiting outside the interrogation room during Ruth's session in case she became distraught and needed psychiatric help. He would evaluate her mental condition after the questioning and help police decide what to do with her.

When Leon returned to his desk, he knew he wouldn't have time to do any extensive research on the case, but he didn't think that would be necessary with Hill leading the questioning. He would watch and listen. He believed he could read people well. He had majored in philosophy and religion in college, and had taken psychology courses for fun. He was an attentive and observant listener.

—m—

Ed left his office at noon and drove home. Thursday was the first day of October, and autumn had already begun working its magic in the neighborhood, despite the muggy temperature. The maples and elms that lined East Indianapolis were fluttering red and yellow in a light breeze.

When Ed opened the mailbox, he found a letter to Ruth from the Poet, just as Hill had predicted. Ed unlocked the door and went inside, then fixed himself coffee and a sandwich. Birds sang in the backyard as he ate. The sky was blue, but dark clouds hovered in the southwest. Ed thought briefly of turning on the gate alarm and video camera but realized the Poet, if he was around, would have noticed that Ed had come home without Ruth.

When he finished his lunch, he smoked a cigarette, then left the house with the letter. He drove to city hall and arrived at the CIB office at 1:30 p.m. A handful of detectives sat quietly at their desks, hunched over papers or talking on the phone as he entered. A few eyes met his and turned away.

Mike Hill rose from one of the desks and met Ed by the bulletin board, where the color drawing of the Poet stared out at the room. Ed handed him the letter, but Hill seemed distracted. He gave Ed only a terse greeting.

Ed had long since given up trying to understand the moody captain. Ed knew Hill had not been happy with him when he had gone over his head to visit LaMunyon last year. Hill had been downright testy at times since then. But Hill had seemed more friendly lately, particularly when Ed had come to him for permission to launch the BTK ad campaign, and their relationship seemed to have stabilized at the level of civility. Today, however, Hill did not appear to be feeling very civil.

Hill handed the Poet letter to a detective, who started for the lab. Ed turned after him, but Hill asked him to wait.

"Let's go in here a minute." Hill nodded toward an interview room near the door, a few feet from where they were standing. "I want to go over some things about the case with you."

Ed walked into a small, drab room with pale yellow walls and thin gold carpeting. The room was dominated by a worn metal table and three wooden chairs. A pair of handcuffs dangled from an iron ring attached to the table. Through a window behind the table, Ed could see the tops of the trees that lined the river and a slice of blue sky patched with gray clouds.

"Just sit over there and I'll be back in a minute," Hill said.

Ed went around the table and sat in a chair beneath the window. He was delighted. The police still cared about the case, he thought. He was anxious to help.

Moments later, Hill came into the room carrying some notebooks and loose papers. Behind him was a younger man whom Ed did not recognize. The younger man closed the door, and he and Hill sat in the two chairs on the other side of the table from Ed.

Hill tossed the letter Ed had just given him onto the table, unopened.

"I know what's in there," Hill said. "I got one just like it."

"Anything new?" Ed asked.

"Nah," said Hill as he spread the notebooks and papers on the table in front of him. "Same old crap."

Ed was impressed by the display of paperwork. It looked like they were really going to get into the case today. He'd probably be late getting back to the office.

Hill introduced Leon and started shuffling through the papers. "Let's see now," he finally said, without looking up, "you were born where?"

The question threw Ed. He wondered why that information was relevant.

"Well, I was adopted in Kansas City as a baby."

"You were adopted?" Hill said, sounding surprised. "That cause you any problems?"

"You mean . . . ?"

"Psychologically. I know that can be tough sometimes."

"Yeah. No, no more than anyone. I don't think it left any permanent scars or anything."

Hill asked about Ed's father, and Ed told him about Elmer and the drugstore. He briefly described the family's move to Bronson and his days in high school.

"Then after you graduated from high school . . ."

"I went in the navy," Ed said. "I was in the navy in the spring, but they didn't call me up until August. Everybody was going off to fight the war."

"I bet they were," Hill said. "I remember my dad going off."

Ed was bewildered. What was Hill doing? Then it hit him. He knew what they were after: him. They had fingered him as the Poet. Ed felt his nerves tingle.

He watched Hill scribble notes on a pad as he answered questions about his navy career, his junior college years, his first meeting with Ruth. His throat was tight, and he had to clear it often as he spoke.

Hill started to dwell on the meeting with Ruth, and Ed was all too happy to correct Hill's impression that he had lived in the boardinghouse at the time Ruth was attacked in 1946, explaining that he hadn't arrived in Fort Scott until the following year.

Hill continued to probe Ed's background with what struck Ed as a studied casualness. Ed answered the questions as calmly as he could, with a growing sense of foreboding.

Hill finally started into the case. He asked about the first phone call Ruth received, about the banner from the Fort Scott newspaper, about the abduction, the first letters, the stabbing, the cutting of the telephone lines. Ed tried to be as forthcoming as he could so they wouldn't think he was trying to hide anything. But he was waiting for the other shoe to drop.

"Phone booth at the telephone office, we get the knife," Hill said, reading from a chronological list of the Poet's activities. He looked at Ed. "You're at work. No way you could have been involved in that."

"I'm afraid not," Ed said, trying a smile.

"Ruth could have put that knife down there," Hill said.

Ed started to open his mouth, but his mind was scrambling.

"Now, I'm looking at it from all the way around," Hill interjected. "I'll give you that."

"Ruth could have put that knife down there."

Ed glanced up at the ceiling. "Not too likely," he said, trying to sound casual. "But I suppose she could have."

Hill continued down the list: the Molotov cocktails, the jar of urine, the wreath burning, the envelope of human feces, the ice picks, the eggs, the firecrackers. "Where were you?" Hill asked each time. "Where was Ruth?"

Ed tried to remember it all. His shirt collar chafed. Why didn't they just get it over with and accuse him?

Hill straightened up from his notes and looked Ed in the eye. "Ed, we started really working on this thing two weeks ago. I know who the Poet is."

Corey Mead

"I hope the hell you do," Ed said.

"But I'm still a little apprehensive about you."

"About me?"

"Would you, to help our investigation, take a polygraph?"

Ed was confused. If they knew who the Poet was, yet were still apprehensive about him, that meant they didn't think it was him. And yet they still wanted him to take a lie detector test. He didn't understand.

But he did feel a sense of relief. "Yes," he said.

"There are some other things I want to talk to you about," said Hill, shuffling through the papers again, "some other things I want to show you."

"I knew it was going to come to this sooner or later," Ed said, shifting in his chair.

"I know who the Poet is. But I got to clear you first. I'm ninety-five percent sure you're not the one, but there's five percent . . . And I'll hit you face up with it."

"That's fair."

Ed waited as Hill continued to look through the papers. He felt as if his nerves were about to snap.

Leon broke the silence. "At any time—when you received a phone call, other than when someone would call and then hang up or not answer—have you ever heard the voice of the Poet?" he asked.

"Not to my knowledge," Ed replied.

"Have you ever been around when letters have been mailed?" Hill said.

"Mailed?"

"Poet letters."

"Have I been around when they've been mailed? Around where?"

"When they were dropped in a mailbox."

Ed's confusion was now total, and he was angry. "No," he said firmly.

Hill locked eyes with Ed and stared at him intensely for a few seconds. Then he decided to take Ed off the hook. He was certain Ed was telling the truth. He had strung out the tension as long as he

216

could, and it was clear Ed wasn't going to crack. Ed seemed genuinely mystified.

"I'm going to show you something that will blow your mind," Hill said. He reached under a stack of papers and pulled out the photograph Detective Rains had taken on Saturday that showed Ruth sticking letters into the drive-up mailbox at the Eastgate mall. Then he slid it across the table to Ed.

"Is that your car?" he asked.

Ed leaned over to examine the photo. "That's our tag number," he said.

"That you driving?"

The photo was sharply focused and in vivid color. Ed could clearly see the car, the driver, and the stores in the background. "Yep. That's Eastgate."

"That's Ruth?" Hill said, pointing at the hand extending from the passenger window to the mailbox, clutching a stack of envelopes.

"It is."

"One of those letters there is a Poet letter," Leon said.

Ed was still trying to absorb all the details of the photo. "Are you positive?" he said.

"Yep," said Leon.

Hill knew the news had not sunk in. "I can verify Ruth has mailed five Poet letters in the last two weeks," Hill told Ed slowly, landing hard on each word.

Ed felt something twist inside his chest. "You've got to be kidding," he said in a small, shrill voice.

"No, I'm not kidding," Hill said. "I wish the hell I was. But I've got to clear you."

Ed felt as if he had just been tossed into a roiling sea. He searched frantically for a life preserver. "Well, what about all this other stuff?" he said, nodding at the papers scattered on the table.

"Ed, you wouldn't believe what we've been doing in the last two weeks," Hill told him. "I've been working down here eighteen goddam hours a day, seven days a week. Ed, I've recovered stuff out of her office in the Poet's handwriting. Out of her desk."

Hill paused. He hadn't been able to keep a trace of excitement out of his voice; it was almost as if he was gloating. He tried to reel his emotions back in and regain his professional detachment.

"You see where I'm coming from?" he said.

Ed continued to stare at the photograph. He felt panic racing around behind his eyes.

"Now, you stop and think," Hill went on. "Every one of these damn things, she could've done."

Then Hill stopped abruptly. He noticed that Ed's face was ashen.

"You want some coffee?" Hill asked.

"I'm gonna have a cigarette," Ed said, almost inaudibly.

Hill left the room and returned to his office, where LaMunyon, Drowatzky, and a few others were waiting behind the closed door. "He's not the one," Hill told them. "He doesn't have anything to do with it."

LaMunyon was not convinced. "He's got to know. He's got to," the chief said.

Hill walked over to a coffee maker on a table by his desk, poured some of the coffee into a Styrofoam cup, blew off the steam, and gingerly took a sip.

"Well, we'll put him on the box," he said, "but he doesn't know anything."

He took another sip and returned to the interview room.

"Here's the problem," Hill said as he took his seat across from Ed again. "We're going to call Ruth in. She's sick. But if she comes in and says, 'Bullshit, Mike. I don't know anything about it' . . ." He shrugged. "That's why we have to clear you."

Then he looked into Ed's eyes, saw the devastation behind them, and softened.

"The lady needs some help," he told Ed quietly. "That's what we're interested in. There's no animosity down here for this three-year caper."

Ed's mind whirled as he tried to reassemble the shattered pieces of his married life. Part of him refused to accept what Hill was telling him. Maybe Hill was lying to him for some reason. Maybe this interview was another ploy to trick the real Poet.

Hill and Leon were discussing Ruth's apparent indifference to the threat against her life and the serenity she had displayed at the hospital the night of the stabbing.

"The nurse said she was 'courageously calm,'" Hill said, reading from a report.

"Not that I know of," Ed said. "I know I wasn't."

Hill showed him the matching tears in the carbon paper found in Ruth's trash and in Sharron LaMunyon's letter. He also showed him the carbon papers from Ruth's office that contained the Poet's familiar printing.

Ed desperately tried to think of something that would clear his wife, but he was left clutching at thin air. "Where did she acquire that vocabulary?" he asked. But it sounded more like a plea.

Hill ignored the question. "We recovered a red bandanna from the trash can and out of her desk. We recovered carbon paper that has been used on Poet letters out of her desk. We recovered one full sheet—and we did it all legally—of carbon paper that had been used. We've known this last week every letter Ruth has sent. The day you went to Topeka, you went to the mail drop in Eastgate and Ruth mailed some letters."

"Yeah, I guess we did," Ed said. "I remember that."

"Five letters were mailed. The helicopter watched you. This last time, she mailed four letters."

Hill showed Ed copies of the four envelopes Ruth mailed on Saturday. He showed the stamps and the results of the fracture comparisons that had been performed in the lab that morning. Ed stared at everything, still trying to process what Hill was saying.

Leon asked, "Is there anything now, in this light, that didn't make sense, or was insignificant before, but that now does make sense, or is significant?"

Ed was numb. Nothing made sense.

"I've hit you with a lot," Hill said softly.

"You certainly have," Ed said.

Hill decided to start searching for a motive. "I'm going to have to ask you a personal question," he said. "Have you ever known her to be unfaithful to you?"

"No," Ed replied.

"Does she know of you ever being unfaithful to her?"

"She can't, because I've never been unfaithful."

"Doctors thought that might have been what set it off."

"I can't say for sure she never has. I can tell you for sure I never have."

"I appreciate that."

"We're not out to hurt Ruth or anything," Hill said. "We have to get this stopped. We have to get her some help."

"I think you're going to have to get me some help, too," Ed said.

Hill waited a moment, then took one last shot. "You're not involved at all? Just don't lie to me, Ed. If you are, tell me."

"Mike, I'm not lying to you," Ed said.

"I just want the truth."

"You got it."

"'Cause, needless to say, you want to get this stopped worse than I do."

Ed looked away. His eyes glazed. "These should have been the best years of our lives," he said.

"They still can be," said Leon. "We want to put an end to this and realize what's going on, what's causing these problems. Then you can go make these the best years of your lives."

"If you agree not to call Ruth, I'll let you call your office," Hill said. "Then we have to get to the KBI. You still willing to take a box to clear yourself?"

"Yes."

—∞—

Hill drove toward the local office of the Kansas Bureau of Investigation, where Ed would take the polygraph test. Ed sat in the passenger seat, quietly groping for ways to defend his wife. He had been overwhelmed by all the information he had been given during the interrogation, but his head had finally begun to clear.

"Maybe," he said, turning to Hill, "she started writing letters just recently in a desperate attempt to get you to do something about the guy who did all that other stuff to her."

Hill watched the road and did not respond.

Ed patted the pocket of his sweat-soaked shirt. "I'm out of cigarettes," he said. "This is no time to quit smoking."

Hill stopped at a convenience store, and Ed climbed out to go buy cigarettes. As he walked up to the door, he saw a row of pay telephones against the wall.

His first instinct was to call Ruth. But what would he tell her? He felt two divergent impulses: he wanted to tell her to run, but he also wanted to ask her if everything he had just found out was true. In spite of all the evidence he had just seen, he still felt that something was missing. Maybe Ruth could explain.

Ed felt Hill watching him. He walked past the phones, entered the store, and bought the cigarettes.

He had one lit by the time he reached the car.

22

RUTH'S INTERROGATION, PART 1

At 5:00 p.m., Ruth replaced the typewriter cover, rose from her desk, slipped her cream jacket over her white, lace-collared blouse, and picked up her white handbag. She unlocked the door to her office, slipped out into the hall, and headed for the elevator. As she walked, she kept looking out for the man with the blond hair she had bumped into by the stairway door a few days earlier.

She was still shaken by the encounter, in which he had tried to get her to help him with a box that did not exist. Ruth often heard rumors floating through the company that the Poet had been seen inside the building, and she wondered if it was finally true. If so, he now knew which floor she worked on, and that was not good news.

She was not certain the man she saw by the stairway was the Poet. He had been bent over at the time, and his face had been concealed from her. She didn't think he had been wearing glasses, but it was hard to tell.

If he was the Poet, then she wouldn't be safe up here anymore.

She would have to take action soon, Ruth thought as she stepped into the elevator. She was angry with herself that yet another day had passed without her making a decision about the bus trip to Oklahoma City. The $120 for the ticket was still tucked away at the bottom of the handbag on her arm.

Why was she making this so difficult? It wouldn't be hard to sneak away from work and walk unnoticed to the bus station. Nobody seemed terribly interested in her anymore, including the Poet, who had been writing lately as if he was saying goodbye to her, a notion she greeted with mixed emotions.

She should have been delighted he was writing about giving up his plans to kill her. Instead, her nausea had increased, and her resolve to kill herself had only become firmer.

She had to die, Ruth thought. It was the only thing to do.

Ruth had a slight headache by the time the elevator reached the lobby. She hoped Ed was waiting for her. She needed to get home and get off her feet. All she needed was to lie down for a few minutes before preparing dinner. Then she would have enough energy to pretend to be happy again. Usually, the worse she felt, the happier she was able to appear to others. And she was feeling so poorly right now that she ought to be a real riot tonight.

"Hi, Ruth."

She glanced up, startled. Lost in thought, she had not noticed Drowatzky standing in the lobby.

"Well, hi," she said, trying to sound warm and enthusiastic. She noticed another officer standing beside him.

"You got time to come to the station with me?" Drowatzky asked. "We have a couple of pictures we want you to take a look at."

"Okay."

Ruth often looked at photos of suspects, although she wondered why she had to go to the police station to do it this time; usually, they brought the photos to her office. Oh, well. She just hoped they had told Ed where she was going so he wouldn't wait forever outside the phone company.

Drowatzky and the other cop walked her to an unmarked car and drove her the few blocks to city hall. Ruth stared out the window as they went. The sun was low, and the sky was filled with gray clouds.

Drowatzky escorted Ruth up to the CIB office. Inside the door, he told her to take a seat outside the interrogation room, then he walked into Hill's office and closed the door behind him.

Seated beneath the sketch of the Poet, Ruth glanced around the room. She wondered about Zortman's retirement party, which was supposed to be taking place that afternoon. None of the men in the room seemed to be in a party mood.

Ruth smiled at a few who looked up at her from their desks. She wondered why none of them smiled back.

Moments later, Hill emerged from his office and greeted her tersely. She noticed his shirt was wrinkled and his tie was loose. She decided the captain had had a rough day. He appeared to be in one of his moods.

He led her into the interrogation room and indicated a chair on the other side of a big metal table. Ruth walked around the table, which she saw was full of papers and notebooks, and sat down. Then a younger man came into the room, closed the door, and sat.

Neither one of these guys is too happy, she thought.

"Well, what you got going?" Ruth asked, trying to sound cheerful.

But Hill, who had just returned from the KBI office, where Ed had passed the polygraph test, was not in a cheerful mood. "There are a lot of questions that people didn't ask when this investigation started," he said, "and I am going to ask them."

"All right."

"I'm going to hit you right up front. I am going to ask you some tough questions. I have already talked to Ed. I had Ed here all afternoon. In fact, Ed is still busy."

"Okay."

"Okay. But to protect yourself and to protect me—this is standard procedure, you know—I am going to have to fill out a rights form."

"Okay."

"You know Detective Leon? This is Jack Leon."

"I met you at your house with Mike Jones one night," Leon said. Ruth dimly recalled him. "Yeah, that's right," she said.

As Hill read Ruth her rights, she thought he was joking. She waited for him to stop reading and give her the punch line. But he kept reading. Soon she felt a small flutter of apprehension. Part of her also felt a sense of relief. It was good to know the police were still taking this thing seriously, after all.

"If you decide to answer questions now without a lawyer," she heard Hill say, "you will still have the right to stop answering at any time. You also have the right to stop answering at any time until you talk to your lawyer. Do you understand that?"

"Uh-huh," she said.

Hill passed the form across the table for Ruth to sign, which she did.

"Okay," Hill said after signing his own name. "Well, why don't we go back to the very beginning? You were born in . . ."

"Richards, Missouri," Ruth said.

Hill asked her about her parents and her early schooling. Ruth was pleased. They were certainly getting into it, she thought. But she suspected she was not going to be looking at any pictures, like Drowatzky had told her.

Hill moved along to the attack in Fort Scott when she was a high school junior.

"You were living at an apartment house?"

"Uh-huh."

"You hadn't met Ed yet?"

"No."

"I know it's hard to relate back to it; that was 1946. Do you remember the day?"

"October 14. My sister's birthday."

"What transpired that evening? You went to school, got out of school . . ."

"I went to school from eight to twelve and worked from three to eleven," she said.

"Where?"

"Telephone company."

"Okay. So you went to school and then you went to the telephone company, and then what happened?"

The day so long ago began to form in her mind again like a thick black cloud, out of which rose the large white boardinghouse entombed by elm trees.

"I went home to eat."

"Go ahead."

Ruth could see herself walk up the three wooden steps, cross the vast expanse of porch, and open the front door. "When I walked in and turned on the light," she said, "the light went off, and this guy said, 'We don't need those lights.' I thought maybe it was my brother or somebody, and I turned around. And he grabbed me by the hair and put me down on the floor."

"How did he put you down on the floor?" Hill asked.

"Just put me down there. And I tried to get away and couldn't," Ruth said. "He started taking my clothes off."

"Did he get all your clothes off?"

"No." But she remembered what he said: "Take your pants off." And she remembered—she would never forget—what she did next: she took them off. On her own.

"What did he get off?" Hill asked.

"He got off my pants," Ruth said, feeling the shame wash over her again.

"You were wearing trousers?"

"I had on a dress."

"Okay. So he got off your underpants. Go ahead."

"And my blouse."

"Okay. What happened next?"

She saw the man tie her hands behind her back and make her lie on top of them. She saw him kneel on her chest and she remembered the crushing pain in her bound hands. He removed a handkerchief and stuffed it in her mouth. The handkerchief had been used. She could taste it again. The memory of that taste almost overwhelmed her.

"He tried to rape me," Ruth said.

"Did he disrobe?"

"No, he had on bib overalls."

"Okay. Go ahead."

"I was fighting him . . ." but he was still kneeling on her and the crushing pain almost immobilized her. She could only squirm helplessly beneath his weight. Then she saw him pull out his penis, already firm, and she began to squirm harder. Suddenly, one of her hands popped free beneath her and she reached for her mouth to yank out the handkerchief, but she scraped him across his stubbly beard and face, and a thumb accidentally went into his eye, making him yelp with pain and lose his erection. He became furious. "You think your ass is so cute, huh?" he sneered. "You think it's too cute for me? Well, you'll get me wound up again because I'll make you move your cute little ass around."

"And it made him mad, and he had some kind of, I don't know what it was, a sharp knife." She could feel the flick of the blade as he slapped it against the back of her legs again. "And he cut me on my legs and on my breasts."

"Where did he cut you on your legs?"

"Just on the backs."

"Low, high?"

"Low."

"Okay. He cut you on your breasts?"

"Uh-huh."

"Very bad scratches? Just superficial, or what?"

"No, they weren't bad at all. Well, they left marks for several years. They are not there now."

"Okay. So . . ."

"Then he said he'd fix me up . . ." Ruth could see herself lying on the kitchen floor, where she had wriggled from the living room during the struggle. Her head was jammed against some cabinet doors under the stove. She could see the man, who was still on top of her, look up, spot the flatiron on one of the burners, and reach for it. But his reach was too short, so he placed a knee on her pubic bone and brought his full weight down on it as he reached higher. She could still feel the sharp pain that shot through her body.

"He turned on the gas and put the iron on and said, 'Now I'll warm your ass and fix your face. If you won't let me fuck you, nobody else will want to.' And he said he was going to cook my face, but he didn't." Ruth remembered the iron glowing red from the heat, and she saw the man bring it down and start moving it up the inside of her left thigh, the heat so intense she couldn't stand it. She twisted violently, felt the iron touch her, and passed out.

"What happened after he burned you?"

"I don't remember."

"Okay," said Hill. "Were you raped that night?"

"No. They never could really tell. There wasn't any semen."

"Did the man remove his penis?"

"Yeah, he had it out."

"How old was this dude?"

"Well, when you are sixteen, you know, people seem older. Uh, thirty-ish, forty-ish, I would imagine. He was just, like, a bum. You know. They had bums then that hopped trains."

"Was there a railroad track close?"

"Yeah."

"Did they ever find anybody?"

"The man next door said there had been a strange person sitting on the porch that weekend. I was off that weekend. He started to go and ask him what he was doing there."

"How long did you live in that home after this assault took place?"

"Not very long."

"After this traumatic thing, how did you feel?" Hill asked.

"Well, I did not handle it very well. I got sick."

"What do you mean, 'got sick?'"

"I would throw up."

"Uh-huh."

"Then my mother came over and stayed with me."

"Mentally, how did it affect you?"

"I don't know."

"Do you still have problems with it?"

"No, I hadn't even thought about it until this brought it up again."

Hill asked about her marriage to Ed, about their move to Wichita, about their two sons, about their work history. Then he asked about the first phone call from the man who demanded money to keep quiet about the 1946 attack, and about the subsequent phone calls.

"Did he ever talk to Ed, or just you?" Hill said.

"Just me," Ruth replied. "He would hang up if Ed answered."

The Fort Scott newspaper banner she had received in her office mail was next.

"It was yellow," Ruth said. "Didn't have a date on it. I stuck it in my desk and took it home and it laid around there, and I finally just tossed it. Probably shouldn't have." She smiled.

"Excuse me," said Leon. "Was that addressed to you?"

"Yes."

"Do you recall reading anything about that incident in your paper?"

"Yeah."

"Did they mention the brand?"

"Oh, yeah. In fact, they put my picture and put 'branded' under it. It was so insensitive, my dad, he was a pretty big man, went to the newspaper and told them to cool it."

Hill and Leon moved on to the confrontations Ruth had had with the man in downtown Wichita and then to the kidnapping incident. They pressed her for details of the kidnapping, going back and forth in her story to establish times and sequences of events. Ruth wondered why they were dwelling on old news. She tried to be patient and helpful, but she was restless and irritated. The tiny room had become oppressively warm, and the wood chair she sat upon was uncomfortable. She felt hemmed in, claustrophobic.

She wondered where Ed was.

Hill wanted to know why she didn't try to escape from the kidnappers' car when it was parked in the bustling Twin Lakes shopping mall. "Didn't people see you?" he asked.

"I am sure they did," Ruth said.

"You didn't try to get away?"

"No."

"Why?"

"Well, how would I get out of that car?"

"Scream, holler."

"I didn't," she said. She could never have done that, she thought.

"Did you ever see a police car?"

"Yeah, one time."

She told of seeing a squad car when the kidnappers stopped at the Twin Lakes mall.

"We had to wait for it to turn. He got very mad and reached down into his boot, and he got this knife and popped it and said, 'You keep your goddam mouth shut. No stupid whore or police lieutenant is going to put me back in jail.'"

"How would he know about the police lieutenant?" Hill asked.

"I don't know."

"Strange."

"I thought so. Then, after we turned—"

"He hadn't been through your purse yet."

"No."

Hill made a note, pleased with himself. He had revealed a major inconsistency: Ruth had always maintained that the Poet learned about Drowatzky when he saw the lieutenant's business card in her purse during the kidnapping. He and Leon were taking her through all these events again to expose such inconsistencies and gather more ammunition against her in case she denied her involvement.

Hill continued to probe the incident. He had her describe how the Poet had hit her in the face with the chunk of concrete, how he had taken her paycheck and other items from her purse, and, finally, how she had escaped in the park while the Poet was relieving himself on the riverbank.

"Did they ever find your property?" Hill asked.

"Zortman got it."

"What did he find?"

"My sweater and my shoes."

Hill stopped and turned to Leon to ask if he had any other questions on the topic.

Leon nodded. He had a lot. Ruth's train had derailed several times, as far as he was concerned. Leon and his kids had often played in the park where she escaped, and he knew it well. He knew the only bushes in the area were on the steep embankment that fell away from the park's grassy playground. It would be difficult to negotiate the embankment even with shoes on, let alone run along it, through heavy bushes, with bare feet. He also knew a short chain-link fence separated the playground from the precipitous embankment. To reach the embankment, Ruth and the Poet would have had to pass through a gate in the fence that was located near the public restrooms. She had not mentioned the gate.

Leon sketched the layout of the park on a yellow legal pad and flipped it around to show her. "Okay. Now, there is a playground," he said, tapping the sketch with his pencil, "and there is a fence that separates the grassy area of the park with bushes that lead down to the river. Do you recall going around that fence?"

"I was around trees," Ruth replied.

"Well, did he lead you into the bushes, then?"

"He just led me down in the grass."

"Was it very steep?"

"Um, not too steep."

"Did you get all the way to the river?"

"Huh-uh. We didn't get very far."

"When you ran into the bushes, did you run farther into the bushes, or back into the park?"

"Park," said Ruth, feeling confused. "No, uh . . . I didn't run into any park, I don't think."

Leon tapped the sketch again. "Right there on Twenty-First Street is a park. There is a street here, there is a bunch of bushes there, and there are the restrooms. The playground is here. But dividing that is a fence. Did he lead you to that gate, into the bushes?"

"I don't remember going through a gate."

"Do you recall being in the bushes where they couldn't see you from the street? Or could you always see Twenty-First Street, no matter where you were?" Leon knew that would have been impossible; the street was too far back from the park to be seen by anyone who was down on the riverbank.

"I could see cars."

"When you ran into those bushes, did you ever lose sight of the cars?"

"I don't think so."

"Okay. Did you run farther into the bushes? If you ran back this way," Leon said, pointing at the playground, "you would've been out there on open grass."

"I just ran along Twenty-First Street in the trees."

"Well . . ."

"The park was on the other side of where he let me out."

"What's important to me is that there are real heavy bushes—"

"I was not in real heavy bushes," Ruth said, irritated.

Which meant she would have had to have run back into the park, a fact that contradicted her previous accounts, a fact she already had denied once during the interview. Leon knew she was totally lost, and he pressed his advantage.

"Okay. The problem I have is, as you ran away from him, as you maced him and he lost sight of you, there is only grass there, and there wouldn't have been any way for him to lose sight of you, unless you just plain outran him."

"There were lots of trees," Ruth countered.

"There are trees, but they are farther south. You would have had to run out of the park and into another park on Twenty-First Street."

"I ran just a . . . I swore I just walked . . ."

"This is three years ago," Leon said, softening. "That's okay."

"I ordinarily—"

"Do you recall," Leon interrupted, "whether or not Detective Zortman mentioned to you that the sweater and shoes were found together?"

"He said he went out and found them out there."

"Did he tell you where he found them?"

"No."

"Well then, when you hid in the bushes, did you fall down at any time, or stumble? It apparently was dark, and it was cold, and you were barefoot . . ."

She did not respond.

"Do you recall falling?"

"No."

Ruth wanted to go home.

—◊—

Ed sat in the orange rocking chair by the grandfather clock, watching glumly as police officers, executing the search warrant on the house, came and went through his living room carrying plastic evidence bags filled with pencils, carbon paper, writing tablets, and other items they had found in the bedroom and in Ruth's corner of the basement.

They did not speak to Ed, nor he to them, although he knew most of them. The officers walked past with grim faces and set the bags by the front door, where they would be collected and taken to the lab for processing.

One of the officers stopped and held a writing tablet in front of him. "You ever seen this before?"

Ed shook his head. "No," he said. "But it could be one of the boys'."

Stay with Ruth as long as you can, he told himself.

23

RUTH'S INTERROGATION, PART 2

"Okay," Hill said. "The next really big thing was Towne East. You guys were going to go somewhere."

"Go on vacation to Colorado," Ruth said.

"Okay. You got home that night from work, you and Ed. Tell me what happened then."

Ruth told of buying the jeans at Dillard's department store and returning to the car.

"Then what happened?" Hill said.

"I heard this guy say, 'Hey, Ruth.' I turned around and I thought, 'Oh, no.' I trucked right on out to the car to unlock it and I had the wrong key in my hand. You don't unlock the door with the ignition key." She tried another smile.

"Had you already put your jeans in the car, or did you still have them?" Hill asked.

"They were in the car."

"Okay. You were trying to unlock the door . . ."

"When I got the ignition key, I had to get it back out. By that time, he was there. He said he didn't know I was going to make it that easy for him."

Ruth could still feel the man's gloved hands around her arms.

"He was trying to get in," she said. "He wanted in the back seat. I should have let him in."

"Why?" said Hill.

"I could have slammed the door on him."

"Uh-huh."

"He was telling me all the time where we were going."

"Where?"

"He said, 'You drive. We are going out on 54 to the Augusta Airport Road.' Then he said, 'You will go to the bridge where it says "Stay out."' He was telling me all this while we were trying to get in the car."

"Then what happened?"

"I was trying to get the door shut."

"Are you in the car then?"

"No. I had one foot in, and I was trying to get the door shut. He was trying to get in the back seat. All you got to do is push the seat, but he was wanting to release the thing. And he put his sack in there. By this time, I thought he was pouring something down my back, and he pushed my head down, and it hit the window while I was trying to get in. I finally got in and got the door shut. I still didn't know I had this knife in my side. I got the car started, and he started to get in, and he got his hand in there some way, and I started off. I couldn't turn the car, and I reached down, and I felt that. But I didn't know then that I had it."

"What did you feel?"

"The knife."

"You didn't know if you were hurt, though?"

"Well, yeah, I knew something was wrong. I couldn't turn the steering wheel."

"How many times were you cut?"

"Once in the back, and three or four times—"

"Stand up," Hill said, cutting Ruth off.

Ruth pushed her chair back from the table and rose.

"Where?" said Hill. "Turn around."

Ruth turned around and pulled up her jacket and blouse to expose the pink streaks that remained from the knife wounds on the lower left side of her back.

"You had one in the upper middle back?" Hill said.

"There was a little one up there."

"And then you had three on the side and some scratches on your arms?"

"Pretty good-sized cut," she said, indicating the wound where a knife had nearly penetrated her kidney.

"How did you handle that? Are you having any problems over that mentally?"

"I don't think so," Ruth said.

"How about the abduction?"

"No. I think if he would just leave me alone, I would be just fine."

Leon spoke up. "I have another way of asking the same questions," he said. "Have you ever had any nightmares about any of that?"

"I have had bad dreams," Ruth said.

"Have you had any bad dreams about the abduction?" he asked.

"No."

"How about the stabbing?"

"Yeah."

"Have you had any bad dreams about phone calls or about letters?"

"No."

"How about when Ed got sick? Have you ever had bad dreams about that?"

"No."

Ruth was uncomfortable with this line of questioning. Why did they care about her dreams?

After a few more questions about her actions following the stabbing, a silence fell over the room. Hill and Leon shuffled through their papers to see what they wanted to talk about next. Hill checked his watch. They had been at it for nearly two hours. He decided it was time.

"Ruth," he began, still moving papers around, "there are some things that have really been bothering me." He looked up at her. "There are several things that have happened out at your house and other places in the city, and I need to know where you were at, what you were doing, where Ed was at, what he was doing. Because, Ruth, either you or Ed could have done every one of these things."

Hill tried to keep his voice even as he spoke, hoping to see a flash of concern in her eyes that would tell him she knew it was over.

Instead, she smiled and gave a quick laugh. "Well, we always said, 'You know, they probably suspect us.'"

"Okay," Hill said. "I was going to have Zortman out at your house on Christmas Eve, '79, because we thought, by the letters, the Poet might try to make a visit. The only people that knew was myself, Zortman, you, Ed, and the family—that knew I was going to have him there at eleven o'clock at night. Ten o'clock, the phone lines were cut. Very strange. Where was everybody?"

"We had Christmas Eve in the dining room," Ruth said.

"Did Ed ever leave your sight?"

"Well, I don't remember. He wasn't in my sight."

"Did you ever go out in the backyard?"

"On Christmas Eve?"

"Uh-huh."

"No, I don't think so."

"You don't remember?"

"I don't think I did. The only thing to go out there for was to take the trash."

Hill moved on, checking his notes. "The phone line gets cut a second time. Who found that, you or Ed?"

"I think I noticed it," Ruth said.

"After the phone line gets cut," Hill continued, "we put an alarm on. The line has never been touched since. We put a camera out there in the back, okay? We lived out there with you for three months, day and night, twenty-four hours a day, even when you guys were at work."

Hill paused to let that sink in. "On the twenty-fifth of January 1980, you get a call at the phone office saying there is something in the phone booth," he said, referring to the butcher knife. "Did you, or did you not?"

"Yeah."

"What was said?"

"He told me to come and get the present."

"Did you put that knife down there?"

"Did I put that knife down there?"

"Uh-huh."

"I am sure I didn't," Ruth said.

"You didn't put that knife down there?"

"No." Ruth did not like Hill's tone.

Hill looked at his notes. "The lock missing from the gate on May 20, 1980. You could have taken that lock, Ed could have taken that lock, or the Poet could have taken that lock, or a neighborhood kid. Do you know where that lock is now?"

"No."

"Don't lie to me at all," Hill said, putting a harsher edge on his voice.

"Well, Mike," Ruth replied with an edge of her own, "I am not lying."

"Okay. Who found the lock missing?"

"I think Ed found it. I don't know."

Hill checked his notes again.

"Urine on the front porch," he said. "Who found that?"

"I did."

"Okay. How was it out there?"

"In a bottle against the door."

"It was just in a bottle against the door? When we got there, it was all over the porch."

"Well, I knocked it over when I went outside."

"Did you put that there?"

"No, Mike," Ruth said, exasperated. "No."

"I told you I'm going to ask some tough questions."

"No, sir, I didn't."

"Did you put that bottle out there?"

"No."

"Did Ed put that bottle there?"

"Well, I don't think so."

"Could he," said Leon, "have put that bottle there and you not know about it?"

"I suppose he could have," Ruth said. "He would have had to go outside to do it."

"Who was the last one to be out on the porch the night before, when you were locking up?" Hill asked.

"Ed was. He always goes out and looks around."

Hill consulted his notes again.

"The beer and the gasoline—November 10, 1980—on the back porch," he said. "Who found that?"

Ruth tried to remember. "I don't know. He found it when he checked . . . I don't know."

"'Set fire to the wreath,'" Hill said, reading from his notes again. "Tell me about that."

"Well, we were in the basement and heard the window break."

"Had Ed been out? Had he been up to the john, or had you been up to the john right before that happened?"

"No. We were watching the *Monte Carlo Show*. I don't think either one of us had been up."

"Who found the ice pick on the front porch, April 1?"

"I think Ed found it."

"Did you put that out there?"

"No."

"Eggs on the sliding glass door," Hill said, gaining momentum. "Who found that?"

"Me."

"Did you do that?"

"No, sir."

"Human deposit on the front porch. Who found that?"

"I did."

"Did you do that?"

"God, no."

Hill nodded to a stack of Poet letters.

"Have you ever written any of those letters?" he asked.

"No, sir."

"Have you ever mailed any of those letters?"

"No, sir."

He landed hard. "What if I called you a liar because I have evidence that shows you have?"

Ruth was stunned and did not speak.

Hill watched her and waited. "It's time to come straight," he said finally. "I have got pictures."

"Mike!" she said.

"Do you want to keep playing your game? You got a problem, lady."

Ruth felt stung, as if she had just been slapped.

"When did I mail a letter?" she said. She was sitting perfectly erect now, her eyes wide and indignant.

Hill reached beneath a pile of papers and pulled the color photograph that showed her mailing the letters in the Eastgate mall on Saturday. He shoved it in front of her.

"When you put them in the mailbox right there," he said, tapping the photo with his finger, unable to conceal his sense of triumph.

Ruth looked down and stared at the picture. Something began to happen in her head. She felt as if a wall of blocks was tumbling out of it, allowing a first glimmer of daylight to penetrate.

"Last Saturday, when you sent the gas bill," she heard Hill saying, "when you sent the department store bill, when you sent the personal letter, you also sent a letter to yourself. You want me to show you?"

Ruth felt ill and filled with shame. She buried her head in her arms on the table. Tears sprang from a deep reservoir of pain inside her and flooded her eyes. Her shoulders began to heave from sobbing. But she made no sound.

Hill did not let up. "Do you want to tell me about it?" he said. "Do you deny it?"

She continued to cry, her head still down, her tears starting to run out over her wrists in tiny rivulets.

Hill softened at the sight of her pain. "Ruthie, look at me," he said, reaching across the table to put his hands on her arms. "Look at me. Ruth, look at me . . . Now, look at me."

Ruth kept her head down.

"I am not mad at you, Ruth," Hill said. "I don't know why you are doing this, but we got to find out why."

She continued to sob silently into her coat sleeves.

Hill straightened and returned to his notes. He resolved to be firm with her.

"I found a bandanna in your trash. I found carbon paper in your trash. I found torn-up paper in your trash that I matched to the Poet." Then Hill looked at Ruth and felt moved, in spite of himself.

"Ruth," he said softly. "Why?"

In a faint, choked whisper, she said, "I don't know."

"Do you need some help?" Hill said.

"Yes."

It was the answer he was hoping for.

"I need two more questions answered," he said. "Look at me. Why did you make up the story about the abduction?"

"I don't know," Ruth said in a barely audible voice.

"Sweetheart, why did you do that?" he said.

"I don't know."

"Why did you stab yourself?"

"I don't know."

"You did stab yourself."

Ruth nodded her head in her arms. But the attack still seemed real to her. She could still feel the man's hands on her, still hear him talking in her ear as she struggled in his grasp. The whole thing seemed so vivid. Surely it must have happened, she thought. But part of her knew it had not.

Hill leaned over. "Why?" he asked softly.

"I don't know."

"The deal in Fort Scott. Why did you make that up?"

Ruth stirred and shook her head in her arms. "I didn't make that up," she said, her voice thick with emotion. That was real, for certain, she thought. Nothing could shake her from feeling that way.

"Okay," Hill said. "You didn't make that up."

"No, sir. I did not."

"Okay. Of all this that I talked to you about, what haven't you done?"

"I didn't set fire to the wreath. I did not do that."

"The paper that was wrapped around the wreath came out of your trash can," Hill said.

"I didn't set fire to the wreath."

Hill let it go.

"Did you do everything else?" he asked.

Ruth nodded, her head still buried in her arms.

"Ruth, I am not mad at you," Hill said, reaching over to her again. "I just want an explanation. Can you give me one?"

It came out like a plaintive wail: "I don't have one," Ruth said, and her shoulders shook more violently.

Hill left to get her some coffee. When he returned, Ruth's head was still on the table.

Leon had not spoken to her.

"Ruth," Hill said, taking his seat again, "something else is very important." He told her about Ed's interrogation. "Did he have any knowledge of this at all?" Hill asked.

"Absolutely not," Ruth said.

"How did you keep it from him? Did you write most of those letters at work?"

Ruth did not respond.

"Where did you write them? At home? Is that what you're saying?"

"Both places," she said.

"Pardon me?"

"Both places."

"Both places. Did you use surgical gloves? How did you keep fingerprints off of them?"

"Just wiped them off."

"With what?"

"A handkerchief."

Hill told Ruth about the intense two-week surveillance she and Ed had been under, and about the search for evidence that was still underway at her house. Ruth told Hill and Leon where she had stored notebooks, bandannas, and other items. Then the two officers tried again to probe Ruth for a motive. Ruth still had not lifted her head from the table.

"I am going to ask you a real personal question," Hill said. "This all started when Ed was in the hospital. Is this what triggered it? Were you and Ed having problems? Do you need that much attention?"

"There is not a nicer person anywhere than he is," Ruth said.

"Okay."

"We never had any problems."

"Do you think he has ever been unfaithful to you?"

"No, sir."

"Have you ever been unfaithful to him?"

"No."

"He doesn't know anything about it?"

"No."

Leon interrupted. "Ruth, did you ever get a phone call from a man who was trying to blackmail you?"

Ruth thought back to that June night three years earlier. She remembered the phone ringing as she climbed up the stairs to the kitchen. She remembered looking at herself in the glass doors that opened onto the patio as she stood by the phone. She remembered the darkness outside and the sense of loneliness and fear she felt as she reached for the receiver.

She did not remember who was on the other end.

"No," she said.

"And when you came up with the banner of the Fort Scott paper," Leon said, "did someone really send it to you, or did you just happen to have it?"

"I had it."

Ruth admitted cutting the phone lines on Christmas Eve in 1979, and cutting the dummy lines that had been installed in their place, but she did not know why she had cut them. She also admitted to putting the butcher knife in the phone booth of the Southwestern Bell lobby.

She could remember doing all that, but it hadn't seemed real at the time.

"The urine on the front porch," Hill said. "Did you pour it out there that morning and then tell Ed? Is that what happened?"

Ruth did not respond. "Ruth, there are no hard feelings between you and me," Hill said, trying to soothe her.

"There should be," she said.

"There aren't. I have no animosity toward you. I want to get everything straightened out; you want to get everything straightened out. Do you not?"

She nodded.

"Okay. Let's get it straight. The urine on the front porch," he tried again. "How did that happen?"

"I just put it out there."

"Was it poured in a bottle, or did you just put it out there?"

"It was poured in a bottle."

"That was your own urine, is that right?"

"Yes."

"The Molotov cocktail—or the gasoline, or the turpentine, whatever it was. How did you do that?"

245

"I took it out of the car," she said.

"How did you get it out of the car?"

"With a hose."

"You siphoned it out of the car. Talk to me about this wreath thing."

"I didn't set the wreath on fire."

Hill moved on. "The ice pick on the front porch. Tell me about it, please."

"I just put it there."

Hill was still talking to the top of Ruth's head. "Ruthie, I'm not mad at you, okay?"

There was no response.

"You put the eggs on the sliding glass door. When did you do that? Before you went to bed, or after Ed went to bed, or what?"

"Before I went to bed."

"Did you just go out and smear them on, or did you actually throw them on?"

"I just put them out there."

"Where was Ed at?"

"In the shower."

"Firecrackers in the mailbox."

"I didn't do that."

"Okay. That was probably pranksters. Human shit on the front porch. Was it yours?"

"That was mine."

Ruth felt completely humiliated.

Hill reviewed his notes.

"Ruth, we got those letters postmarked from Oklahoma. Do you remember that? How did those letters get an Oklahoma City postmark?"

"I just mailed it down there."

"Is that when you guys went . . ."

"God, I wish I was dead," Ruth moaned.

"No, you don't. No, you don't. That's when you guys were going to Colorado? You drove through Oklahoma?"

"No."

"Well, how did those letters get to Oklahoma?"

"I just sent them to the post office and asked them to mail them."

Hill was stunned. It was so simple. "Oh," he said.

"Oh, God," Ruth moaned.

Hill moved on. "You say the deal in Fort Scott was actually true. You swear to me that was actually true. But there is something you didn't bring up. The first time you talked to us you said he put something over your nose. You didn't say anything about it this time."

"Well, he did."

"Okay, he did."

Next, Hill asked her if she had ever bumped into a man on the street in downtown Wichita, and she insisted she had.

"Somebody just tried to make a pass at you?"

"I guess."

"Can you tell us what brought this thing in Fort Scott back? Do you like publicity? Is that what you wanted?"

"No."

"Why did you do it?"

Ruth had no idea. She shook her head.

"Are you glad it's over?" Hill asked.

"Yes," she said.

"The kidnapping. What did you do for all those hours? How did you get up there?"

"On the bus," she said. But she still could hear the car squeal to a stop behind her, feel the man grab her and kick her and shove her into the back seat. She could still see the junk in the back seat and remember the dizzying ride through the city streets. It all seemed so real.

Ruth could not lift her head. She kept it buried in her arms, as if she was hiding from the two officers. She felt a deep sense of shame. Her limbs felt mechanical, numb. She felt dead. If only she was.

"Where did you spend all the time?"

"Twin Lakes."

"How did you hurt your leg? You had a bruise on your leg."

"I don't know. I must have hit something."

"Were you ever at the park we were talking about?" Leon said.

"Yes."

"That is where the sweater and shoes were found. Did you ever go back into those bushes?"

"No."

"You rode the bus to Twin Lakes," Hill said, "then you planted that stuff, then called us. Is that right?"

"Called Ed," Ruth said.

"The deal where you cut yourself—where did you get the knife?" Hill said.

"I don't remember."

"Where did you get the wine bottle?"

"I don't know."

"Where did you get the glove?"

"Had it at home."

"Ruth," said Leon, "I realize there are a lot of things you don't want to talk about, but I think we could solve some of this if we could just get down to how you feel."

"I wish I was dead," she said.

"No, Ruth," said Hill. "Right now it seems like the world has come to an end, but it has not, Ruth. It hasn't."

"When you were doing these things," said Leon, "do you recall seeing yourself doing them?"

Ruth did not respond.

"Do you recall what was going through your mind when you were writing a letter?" Hill asked. "Were you angry? Were you sad?"

"I don't know."

"You don't know. There are a lot of questions you can't answer, is that what you're saying?"

She nodded.

"After you had mailed a letter, did you feel better?" Hill asked.

"I wished I hadn't done it," she said.

"Why, or what, made you start saying you were getting phone calls?"

"I don't know."

"Were you afraid of losing Ed?"

"No."

"Did you think Ed was going to die?"

"No."

"Ruthie, have you told me everything, or are you still holding back?"

"I don't think I'm holding anything back."

"Do you think you *need* to see a doctor now?"

"I am sure I do."

"Do you think you need to see one tonight? I'll be quite frank with you. I have been concerned you might hurt yourself."

"I must be crazy," she moaned.

"No, you are not crazy," Hill said. "There is help."

"I can never face Ed again."

"Yeah, you can."

"He is the nicest person I have known."

"You are just ill, Ruth," Hill said. "You only have a disease, just like any other disease in the body. Okay? There is treatment for it."

"I can never face Ed again."

"You haven't done anything except be ill."

"Yes, I have. I'm a bad criminal."

"No," said Hill. "It is not the same. I guarantee you it is not the same."

Hill decided it was time to bring in Schrag.

—m—

When Schrag entered the room, Ruth's head was still down.

"Hi, gal," he said, trying to sound chipper. "Would you look at me? Huh?"

Ruth didn't move.

"Do you know who I am?" he asked.

No response.

"Well, look."

Finally, Ruth lifted her head.

"Now do you know?"

Ruth recognized the man who had hypnotized her, the man she had gone to for help once, only to find herself unable to open up to him.

Schrag smiled. "Don't hide your face. It's okay," he said. "How do you feel now?"

"Bad," she said.

"Don't feel badly," he said, settling in the chair Hill had vacated. "What would you like to do now?"

"Go home and just die," Ruth said, and she buried her head in her arms again.

Schrag doubted he would get much out of her in this condition. But his primary fear had been alleviated when Hill had told him outside the room that Ruth had confessed to being the Poet. It meant she was not a dual personality, where two or more separate and distinct emotional systems and thought processes coexist in one person, each unaware of what is happening in the other. Had she been a multiple personality, the part of her that was Ruth most probably would not have known what the other part of her was doing as the Poet. But she had known, and so she seemed to be a unified personality.

Nor did Schrag believe that Ruth had consciously perpetrated a hoax. Schrag believed she had an illness that fell under a broad category known as dissociative reactions, which are characterized by fugue states and partial amnesia. Typically, they occur in egocentric, immature, highly suggestible people who are faced with some conflict they can't escape. Some avoid their conflicts by getting sick. But those suffering from dissociative states avoid their conflicts by forgetting them. They want to run away from them, but they see that solution as cowardly, and eventually the conflict becomes so unbearable that they repress it in their subconscious.

Often they repress large segments of their personality, as well, while allowing the more congenial side of themselves to carry on. That's why Ruth seldom showed any rage or fear during her ordeal and always appeared nice and jovial, Schrag thought. She was denying her own feelings in order to behave as others expected her to. That was also why she functioned normally at work and at home while the Poet was assaulting her from within.

Ruth, Schrag felt, was suffering from an uncontrollable impulse disorder that arose out of some unresolved conflict in her past. She had repressed something hideous that had happened to her, and it had been bubbling for years in a poisonous pool of guilt and rage in her subconscious mind. The Poet's letters, he thought, as well as the acts of vandalism at her house, were expressions of that guilt and rage. Part of her mind knew what she was doing, but the greater part blocked it out.

And she could not stop. At least, not on her own. It had been a compulsion. Every time Ruth had written a letter or committed some other act as the Poet, her underlying feelings of guilt and rage had been temporarily alleviated, but because she hadn't understood and dealt with those feelings, she had been compelled to write again or commit some other act. It was a vicious cycle that could only be broken when she was caught.

"Did you ever have any understanding as to why any of this was happening?" he asked Ruth.

She didn't respond.

"Can you describe to me how you felt when these things were happening? What did you feel like inside?"

She still didn't respond.

"Describe anything that comes to your mind."

Nothing.

"If I were to give you a piece of paper now and say you are the Poet, would you write a letter as if you were the Poet? Could you do that now?"

Ruth shook her head.

Schrag realized she would not be able to write a letter as the Poet on command, because she wasn't experiencing the necessary emotions. Ruth might not even remember writing the letters at all, even though she knew she had. People suffering from her type of disorder keep the forgotten information stored in the subconscious. For the same reason, Ruth also was probably still able to remember the stabbing and kidnapping incidents in vivid detail, just as she described them to the police, even though she realized both were figments of her imagination.

"Did you ever, years back, or in the last two or three years, wonder that maybe something was wrong?"

"Yes," Ruth said.

"It was kind of like you were doing something that you really couldn't control, like you had to do it, right?"

"It seemed like I had to do it," she said.

"And after you did it, how did you feel?"

"Relief."

"It kind of got rid of a lot of feelings inside you."

"I tried to figure it out one time," Ruth said. "When that thing happened in Fort Scott."

"Uh-huh."

"One of the policemen was so bad." Then she felt a pang in her heart. "And these here were so nice."

Schrag pressed for details about the Fort Scott attack, but Ruth found it too painful to discuss again. She only wanted to tell him that the police who had questioned her that night hadn't believed her story, and that one of the cops had rudely stuck his boot out to lift her leg so he could see the wounds from the iron on her thighs.

Schrag knew the story, knew that the police in Fort Scott hadn't thought the attack had happened, at least not the way Ruth had described it. But he also knew that what happened during the attack was less important than Ruth's reaction to it. To her, the attack was real in all its sordid details, and she had felt dirty, abused, and humiliated by it.

Moreover, the brands on her thighs, with their obvious sexual connotations, had, in her own mind, marked her for life as someone who had been violated. She also knew the entire community felt the same, thanks to the Fort Scott newspaper, which had run her photo on the front page with the word "branded" beneath it. As a budding young woman of sixteen, the label must have hurt and shamed her.

No doubt she also had suffered from the age-old belief that women who are sexually assaulted somehow "asked for it," a notion that the Fort Scott police, by their actions and attitudes during their interrogation that night, had reinforced.

The rudeness and insensitivity of the police in Fort Scott in 1946 unquestionably inspired the Poet to retaliate by tormenting the police in Wichita more than thirty years later.

Schrag did not believe the Fort Scott attack was the primary cause of the Poet. Her reaction to whatever had happened in that boardinghouse must have been triggered by something that had happened to her before, perhaps in her early childhood.

He doubted he would discover what that was in a short interview, but maybe he could find out what had set off the Poet after all these years.

"Then you grew up and got married, and all that was forgotten," Schrag said. "Or was it? Did it still bother you?"

"It did."

"When did you start to think about it again? Did you begin dreaming about it or anything?"

"I can't tell you that. I don't know."

He asked her about the first phone call she received from the person who wanted to blackmail her. She again denied receiving such a call and could not recall feeling emotionally disturbed around that time.

In his own mind, Schrag disagreed with her. He thought Ed's collapse had been a stressful event in her life. Ruth, worried that Ed had suffered a heart attack, probably had started wondering what would happen to her without him.

Ruth's mother had moved to Wichita in recent years, bringing the unpleasant memories of the past with her. Ruth also must have had many unresolved feelings about her mother because of how she had treated her after the Fort Scott attack, and she may have wondered how her mother felt about her.

All these factors could have combined to weaken Ruth's repression and bring the Poet closer to the surface.

Although she had now said she never received that phone call, the incident seemed real to Ruth at the time. Again, what had happened that night was less important than her reaction to it.

"Was there anything else that happened to you in your life at that time?" Schrag asked her.

Ruth shook her head.

"Why was it that it kind of kept growing, then?"

She did not respond.

"You came to my office and did the hypnosis," Schrag said. "What did you think about when I asked you to describe this person? You gave the details—the eyebrows and so on. What were you thinking of? Any person?"

"I was thinking of the man I saw on the street," Ruth said.

"Were you aware you were doing that?"

"I had to have been."

"Maybe you didn't know then."

"I guess I'm just crazy," Ruth said.

"No," said Schrag. "Maybe part of your mind doesn't remember what the other part thinks."

She probably really had run into some guy downtown, Schrag thought. The man probably had made a pickup attempt, and that had finally led to the birth of the Poet, because it had further weakened Ruth's repression by stirring up all those unresolved feelings about herself and her sexuality. At that point, the Poet must have become an uncontrollable impulse in her head. Thus her description of the Poet was a description of the man who had bumped into her after work as she had walked to Henry's department store to meet her husband.

"Did you ever think, when you came to my office, to pull me aside and say, 'I need to talk to you'?" Schrag asked.

"I wish I had," Ruth said into her arms, her head still buried in them.

"Were you too scared to do it, or what?"

"The time I went down there to talk to you, I thought, 'I don't know what I'm going to do,'" Ruth said.

Schrag remembered when Ruth had come to him alone, without police, a meeting he had found curious and unrewarding.

"Who made that appointment, you or Ed?"

"He did."

"I don't know if I kept very many notes about that, but as I recall, Ed said this thing was upsetting you. Had it really been upsetting you that week?"

"I was wanting someone to stop me."

"In some way, you knew there was a part of your mind that was doing something wrong."

"I thought I'd never do it again," she said, "then I couldn't wait to do it again."

"It was obsessive . . . a compulsive thing, wasn't it? You had to do something over and over, and you felt guilty about it. When it was done, you felt relieved, right? And you told yourself, 'I will never do it again.' Then it wasn't but a few days later and you actually had to do it over, right?"

"I don't think I'm basically a really bad person," Ruth said.

"Of course you aren't," Schrag said. "If you were a bad person, you wouldn't be telling us this. You would be lying about it."

"I did lie."

"I mean, right now. Are you lying now?"

"No."

"Okay. You are a good person, but during those times, there was a force within you that made you do this, which you really didn't understand. Or do you?"

She shook her head.

"I had thoughts in my mind over and over about how bad it was going to be at this point," she said.

"You thought in your mind that at some point you were going to get caught?" Schrag asked.

"I knew I would."

"But you feel relieved, don't you?"

She nodded.

"Well, see, that's the whole secret. Now you can get well. Did you know that?"

She did not respond. She was not so certain about that. She was more certain she wanted to die.

"You're real tired," Schrag said. "What would you like to do now? What about going to the hospital?"

"No."

"You don't want to do that? What if Ed wants you to go and rest? How would you feel about that?"

"No."

"You don't just want to go home, do you?"

Ruth nodded in her arms.

"You mean you just want to go home and go to work tomorrow and forget the whole thing?"

"No," she said.

"What do you want to do?"

"I don't know."

Schrag thought a moment.

"What was the worst of everything you did, Ruth?" he asked.

She was silent.

He tried again. "What was the very worst you did?"

Finally, Ruth looked up, her face a pattern of red blotches where it had been resting on her arms. She looked at Schrag with moist eyes.

"Everybody believed me," she said.

24

THE AFTERMATH

After her interrogation, Ruth was taken to St. Joseph Medical Center, where she signed herself into the psychiatric ward. Hill went to a probate judge the next day and signed involuntary commitment papers against her, as well.

A few days later, Ruth was transferred to Wesley Medical Center to spend the remainder of her thirty-day commitment. During that time, she agreed to seek long-term therapy from a Wichita psychologist named Dr. Andrew Pickens.

On October 12, Pickens filed a preliminary report based on six hours of consultation with Ruth. His report largely confirmed Schrag's assessment. He called Ruth's illness an "atypical impulse disorder with dissociative and repressive features." Ruth, he wrote, had repressed certain unacceptable sexual and aggressive feelings until the stress of her husband's hospitalization and the interaction with the strange man in downtown Wichita had weakened the repression and brought those feelings closer to the surface.

Ruth's actions as the Poet, Pickens wrote, had been partially conscious—but largely unconscious—attempts to gratify and defend against her feelings.

She had been aware she was committing those acts, but she didn't know the reason why. Pickens also pointed out the compulsive nature of Ruth's actions.

On November 6, based in part on Pickens's report, the Sedgwick County District Attorney's office issued a statement announcing that no criminal charges would be filed against Ruth. The district attorney decided that her actions as the Poet "were not malicious or deliberate but were the result of a psychiatric problem for which care and treatment and extensive psychotherapy are being obtained for Mrs. Finley."

The Wichita Police Department agreed with the decision. "It doesn't do us or the community any good to prosecute her," Hill told the press.

On the same day, Ruth released a statement of her own to the media:

> I think I may have died and gone to hell. I think I'm coming back, though, thanks to the kind nursing staff and doctors at the Wesley Medical Center psychiatric unit and to an understanding family who stood by me, especially Ed and my loyal and dependable sister, Jean.
>
> I'm equally grateful to the fine officers of the Wichita Police Department, who in the end saved me from either a mental breakdown or my own self-destruction. It's been a nightmare for all involved.

Ruth's mother, Fay Smock, who had lived in Wichita throughout the Poet case, was asked what she thought about how it had ended.

"I was crushed," she said. "There was no sign of anything. We just never thought of such a thing. But I always prayed for him to be caught and put where he belonged, and I believed he should get treatment if they decided he was crazy. The prayer still goes. I just put her in the Lord's hands. He'll take care of her."

Fay's initial comment when she first learned Ruth was the Poet had been slightly less sympathetic. When Jean broke the news to Fay that Ruth was being committed to the hospital for treatment, Fay responded, "But who's going to do my laundry?"

—⁂—

Ruth's nightmare did not end with her commitment. She continued to be plagued by the Poet in the hospital.

He came to her hospital room one night. She was asleep in her bed when suddenly the lights came on. Ruth rolled over and there the Poet was, standing over her, breathing hard and grinning in triumph.

Ruth screamed and the Poet ran out of the room as the tall figure of an orderly appeared over her. The orderly did not seem to see the Poet run past him out of the room.

Ruth began to think the Poet was real again, and she wondered if she had confessed to police in error. Maybe the man really had kidnapped her, stabbed her, and written her all those letters. She had some memory of writing letters in the basement by the washing machine, but she could not remember writing so many. Nor could she imagine how she had done everything else the Poet was supposed to have done. Perhaps he existed after all, she thought. She wanted nothing more than to get out of the hospital, find him, and kill him.

And then kill herself. She still had to die, she thought. She was worthless to anybody now. Even though Ruth entertained thoughts that the Poet might be real, she had occasional flashbacks of things she had done in his name, and she would be flooded with humiliation, which would renew her determination to end her life. Not only had she humiliated herself, Ruth thought, she had embarrassed Ed, her brother and sister, her children, and, once again, her mother.

Her mother. Ruth had conflicting emotions about her mother. They fluctuated between love, hate, and guilt. In the weeks before the interrogation, she had begun to gripe about Fay to Ed. Every Sunday, she and Ed took Fay to church with them, and often, sitting beside her in the pew, Ruth had felt an urge to strike her.

She did not understand why she felt as she did. Perhaps it was because she sometimes felt as if her mother hadn't wanted her in the first place, not after Morris's difficult birth. Perhaps it was because she sometimes suspected her mother had hoped for another boy; Fay had planned to name the next one Albert Joe, after Carl's father.

Perhaps it was the way her mother had treated her after the attack in Fort Scott, locking her up in the house for a week without letting her speak to anyone. She felt as if her mother had been embarrassed by the incident; she seemed to regard it as a personal annoyance. Her mother had always seemed embarrassed by anything Ruth had done wrong.

Fay did not believe in counseling for Ruth after the attack. Ruth once overheard her telling somebody that Ruth might need shock therapy, and that had frightened her, but no such treatment had been forthcoming, no treatment of any kind.

Ruth sometimes wondered if her mother had believed her story about the attack. Fay had seen the cuts on Ruth's legs that night. To her, the marks looked even and parallel, as if done carefully and deliberately by a bobby pin. They did not look like wounds from a man who had wildly slashed at her daughter's legs with a knife during a struggle. Fay had never said anything to Ruth about that, but Ruth had sensed her suspicions. She wished her mother had wanted to talk about it, but she seemed to want to forget the whole thing, and she wanted Ruth to do the same. Ruth had always wondered why her mother had never spoken with her about it.

And she wondered something else: Why, when she went on those crying jags as a tiny young girl, didn't her mother ever ask her what was wrong?

Not that she could have told her. She didn't know then and she didn't know now.

But in the hospital, Ruth had dreamed one night that she was four years old again. In her dream, the four-year-old Ruth was having a dream of her own, about a man in bib overalls raping a little girl.

The four-year-old Ruth awakened from her dream screaming, "He's killing her, he's killing her!" which in turn woke the adult Ruth.

In the light of morning, Ruth felt a need to rush to the little girl and protect her. It was the same feeling she'd had after a dream in which the same man had threatened to throw the little girl off a bridge—the bridge in Ed's painting that hung at the bottom of the basement stairs, the one that spanned the Marmaton River near her home in Richards.

Ruth continued to be assaulted by flickering images of her past. She thought about the neighbor man who had lifted her up at the water well one day when she was little, making her cry and causing her dog, Stubby, to lunge at him. She had sudden glimpses of the man's house, but she couldn't sustain those glimpses; it was as if her mind was holding up flash cards of her past and taking them away again. But it began to occur to her that she had been inside the man's house. In one glimpse, she saw a bedroom at the back of the house. In another, she saw a little girl tied to the posts of the bed.

She could not see what happened next, but she thought she could see a woman holding the little girl on her lap when it was over. The woman was washing the little girl and comforting her. The little girl was naked except for a pair of scuffed leather shoes.

Ruth held on to the image of the shoes. She considered the shoes for some time.

Thinking about them one day weeks later during a therapy session with Dr. Pickens, she suddenly blurted, "Shoes, screw. Sold her ass for a cookie at only four. Now that makes her a whore."

25

1933

Ruth Smock, a golden-haired child of three and a half, is clinging to her mother's dress. It is after church on Easter morning. They are standing in the front yard of the Smock farmhouse southwest of Richards. The branches of the catalpa trees are swaying in a gentle breeze overhead, and the sun is trying to work its way through a thin layer of wispy white clouds. Crickets surround them, singing their own tiny hymns. And the man is there, too.

He is standing in front of Ruth, looming over her like a silo, standing there in his bib overalls, talking to her mother, asking would it be okay to take Ruth to his house so his wife can see Ruth's pretty new Easter dress.

Ruth is hanging on to her mother's dress, trying to tuck herself in behind it and disappear. She does not want to go to the man's house, but she cannot make the words come out, cannot say that to her mother, who is smiling at the man now, saying, sure, it would be just fine if Ruth went over and showed off the new dress to his wife, Ruth thinking, no, no, no, don't make me go.

Her mother is looking down at her and Ruth is shaking her head and starting to cry. Her mother is scolding her and telling her to go on, go to the man's house, what's the matter with you, why are you being such a baby?

The man is reaching down and taking Ruth's tiny hand in one of his huge, dirt-stained hands and tugging her loose from her mother's skirt, then picking her up in his arms. She can smell the familiar scent of tobacco on the man's breath and see the heavy, black beard stubble on his face. She is overcome with fear and is crying harder, but he is carrying her to his car out on the dirt road in front of the house, and her mother is staying back by the house, not coming after her to bring her back and save her.

The man is opening the passenger door and putting her on the front seat, then slamming the door, leaving her sitting there alone. He is walking around the car, climbing in behind the wheel, closing his door, and the two of them are together now, sealed off from the rest of the world, Ruth terrified and hysterical, sitting beside this awful man inside this big machine.

She wants to escape but there is nowhere for her to go but the back seat, and she is scrambling over the top of the front seat to get there when she feels him grab her by her feet. Then she is falling into the back seat, feeling her shoes come off in the man's hands.

She cannot see the road from the back seat, but she knows the man's house is not far. She has made this trip before. She knows it will not be long before the little girl gets hurt again. Maybe this time she can help her.

She is feeling the car turn and slow, then stop, then hearing the man get out and walk around to her door. It is opening and the man is reaching for her, but she is slithering beneath the man's hands and leaping to the ground. She is trying to run, but she is in a field of weeds and the weeds are full of stickers. Without shoes on, it hurts, and she is feeling a stab of pain in her foot and falling down. The man is there quickly, picking her up and telling her to "c'mon," then carrying her into the big red barn and laying her on her back in the dirt and taking off her dress.

Ruth is feeling herself floating up to the sky. She is floating higher and higher, all the way up to heaven, changing into an angel with big white wings. She is hovering over the barn, watching the man who is lying on top of the little girl, making the little girl cry. Ruth wants to fly down and rescue the little girl, but she is hanging up there, suspended in the sky, and all she can do is watch.

When it is over, Ruth is lying on the ground inside the barn again, naked. She is crying because she could not help the little girl.

The man is angry with her for making so much noise. He is grabbing her hands and yanking her to her feet. He is taking her out the back of the barn, Ruth pulling against him, being dragged, screaming, her eyes shut.

Then they are outside and she is being thrown to the ground. She feels her face being shoved into something wet, sticky, and smelly, and her screams are stifled. He is holding on to the back of her head, pushing it deeper into the gooey stench. Then she is opening her eyes and staring into the carcass of a dead animal, the man telling her, "Maybe you'll learn to keep your mouth shut."

She is violently ill, vomiting, the man standing over her, waiting. Then he is picking her up and taking her inside the house.

He is washing her face, saying he is sorry for what he did, then helping her put on her new Easter dress, Ruth sobbing and calling softly for her father, certain that he and her mother know what has happened but don't care, that maybe they even wanted it to happen, maybe even wanted her to die.

—∿—

Ruth's aunt had given her a clothbound book of nursery rhymes by then. Ruth could not read, of course, but her aunt had read some of the poems to her and she had become fond of the nonsensical verses. But one day as she played with the book in her front yard, she suddenly realized all the poems in the book were about her. She even saw her picture on the cover of the book. In the picture, one of her blond curls fell over her forehead, and she was sucking her thumb.

She felt she must destroy the book because the verses were telling the truth about her, saying bad things about her, and if anybody found the book and read it, they would find out what a bad little girl she had been. She found a place and hid the book there so nobody would know what she had done.

It was all because of that man, Ruth thought. He made her do things she didn't want to do, things that ended up hurting the little girl she knew. But she believed what happened to the little girl was all her fault.

After another time in the barn, when the little girl had been hurt again as Ruth watched from the sky, he had walked over to a milk stool by the barn door and then sat on it for a while with his head in his hands. It seemed to Ruth as if he was crying. She had walked up to him and patted him on the shoulder, trying to comfort him, as if it was her fault he was crying, but as soon as she touched him, he grabbed her, put her on the ground, and hurt the little girl again.

Ruth knew she could not tell anybody about the little girl because then they would find out how bad she had been, leaving her alone with the man. Besides, the man told her not to tell anybody, and she always did as she was told.

The man had made the point quite clearly to her one day at her grandmother's house in town. She was playing with a doll in the front room when he dropped by for a visit. When she saw him walk in the door, she burst into tears, and he took her hand and whispered to her to shut up. Later, he took her outside, grabbed the doll out of her arms, yanked the doll's head off its body, and told her, "This is what happens to little girls who don't do what they're told."

Ruth had seen chickens killed on the farm like that, and she knew she didn't want to die that way, floundering around without a head, so she hadn't said anything and had always done what the man wanted.

But she knew her parents knew what was happening, because they were parents and they knew everything. They must have suspected something the night they went for supper at the man's house. The man had picked her up after the meal and taken her to the bedroom while her parents were in the kitchen visiting with his wife. He had tied her hands to the end of the bed with a rope and walked out of the room, leaving her lying there helpless, crying. After a while, her parents had come into the room, found her, and untied her.

"Now, don't you cry," her mother had told her. "He was just playing a game with you."

She wondered why her mother and father didn't stop what was happening.

Then one night, much later, she thought she overheard her mother and father talking about it in the kitchen.

"He wouldn't do anything like that," she heard her father say.

"Well, go ask him," her mother said.

That was all she heard.

But the man stopped what he was doing after that.

Ruth didn't know how long it had been going on, had no idea how much time had passed since that first time in the neighbor's house. When her father had dropped her off. When he had driven by the man's house with Ruth in the car, when the man had offered to babysit her while her father ran errands, when her father had said, "Fine."

The man scooped her off the front seat and carried her in his arms into his house. He took her to the bedroom and sat her on a chair. "Let's play a little game," he said, pulling out a skeleton key that hung from a lanyard. "It's called Find the Key."

He dangled the key in front of her face and told her to find it. Silly, she thought. There it was, right in front of her. She giggled.

Then he dropped the key down the front of her pin-striped overalls. She reached down inside the overalls and fished it out, then handed it back to him, still giggling.

Next, he put the key in a pocket in his overalls and told her to find it again. She reached inside his pocket and brought it out.

Then he dropped the key down her overalls again. Only this time, he decided, it was his turn to find it.

He took off her overalls, then he took off her panties.

He took her to the bed and she started squirming and crying. He tied her hands to the metal bed frame, the juice from a plug of tobacco he had been chewing oozing from the corners of his mouth. He moved on top of her, grabbed a pillow, jammed her face to one side, and covered it with the pillow.

With her head pinned in that position, Ruth was left staring at a large box in the corner of the bedroom that appeared to be filled with lacy material.

And then . . .

She floated into the sky. Floated up to heaven. Became an angel in white, staring down at a bed where a little girl lay screaming in pain as a man in overalls with tobacco juice streaming from his mouth writhed on top of her. She could almost feel the little girl's pain and she wanted to help her, but she was unable to reach her from so high up.

She could only watch helplessly as the man raised himself off the little girl, moved up to her mouth, and inserted something in it, forcing the little girl to taste her own blood.

She could feel the little girl's nausea, and it was almost as if she herself was the one who now began vomiting onto the bed.

But she knew it wasn't her. She knew this was happening to someone else. She was safe up there in the sky, even though it was her fault that the little girl had to go through all this.

She wanted to swoop down and save her. But she also hated her.

She could not imagine what the man had done to the little girl, but she knew it was bad because the little girl had struggled so much.

She had struggled especially hard when the man had tried to get inside her mouth. It had not been easy for him to do that. First, he'd had to knock the pillow off her head, then he'd had to hold her head still with one hand as, with the other, he removed the soiled red bandanna he had shoved inside her mouth to keep her quiet.

EPILOGUE

Following her hospitalization, Ruth began therapy with Dr. Andrew Pickens on an outpatient basis. They met two hours a week off and on for the next six years.

Pickens practiced a form of therapy called "psychoanalytic psychotherapy" in which doctor and patient simply talk with each other, the patient doing most of the talking as the doctor, serving as a "blank screen" upon which the patient can project his or her emotions, listens and guides the discussion. Ruth and Pickens worked together a total of five hundred hours before Ruth could understand, accept, and deal with the fact that the little girl who had been raped in 1933 as Ruth had watched from heaven was Ruth.

In essence, she had to make peace with the "little girl" within her. She had to save her from the past, accepting her into her total personality. Ruth had put the "little girl" on hold for forty-five years, until the "little girl" had burst forth as the Poet, screaming in rage for release.

The dissociative state of consciousness she entered as the Poet was similar to what she did to escape the rapes as a little girl, by floating up to what she perceived as heaven. But it was a more complete dissociation. As the Poet, she left herself and in a sense became another person; although it wasn't a coherent person, it wasn't a separate personality.

Although she had flashbacks to some of the things she had done as the Poet, she could not remember everything, and some of the incidents, notably the stabbing and kidnapping, continued to seem real to her during therapy, and still do. (She later remembered she had stabbed herself by wedging the knife between two sinks in the gas station bathroom and backing hard against the blade.)

Ruth's intent as the Poet was to get help, just as she had wanted to get help for the little girl back in 1933. She was reexperiencing the same feelings of helplessness and hostility she'd had as the little girl. However, although she wanted to get help, she did not want to reveal what it was she needed help for because she did not want to relive those painful experiences. And so the Poet continued to harass her.

It is possible that she would have killed herself had the police not stopped her. In many ways she had been trying to kill herself from the moment she was first raped.

What really happened on that October night in the Fort Scott boardinghouse when she was sixteen remains open for speculation. Ruth insists she was attacked and branded by a man just as she described to police, although the physical evidence gathered by the officers at the scene and observations by doctors who treated her suggest she was home alone that night and probably used the iron on herself.

But what really happened is less important than what Ruth thought had happened. To her, the attack was as real as it was brutal, and it served to re-intensify the feelings she had experienced as a little girl.

Ruth continued to write poems during her therapy. Encouraged and guided by Pickens, she continued to let the little girl express her emotions. As an adult, she was able to give voice to feelings she could not express as a child.

Ruth returned to work shortly after her commitment and continued to work for the phone company until her retirement in April 1991. She and Ed remained happily married in Wichita, finally enjoying "the best years of their lives."

Ruth discovered in therapy that she was the only one who could save the little girl. It took years, but Ruth eventually grew closer to the girl and began to accept her back into her total personality. She even lay on the floor, imagining the little girl lying beside her. Finally she sat on the couch with her one day and allowed the little girl to become part of her.

After the decades of trauma, Ruth's story had a happy ending. She never wrote poetry again.

Acknowledgments

My deepest gratitude to Oli Munson and Laura Van der Veer for championing this project from the start, and for their faith and support during its lengthy gestation. I am also eternally grateful to Fred Mann for sharing his voluminous and absolutely essential research materials with me. This book could not have been written without Fred's work—it is his book as much as it is mine.

As always, I would like to thank my family and friends for all of their support, as well. And my gratitude to the entire team at Little A, including Karah Nichols and expert proofreaders Amanda and Laura, for their outstanding work on this project.

About the Author

Photo © Gary Sloman

Corey Mead is an associate professor of English at Baruch College, City University of New York. He is the author of four books, including *The Hidden History of the White House* and *Angelic Music: The Story of Benjamin Franklin's Glass Armonica*. His work has appeared in *Time*, *Salon*, *The Daily Beast*, and numerous literary journals.